Com Permanent Workplace Injuries

A Study of the California System

Mark A. Peterson

Robert T. Reville

Rachel Kaganoff Stern

with

Peter S. Barth

Prepared for the
Commission on Health and Safety and Workers' Compensation

RAND

The Institute for Civil Justice

THE INSTITUTE FOR CIVIL JUSTICE

The mission of the Institute for Civil Justice is to help make the civil justice system more efficient and more equitable by supplying policymakers and the public with the results of objective, empirically based, analytic research. The ICJ facilitates change in the civil justice system by analyzing trends and outcomes, identifying and evaluating policy options, and bringing together representatives of different interests to debate alternative solutions to policy problems. The Institute builds on a long tradition of RAND research characterized by an interdisciplinary, empirical approach to public policy issues and rigorous standards of quality, objectivity, and independence.

ICJ research is supported by pooled grants from corporations, trade and professional associations, and individuals; by government grants and contracts; and by private foundations. The Institute disseminates its work widely to the legal, business, and research communities, and to the general public. In accordance with RAND policy, all Institute research products are subject to peer review before publication. ICJ publications do not necessarily reflect the opinions or policies of the research sponsors or of the ICJ Board of Overseers.

Robert B. Shapiro, Chairman and Chief Executive Officer, Monsanto
Company

Bill Wagner, Wagner, Vaughan & McLaughlin

Paul C. Weiler, Henry J. Friendly Professor of Law, Harvard University
Law School

PREFACE

This volume contains a technical discussion of a comprehensive empirical analysis of the permanent partial disability component of California's workers' compensation system. Established early in this century, this system processes hundreds of thousands of claims from injured workers every year and pays out billions of dollars in benefits. It has been widely criticized as complicated and providing minimal compensation at high costs.

Reform legislation in 1993 established the Commission on Health and Safety and Workers' Compensation, a politically balanced body meant to oversee and deal with possible changes in the system. One of the commission's charges was to evaluate the system's permanent partial disability component. The evaluation was conducted by RAND's Institute for Civil Justice.

The results of this evaluation should be of interest to a wide variety of participants in California's workers' compensation system, including employers, insurers, attorneys, and employee groups. The study findings will also be useful to workers' compensation experts in other states that are considering changes in their workers' compensation systems.

In light of these diverse audiences, we present our findings in several forms. This volume provides the technical details of our methods and findings. A summary of the evaluation can be found in *Findings and Recommendations on California's Permanent Partial Disability System: Executive Summary*, Rachel Kaganoff Stern, Mark A. Peterson, Robert T. Reville, and Mary E. Vaiana, MR-919-ICJ, 1997.

The study was a collaborative effort. Mark A. Peterson led the research. Robert T. Reville was responsible for the wage loss analysis. Rachel Kaganoff Stern led the qualitative analysis of the workers' compensation process. Peter S. Barth conducted the multi-state comparison.

For more information about the Institute for Civil Justice, contact:

Dr. Deborah R. Hensler, Director

Institute for Civil Justice

RAND

1700 Main Street

Santa Monica, CA 90407-2138

TEL: (310) 451-6916

FAX: (310) 451-6979

Internet: Deborah_Hensler@rand.org

A profile of the ICJ, abstracts of its publications, and ordering
information can be found on RAND's home page on the World Wide Web at
http://www.rand.org/centers/icj.

CONTENTS

FIGURES

TABLES

ACKNOWLEDGMENTS

We would like to extend our sincere thanks to Christine Baker, the Executive Director of the Commission on Health and Safety and Workers' Compensation, for her expert guidance and support throughout this research project. We are also grateful to the members of the Commission on Health and Safety and Workers' Compensation and the advisory group on workers' compensation, many of whom spent considerable time responding to our questions and providing research advice and direction.

The Workers' Compensation Insurance Rating Bureau (WCIRB) and several California state agencies assisted us by providing us with data and helping us to understand the databases. Dave Bellusci at the WCIRB was enormously helpful, as were Michele Bunds and Rich Kihlthau at the State of California Employment Development Department (EDD). We also thank Blair Megowan and Del Gaines at the Disability Evaluation Unit; Ted Sorich, Jim Culbeaux, Russ Roeckel and Elizabeth Nisperos at the Department of Industrial Relations Data Processing; Walt Gladwin at the WCIRB; and Dave Jones at the EDD. We are grateful to the many members of the broader workers' compensation community who agreed to participate in our qualitative interviews.

John Burton at Rutgers and Bob Schoeni at RAND reviewed our report and their suggestions improved it immeasurably. Sue Polich prepared the complex data files for analysis and provided invaluable assistance throughout the study.

Finally, we thank Frank Neuhauser at Berkeley and our RAND colleagues Lloyd Dixon, Deborah Hensler, Dan McCaffrey, Erik Moller, Mary Vaiana, and Pat Williams for their contributions to the project. Any errors that remain are our responsibility.

LIST OF ABBREVIATIONS

AMA	American Medical Association
AME	Agreed Medical Examiner
AOE	Arising Out of Employment
C&R	Compromise and Release
COE	In the Course of Employment
CPI	Consumer Price Index
CWCI	California Workers' Compensation Institute
DCBS	Department of Consumer and Business Services (Oregon)
DEU	Disability Evaluation Unit
DI	Disability Insurance
DIA	Division of Industrial Accidents
DWC	Division of Workers' Compensation
EDD	Employment Development Department
EGR	Expected Growth Ratio
ERC	Economic Recovery Compensation (Minnesota)
F&A	Finding and Award
IAB	Industrial Accident Board (Texas)
IC	Impairment Compensation (Minnesota)
IIB	Impairment Income Benefit
IMC	Industrial Medical Council
IME	Independent Medical Examiner (Colorado)
IQR	Interquartile Range
LWEC	Lost Wage Earning Capacity
MMI	Maximum Medical Improvement
P&S	Permanent and Stationary
PPD	Permanent Partial Disability
PTD	Permanent Total Disability
QME	Qualified Medical Examiner
SCIF	State Compensation Insurance Fund
SIB	Supplemental Income Benefit
SSI	Social Security Insurance

SSN	Social Security Number
Stip	Stipulation with Request for Award
TD	Temporary Disability
TPA	Third Party Administrator
TPD	Temporary Partial Disability
TTD	Temporary Total Disability
TWCC	Texas Workers' Compensation Commission
UCB	University of California at Berkeley
UI	Unemployment Insurance
USR	Uniform Statistical Reporting Plan
VR	Vocational Rehabilitation
VRMA	Vocational Rehabilitation Maintenance Allowance
WC	Workers' Compensation
WCAB	Workers' Compensation Appeals Board
WCIRB	Workers' Compensation Insurance Rating Bureau
WCRI	Workers' Compensation Research Institute
WL	Wage Loss

1. INTRODUCTION

Born of a compromise between labor and employers in 1911, the California workers' compensation plan has evolved into a system that is as overly complex as it is vast. Over 300,000 workers each year receive benefits for work-related injuries resulting in billions of dollars in paid benefits, and insurance premiums that peaked in 1994 at $9 billion, but by 1996 had fallen to $6 billion. Buffeted by significant legislative reforms in 1989 and 1993, as well as frequent and ongoing administrative changes implemented by the Division of Workers' Compensation, system participants complain that confusion, complexity and delay are the main constants in the California workers' compensation system.

The cumulative result of the recent legislative changes is a system that is much changed and in many ways improved. Yet many complain that the problems of yesterday linger on--in some cases worse than before. The number of claims and paid benefits are down and total premiums paid are down dramatically. Policy changes in medical-legal fee schedules, adjustments in the compensability of certain types of claims, greater vigilance in the fight against fraud, broad changes in the nature of the California workforce (a continued shift out of manufacturing, into the service sector), as well as changes in the overall health of the California economy all clearly contributed to the decline in benefit and premium payments.

While welcome, reduced payments are not the only measure of success for the workers' compensation system. Notably missing from recent evaluations of the permanent partial disability (PPD) system in California is a rigorous evaluation of the adequacy and equity of indemnity benefits. While the recent reforms of the workers' compensation system may have accomplished much in the way of reducing the overall cost of the system to employers--measured in terms of insurance premiums and benefit payments--they did little to reduce the transaction costs associated with administering the system. Litigation and the costs associated with settling cases through the Workers'

Compensation Appeals Board (WCAB) have increased steadily--even in the
post-reform period. Expenses associated with managing the Division of
Workers' Compensation continue to rise. So, as benefits and premiums
paid decline, the expenses associated with running the system continue
to climb even today. California's workers' compensation program
provides workers with relatively little compensation but a lot of
"system." After nearly a decade of reform the question remains, where
do we go from here?

In July of 1996, RAND was asked to address the complicated,
politically intricate question of how the California workers'
compensation permanent partial disability system might be reformed to
improve its adequacy, equity, and efficiency and how the system might be
brought better in line with the constitutional mandate upon which the
original labor/employer compromise rested. Following this introduction,
our report will address these important questions in seven sections.
Section 2 will provide a general description of the California workers'
compensation system, and will focus more narrowly on the structure of
the permanent partial disability system. This section will outline the
constitutional mandate underpinning the system and address at a general
level how recent legislative changes have restructured the way in which
benefits are determined and then paid. Section 3 presents an analysis
of five other states that have recently implemented significant reforms
to their workers' compensation systems. Section 4 will address issues
of process, participant values, and participant experiences with recent
reforms through a set of qualitative interviews. Sections 5, 6, and 7
report quantitative analyses using data on claims from the Workers'
Compensation Insurance Rating Bureau (WCIRB) and the Disability
Evaluation Unit (DEU), linked to wage data from the Employment
Development Department (EDD). Section 5 analyzes the adequacy of
indemnity benefits in California. We estimate the loss of wages over
the years after the injury for PPD claimants from 1991-1993, and the
fraction of wage loss replaced by indemnity benefits. Section 6
evaluates the disability rating. We examine whether the rating predicts
wage loss, and whether there are differences in replacement rates by
disability rating. We also examine the consistency of rating by

comparing ratings for the same claim by insurance adjusters and by the DEU. Section 7 explores claims processing, focusing on differences between high- and low-rated claims. Section 8 concludes the report--summarizing results and detailing a set of policy reform proposals generated by the qualitative and quantitative analyses completed during this study.

2. THE HISTORY OF WORKERS' COMPENSATION IN CALIFORNIA

Workers' compensation programs were an outcome of the Progressive Era when reformers responded to both labor and employer concerns about high rates of work-related injuries, insufficient compensation to injured workers, and continuing employer uncertainty as to how to predict the costs related to these injuries. Reformers in California first adopted a voluntary plan under the authority of a 1911 constitutional amendment; however, it attracted few takers in the employer community, so two short years later California turned instead to a program that was compulsory. The Boynton Act, passed in May of 1913, required that employers provide workers' compensation benefits to their employees, with some exceptions (the agriculture sector was exempted from the system until 1959).[1]

The Boynton Act also established the State Compensation Insurance Fund (SCIF) in an effort to insure that all employers would be able to procure workers' compensation insurance at fair rates. The Boynton Act was a compromise between employers and labor. In exchange for limited but certain damages under a statutory compensation system, injured workers gave up the right to sue their employers for full but uncertain damages under tort liability. Conversely, employers agreed to pay benefits for all workplace injuries and illnesses, regardless of fault, but were granted protection against unpredictable, subjective, and possibly excessive tort judgments.

PERMANENT PARTIAL DISABILITY PAYMENTS

With the enactment of the Boynton Act, an essential element of the California workers' compensation scheme has been the required payment of permanent disability benefits, including compensation for permanent partial disabilities (PPD). Despite this seemingly straightforward directive, debate over the magnitude and necessity of such awards has simmered since the inception of the benefits system, beginning with the

---

[1]California Workers' Compensation Law, 5th Edition, Issue 0 (1994), pp. 1-4.

very definition of the term "disability." The current controversy over the determination and delivery of permanent partial disability awards dates from the benefit structure first devised by the Industrial Accident Board before World War I and incorporated into the statutory and administrative structure of the system ever since. Court decisions as to how the law and regulations should be applied have also played a key role in the development of PPD indemnification. As many commentators have noted, the permanent disability compensation system poses difficult questions of equity, adequacy, and efficiency, yet the permanent disability scheme lies at the very heart of the constitutional mandate to provide benefits to injured workers in a manner that is "expeditious, inexpensive, and without encumbrance of any kind."

By statute, the workers' compensation laws must be liberally construed in favor of providing benefits. Labor Code 3202 provides:

> The provisions of Division 4 and Division 5 of this code
> [workers' compensation and safety provisions] shall be
> liberally construed by the courts with the purpose of
> extending their benefits for the protection of persons injured
> in the course of their employment.

This provision has been interpreted to apply equally to the courts and to the Workers' Compensation Appeals Board (WCAB); to factual issues as well as to statutory construction. Any reasonable doubt as to whether a disability is compensable is required to be resolved in favor of the employee.

The concept of "adequate" compensation has been a central issue in the debate surrounding the payment of permanent partial disability benefits in California. The originators of the California system wanted to compensate injured workers for their lessened capacity to compete in an open labor market, without providing benefits that were so generous that employees would lose their incentive to return to work. This balance was to be reached by paying workers two-thirds of their pre-injury wages (up to a set maximum). At this payment level, workers would need to return to work to maintain their pre-injury standard of living, while at the same time receiving compensation for their lost ability to compete.

In California, injured workers who must take time off work as a result of a workplace injury receive temporary disability payments in the initial period that they are off work, undergoing medical treatment. "Temporary disability" is defined as an incapacity to work that is expected to be cured and that results in a wage loss. Temporary disability payments are calculated based on actual pre-injury wages. Workers are compensated at a two-thirds replacement rate up to a set maximum ($336 a week prior to all of the reforms, adjusted upward in 1994, 1995, and 1996--now set at $490 a week). Temporary disability payments cease when the worker returns to work, or when they are declared "permanent and stationary" (P&S), meaning their condition is unlikely to improve further, even with additional medical treatment.

Once a worker with some level of permanent disability returns to work, or is declared permanent and stationary, he/she will begin to receive permanent disability payments. Permanent partial disability payments are meant to replace wages lost as a result of the industrial accident or illness. Unlike temporary disability payments which are paid when a worker is out of work and can be based on actual pre-injury wages, permanent disability payments have to be predictive. PPD benefits are paid before and must anticipate much of the worker's wage loss. Knowledge of actual, long-term, post-injury wage losses is not available as a base for the calculation. Instead, California uses a permanent disability rating schedule. To determine an initial disability rating for each injured worker, the rater draws on medical reports from either treating or forensic medical evaluators (depending on the specifics of the case) in order to apply a complex schedule. The ratings are adjusted for age and occupation to determine the final rating.

The extent of a worker's permanent disability determines how long disability payments last. The higher the PPD rating, the larger the payment. However, amounts of weekly payments are not affected by disability ratings. Permanent partial disability payments have a ceiling of $230 per week (for those who are between 70 percent and 99.75 percent disabled), which is far below the rate used as the maximum for temporary disability payments. This disparity between TD and PPD payment maximums is an important issue in California. The financial imbalance may provide incentives to injured workers to stay on temporary disability longer than they might otherwise, since their payments will drop when they shift to permanent disability.

THE COMPLEXITY OF PPD RATINGS

Virtually every form of disability is listed in the Schedule for Rating Permanent Disabilities--and a significant number of disabilities that had previously been unrated were added to the schedule with the revisions published in January of 1997. The schematic definitiveness of the PPD schedule masks its true complexity. As noted more than a decade ago by the 1986 Joint Study Committee on Workers' Compensation, the current system at best seems to be "an expensive means of determining an essentially arbitrary amount of permanent disability compensation." The rating schedule is treated as sufficiently exact as to be deemed prima facie evidence of amount of disability in any compensation proceeding, but in practice--and for a variety of reasons--this computation is the source of many disputes.

First, subjective factors and competing values enter into the calculation of the ratings themselves. California includes as ratable factors subjective symptoms such as psychological impairment and pain, frequently disputed disability elements that some other states ignore in order to reduce disputes. In addition, there is historical disagreement as to whether such awards should be designed to compensate, solely, loss of earnings (either actual or estimated) or personal loss and lifestyle impairment as well. The California Legislature has never provided a statutory definition of "permanent disability," leaving the task of defining the purpose and boundaries of benefits to the administrative and judicial branches of government.

Second, every factor that the schedule uses to determine disability ratings can be disputed in at least some claims. Even the most basic issues can be disputed. For example, a worker's "occupation" at the time of the injury, a fundamental component of the ratings determination, may be subject to dispute, particularly when the actual work tasks of the employee differ markedly from a formal job description. Combined effects of multiple disabilities resulting from a single injury, from job-related and non-job-related causes, or from successive industrial injuries may add more contention.

Third, procedures intended to reduce litigation may have, over time, actually increased it. If the parties (including the insurer) are unable to resolve the claim through "informal" procedures (which may include discovery and exchange of medical evidence), an application for adjudication is filed with the WCAB, indicating that a bona fide dispute exists. In 1989, in an attempt to conserve the limited resources of the WCAB and to encourage the parties to avoid actual litigation, numerous reforms, such as mandatory settlement conferences, were legislated. However, the basis for the award of PPD benefits--residual impairment-- may transform the adjudication process into a contest between competing medical evaluations. One observer has called this the "dueling docs syndrome" and has concluded that significant resources from the workers' compensation system go to support this kind of litigation.[2]

Finally, litigation may be further exacerbated by a statutory provision that entitles an employee to reimbursement for medical-legal expenses reasonably, actually, and necessarily incurred in making a claim. Medical-legal expenses can include costs for x-rays, laboratory fees, diagnostic tests, medical records, medical reports, medical testimony, and legal fees necessary to prove a contested claim. The choice of the medical-legal provider is up to the employee, but may be contested by the employer or the insurer. Both the 1989 and 1993 reforms attempted to deal with many of these issues, particularly those in the medical-legal arena. A detailed discussion of the two reform bills is included at the conclusion of this section.

ADEQUACY OF CALIFORNIA PPD PAYMENTS

Many critics of the California workers' compensation system argue that PPD payments in California provide insufficient benefits to injured workers. In 1989, before the recent statutory reform cycle, PPD payments for injured workers with disability ratings below 24.75 percent were a maximum of $140 per week. This differed little from the weekly

---

[2]Barth and Telles (1992), p. 83.

maximum payments of $148 for injured workers with disability ratings from between 25 and 99.75. After the reforms, the benefit maximum was gradually increased but only for injured workers with disability ratings above 15.[3] PPD maximum benefits for workers with ratings below 15 percent have not changed since 1983. Although these payments are meant in part to replace lost wages at a two-thirds replacement rate, none of these rate increases were based on studies of the actual amount of wages lost by workers with varying disability ratings. A new rating schedule, designed to address inconsistencies in the rating system, as well as to more fairly compensate particular areas of injury, went into effect in January of 1997. Again, although a great deal of research and study went into developing this revised schedule, no attempt was made to systematically analyze how disability benefits are related to workers' actual post-injury wage losses. Our analysis in Section 6 suggests that these statutory and administrative revisions of the schedule and benefit increases were insufficient for workers with low ratings. In particular, we find that workers with disability ratings below 20 suffer significant uncompensated wage losses.

1989 AND 1993 REFORMS

The 1989 and 1993 statutory reforms implemented major changes in the area of workers' compensation. The first bill was the Margolin-Greene Workers' Compensation Reform Act of 1989. One of the central goals of this bill was to substantially reduce medical-legal expenses. Medical-legal expenses are those associated with completing the medical evaluations necessary to provide input into the disability rating process. Forensic medical costs had steadily increased prior to the 1989 reforms. Cost increases were attributed to two main factors: escalating fees for individual medical-legal reports and the "dueling doc" cycle. The Margolin-Greene Act addressed both. First, fee schedules were adopted which set limits on the cost per forensic medical evaluation. The Industrial Medical Council (IMC), a new organization established to replace the Medical and Chiropractic Advisory Committee, was given ongoing responsibility for setting medical-legal fees.

---

[3]See Labor Code 4653, 4453, 4654, 4655, and 4658.

Second, for disputed claims, medical evaluation reports were limited to one per medical specialty.

As the reformers hoped, these new fee schedules and limits on the number of evaluations deemed compensable have significantly reduced medical-legal costs in the workers' compensation system. However, these tighter strictures on medical-legal expenses may have contributed to another problem--a near explosion in filings and backlogs of medical liens. The WCAB has been forced to establish special court lien units to handle this increased caseload.

The reforms set up a series of procedures, presumptions, and periods of exclusivity in an attempt to limit the number of competing medical-legal reports. First the statute states that the report and conclusions of the "treating doctor" shall have a presumption of correctness. Employers have exclusive right to designate a worker's treating doctor during the first 30 days after a claim is filed (unless an employee predesignated a doctor for this purpose). Unrepresented and represented claimants unhappy with their employer's choice of treating physician must wait until the window of employer control over treating physician choice expires before changing their treating physician. If an unrepresented claimant has already been evaluated as P&S by an employer-chosen treating physician during the 30 days, they do not have the option of switching to a new physician of their choosing. In such situations, unrepresented claimants can only choose a new doctor from a panel of three qualified physicians provided to the claimant by the IMC and drawn from a list of Qualified Medical Examiners (QMEs) with an appropriate specialty and geographic location. This panel of three QMEs is often referred to as the "doc-in-the-box." QMEs are required to pass a state exam designed and administered by the IMC. It was hoped that QMEs would function as informed, neutral experts who would bring objectivity to the medical evaluation process. However, the QME exam has been criticized as insufficiently rigorous. Critics assert that doctors with questionable forensic medical skills and credibility took and passed the QME exam, and now have the added status of being state-qualified doctors.

Passage of the Margolin-Greene Act brought with it a number of administrative changes, including the renaming of the Division of Industrial Accidents (DIA) as the Division of Workers' Compensation (DWC). New requirements were placed on insurers regarding the timeliness and adequacy of indemnity payments. Insurers and self-insured employers were required to begin temporary total benefit payments within 14 days of first notice that an injured employee was temporarily unable to work. The statute called for an automatic 10 percent penalty if the insurance company failed to make timely or adequate payments. The newly formed DWC was instructed to establish an audit unit responsible for enforcing standards for payment timeliness and adequacy, with authority to assess automatic or larger penalties and sanctions, up to license revocation, if an insurance company failed to improve its payment processes.

The statute increased maximum benefits for temporary total, permanent total, permanent partial disability, and death benefits, except for PPD benefits where partial disability ratings were below 25 percent. Benefit increases were estimated at about $1.4 billion per year.

The Act made a number of adjustments in dispute resolution procedures used by the WCAB. First, mandatory settlement conferences were required for cases in which backlogs prevented hearings from being held within 110 days. Second, in an effort to ensure that bona fide disputes existed, the new law required tougher standards be met before claimants could file a claim in the WCAB. Claimants had to establish that efforts had been made to resolve the dispute, including providing the conflicting medical reports, or other supporting materials.

Two commissions were established to look into whether or not additional reforms were warranted in a number of policy areas within the workers' compensation system. First, an Insurance Rate Study Commission was approved and given authority to evaluate the ratemaking procedures used to govern workers' compensation insurance providers in the state. Second, a Commission on Workplace Health and Safety was set up largely to review and provide funding for projects addressing labor- or employer-sponsored workplace illness and accident prevention programs.

Funding for these projects was to come from audit-generated penalties assessed on both insurers and self-insured employers.

Minor clean-up legislation was passed in 1990, and again in 1991, but the next major policy revision did not arrive until 1993. These reforms, known as the California Workers' Compensation Reform Act of 1993, much like their 1989 predecessor, were quite broad in scope. Many stakeholder groups felt that the 1989 reforms had not gone far enough. Preliminary data available at the time of the bill's passage showed a system that was still very expensive and cumbersome. Given the inherent lags in the availability of quantitative data concerning system outcomes, some critics of the 1993 reforms assert that they followed too closely on the heels of the Margolin-Greene Act. These critics note that there were in fact significant reductions in costs (such as total benefits and premiums paid) in the period 1991-1995, which were not fully apparent at the time of the second system revision.

The California Workers' Compensation Reform Act of 1993 included the following major provisions:

1. Placed a $16,000 cap on vocational rehabilitation payments.
2. Authorized the use of managed care (subject to certain guidelines) in workers' compensation.
3. Further reduced medical fee schedules.
4. Limited the number of compensable medical-legal evaluations in disputed claims to one per side.
5. Raised the standard for compensable stress claims--requiring that work-related stress amount to over 50 percent of the cause of the psychiatric injury in order for it to be classified as compensable.
6. Raised the standard for post-termination claims--eliminating compensation for claims filed after the termination date for which no notice of the claim was made prior to the time of termination.
7. Eliminated coverage for stress claims that resulted from "good faith" terminations.
8. Toughened fraud prevention measures.

9. Abolished the minimum rate law for workers' compensation insurance providers--shifting instead to a system of open rating.

10. Provided for the development and implementation of a number of "carve-out" programs--which were to be collective-bargaining-based alternatives to the main workers' compensation system.

11. Created the Commission on Health and Safety and Workers' Compensation--a Commission whose mandate is to work with both labor and employers to monitor and evaluate the workers' compensation system.

12. Phased in increases over a three-year period, in the maximum weekly temporary total disability (TTD) payment (from a pre-reform level of $336 per week, to $490 in 1996).

It is still too early to assess the full effect of the 1989 and 1993 reforms. Cases operating under the pre-1989 rules are still in the system and many "window period" cases, those subject to the 1989 rules, rather than the newer 1993 rules, are still open. The California workers' compensation system has been much reformed in recent years, and remains in flux today.

A SIMPLIFIED OVERVIEW OF A PERMANENT PARTIAL DISABILITY CLAIM

Although no two permanent partial disability claims are alike, it is possible to distill the permanent disability claims process down to a simplified core. The following description is an introductory foundation for readers less well-versed in the specifics of the California workers' compensation system. Readers with a great deal of experience in the intricacies of the California claims process may wish to proceed directly to the conclusion of this section.

Workers who suffer either a workplace injury or illness must first inform their supervisor that such an event has taken place. Verbal notification is sufficient in the immediate days after the event, but for injuries after 1/1/94 written notification must be given to the employer as well. In addition, claimants must now file an Application for Adjudication of Claim with the Workers' Compensation Appeals Board.

Employers and insurers vary in their own internal paperwork
requirements.

All workers attesting that they have a workplace injury or illness,
whether or not it is admitted by the insurer/employer, are entitled to
initial medical treatment--such that a medical diagnosis can be
completed. Workers who cannot return to work immediately are entitled
to temporary disability payments. These payments fall into two
categories, temporary total disability payments (TTD) or temporary
partial disability payments (TPD). TTD payments are made indefinitely,
until either (1) the injured worker can return to work, or (2) the
injured workers' condition is deemed permanent and stationary (P&S) by a
treating physician, meaning that the worker's condition is unlikely to
improve even with additional medical treatment. TPD payments are made
if a worker can return to work, but only for limited hours, or with work
restrictions. TTD payments are made based on a worker's actual earnings
at the time of the injury. The payments cover two-thirds of the
worker's actual wages, up to a set maximum. TPD payments cover two-
thirds of the difference between the worker's earnings in a modified
work capacity and his or her pre-injury wages.

Employers have 90 days in which to admit or deny a claim. Claims
not denied at the 90-day mark are automatically treated as admitted.
Employers have control over the choice of treating physician for the
first 30 days (unless employees have pre-identified a workers'
compensation doctor). After the first 30 days, employees who have
retained counsel can switch to the doctor of their choice.
Unrepresented claimants may also change doctors, but they do not have
free choice as to which physician they see. Instead, unrepresented
claimants are required to choose from a panel of three qualified medical
examiners (QMEs) identified by the IMC.

Employees continue to get medical treatment, and temporary
disability payments if they cannot work, until they can return to work,
or until their doctor determines that their condition is P&S. Claimants
with permanent disabilities are given a disability rating based on an
evaluation completed by the treating physician, or by a forensic doctor.
On the basis of the P&S report, submitted by the treating doctor or a

forensic doctor, a disability rating can be calculated for workers with permanent disabilities. Ratings are usually calculated by insurance adjusters, or a rater with the state's Disability Evaluation Unit, but can also be calculated by the applicant lawyer. In disputed claims, more than one medical-legal evaluation may be completed, and additional rating evaluations may be completed based on the competing evaluations.

Claimants and insurers/employers may initiate litigation at any time during the claims process. Disputes can arise over whether or not the claim is industrial in nature; the extent of apportionment (responsibility) of the injury to the workplace and, therefore, the employer/insurer; the amount and kind of medical treatment or evaluation that is appropriate and fair; the extent of residual permanent disability; late or inadequate payment advances (before the claimant is P&S); late or inadequate permanent disability payments; and many other reasons.

Both unrepresented and represented claimants have a number of options in choosing how to close their claim. They may elect to settle their case through a compromise and release (C&R), in which case they will get both their indemnity benefits and some estimate of their future medical expenses in a lump sum payment. Alternatively, claimants may settle their claim with what is referred to as a Stipulation with Request for Award (Stip). In these cases indemnity payments are paid out over time, and future medical expenses related to the industrial injury or illness are the ongoing responsibility of the insurer/employer. If a represented claimant cannot reach a settlement agreement of either type, and the case goes to trial at the WCAB, the judge will issue a decision called a Findings and Award (F&A). Unrepresented claimants who cannot reach a settlement may choose to represent themselves in the court process, in which case the decision reached in their trial will also be called a Findings and Award.

Claimants with permanent disabilities must be rated in order to determine the level of indemnity payments to which they are entitled. As stated above, this rating can be completed based on the evaluation of a treating physician, although in litigated cases it is generally done on the basis of a medical-legal evaluation completed by a forensic

doctor. The rating itself can be completed by a WCAB judge, a lawyer,
an insurance adjuster, or a rater working within the state's disability
evaluation unit (DEU). In recent years because of considerable backlogs
at the DEU, insurance companies and self-insured employers were allowed
to use private outside raters to complete the disability rating. This
practice is no longer encouraged by the DWC. Disability ratings involve
a relatively complex calculation with different numerical weights
attached to medical findings (both objective and subjective). This
number is then adjusted by the age and occupation of the injured worker.
The resulting final rating then corresponds with a number of weeks of
indemnity payments. The actual amount of payment (rather than the
number of weeks of payment) is determined by the worker's pre-injury
wage--up to a set maximum. The maximums vary by level of disability--
with those with higher disability ratings eligible for higher maximum
payments.

In addition to indemnity payments, permanently disabled workers may
be eligible for vocational rehabilitation payments. These payments are
now capped at $16,000 and vocational rehabilitation programs must be
completed within 18 months after they are approved.

Throughout the process described above, there are many specific
paperwork requirements imposed on both injured workers and
employers/insurers. These requirements affect both litigated and non-
litigated claims (although not in exactly the same way). With the many
changes brought on by the 1989 and 1993 reforms, paperwork and process
requirements can vary a great deal depending on the date of injury.[4]

CONCLUSION

The previous description of the historical evolution of workers'
compensation policies in the State of California, as well as the brief
outline of how individual permanent partial disability claims are
processed, lays an important foundation for the research, analysis, and
policy recommendations that follow in the next four sections. As this

_____

[4]This summary description of the workers' compensation claims
process in California was informed by our many qualitative interviews
with system participants, as well as by the Nolo Press guide for injured
workers (Ball, 1995).

history noted, the workers' compensation system in California is a complicated, fluid enterprise. Important changes in the California workers' compensation system are recent enough that the full effect of those changes cannot be readily measured as yet, particularly through available quantitative data sources. System outcomes are driven by concrete factors such as benefit payment schedules, rules for vocational rehabilitation programs and the state's disability rating schedule. In addition, less concrete issues such as widely accepted but more informal claims processing procedures, understandings about how to handle unscheduled injuries, and regional variations in accepted practice play a critical role in driving system outcomes. Some of these factors are best measured and evaluated through qualitative research methods, and others are more appropriately assessed through quantitative statistical analyses and economic models. For these reasons we elected to take a multifaceted research approach so that we could assess the permanent partial disability system from a number of different vantage points.

The research tools employed in this study fall into six categories. First, we completed a review of the relevant literature on workers' compensation and related issues. This literature is referenced, where appropriate, throughout the report. Second, we looked at recent workers' compensation reform efforts in a number of other states. This analysis is presented in Section 3. Third, we completed a series of qualitative interviews of system participants. These interviews are summarized in Section 4. Sections 5, 6, and 7 present the results of our quantitative research. These sections report statistical analyses based on claims data from the Workers' Compensation Insurance Rating Bureau (WCIRB) linked to ratings data from the DEU and wage data from the EDD. In these sections, we report our wage loss study, which looks at the post-injury wage experience of workers who experienced industrial accidents or disease, as well as looking at the relationship between the disability ratings given to injured workers and their post-injury wage losses. Finally, we interviewed a set of senior-level system stakeholders in order to test our initial research conclusions, as well as policy recommendations, before we drafted our report.

3. OTHER STATES' EXPERIENCE WITH PPD PROGRAMS

INTRODUCTION

The purpose of this section is to describe other states' experience with permanent partial disability (PPD) programs. We begin by reviewing the general goals of PPD programs and the three fundamental approaches to PPD compensation. We then describe in some detail five states' experience with PPD programs. Texas, Colorado, Minnesota, Washington, and Oregon were selected because characteristics of their PPD systems, before and after recent reforms, provide potential insight into alternative methods of compensating PPD cases. We conclude our discussion by drawing some generalizations from these state-specific experiences.

GOALS AND APPROACHES OF PPD SYSTEMS

Goals

Although states use different approaches to compensating permanent partial disability claims, the goals for PPD programs do not vary greatly. States may rank their goals differently and seek to meet them in different ways, but all states would like their PPD programs to achieve the following:

- **Promptness**--This goal is achieved when workers entitled to PPD benefits receive them shortly after any temporary disability benefits (most often called Temporary Total Disability [TTD]) end. Promptness can also refer to the time that it takes to determine the amount of any entitlement.

- **Low Employer Costs**--States do not want the costs of their workers' compensation programs to burden employers. This concern has probably never been more important than over the past decade, when many states witnessed explosive increases in the costs of workers' compensation for their employers. And in many states, the costs of permanent partial disability are higher than for any other type of indemnity benefit under workers' compensation.

- **Fairness and Adequacy**--There is considerable room for debate over the meaning of fairness as it applies to workers' compensation. Minimally, states seek to adhere to the principles of horizontal and vertical equity. The former is achieved when persons with equal circumstances receive equal outcomes. Vertical equity exists when treatment differs appropriately among persons whose circumstances differ, i.e., there is a larger benefit paid to the person with the more serious loss. Adequacy is related to the degree to which benefits replace the earnings lost due to the disability.

- **Ease of Administration and Low Transactions Costs**--Most jurisdictions find it difficult to administer their PPD programs. Frequently, the very structure of the program makes controversy and litigation commonplace. Increased complexity and controversy often lead to increases in system costs without corresponding increases in benefits to disabled workers.

- **Prompt Return to Work**--Not all states necessarily include return to work elements in their workers' compensation programs. However, all jurisdictions seek to eliminate or minimize program features that discourage persons from returning to their employment when their medical condition warrants it.

Approaches to PPD Compensation

All states use one or a combination of three fundamental approaches to PPD compensation: (1) impairment, (2) the loss of wage earning capacity, or (3) wage loss. Each approach has strengths and weaknesses. A number of states have combined approaches in an attempt to overcome the shortcomings of a single approach.

Impairment. Certain jurisdictions compensate PPD claimants primarily or entirely on the basis of their impairment, utilizing the degree of medical (functional) loss that the worker has sustained to determine the level of benefits.[1] Thus, in an impairment-based state, persons who sustain the loss of a thumb are compensated to the same degree regardless of the effect that the loss has had on their livelihood.

States that compensate on an impairment basis may modify the benefits paid depending on a claimant's individual circumstances. A modification found in most states is to vary the benefit paid with the worker's pre-injury earnings. In its purest form, a benefit would be based solely on the type or degree of impairment. For our purposes, we will consider the impairment approach to allow for modifications based on the pre-injury earnings level and on the worker's age.

Most states (although not California) have a schedule of impairments embedded in their workers' compensation statute. These schedules commonly apply to body extremities (fingers, hands, arms, toes, feet, and legs), to the eyes, and in some cases to hearing and other parts of the body. The schedules provide explicit benefits (either in numbers of weeks or in dollar amounts) for the loss or loss of use of one of these listed body parts. Such scheduled benefits are examples of impairment-based benefits. This observation is important: Some persons argue that an impairment-based system should not be used in their state, not recognizing that an existing schedule of benefits for the extremities is impairment-based.

The major criticism of an impairment-based PPD system is that it does not take account of differences in individual claimants that can result in widely varying economic outcomes despite similar impairments. For example, in the case of a conventional, scheduled injury, the loss of a small piece of a finger may have no economic consequences for an economist but will have a devastating effect on the earnings of a pianist. The large difference in outcome need not be the result, simply, of occupational differences. It is not difficult to imagine that an equivalent back impairment to two workers of the same age and occupation could lead to vastly different economic outcomes.

---

[1]Here and throughout this report, impairment refers exclusively to medically determined loss of physical or mental function, and disability refers to non-medically determined loss, i.e., the social/economic loss.

Differences in personal temperament, in family support, or in the economic conditions of the community in which a person lives may contribute to these variations in outcomes. A benefit based solely on the degree of impairment, or even one modified by age or occupation, may not adequately compensate some workers.

Supporters claim several advantages for an impairment-based scheme, including the assertion that it can deliver benefits based on uniform and objective criteria. However, there is no guarantee that a particular impairment-based system will be administered in a manner that assures uniform and objective results. Additionally, very little empirical work has been done thus far to test whether impairment-based schemes currently in use actually generate objective outcomes. Supporters also suggest that an impairment-based system does not give a worker an incentive to delay or postpone returning to work. Since the worker's benefit is based on medically determined criteria that are permanent in nature, the impairment rating and the PPD cash benefit are not affected by the worker's employment or earning status.

Loss of Wage Earning Capacity. Some states set PPD benefits based on the lost wage earning capacity (LWEC) of the worker, sometimes in combination with an impairment-based scheduled injury. Jurisdictions that use LWEC do so with a view to *projecting what the future economic effect of the permanent disability will be.*

A typical LWEC approach rates disability in the following manner. The injured worker may be given an impairment rating prepared by a treating doctor, a forensic medical person, a "neutral" doctor, or some combination of these. This medically determined rating serves as one input in the process of determining a disability rating. Typically, the impairment rating serves as a lower bound of the disability assessment.

The disability rating will be increased from that impairment level as the claimant demonstrates that his/her future earnings are likely to suffer as a consequence of the condition. To make this claim, the parties consider variables such as the person's age, working experience, education level, language skills, and the condition of the local labor market.

In addition to these factors, one criterion that appears to affect the disability rating is the post-injury work experience of the claimant up to the point when the disability determination is made. The size of the PPD award can be significantly affected by the amount of time that passes between the injury and the point that maximum medical improvement (MMI) is reached, and by the employment and earnings success or failure in the time span between injury and MMI and disability determination.

How can one determine the future economic effect of an impairment? In principle, ratings could be developed empirically--i.e., set ratings to reflect actual wages historically lost by workers in certain categories. But no LWEC system has yet been set this way. Rather, a number of practices have been developed to deal with what are intrinsically subjective evaluations. In some cases experienced persons representing the applicant and the insurer "know" what such cases are worth. They can agree to settle on the value of a PPD claim based on previous settlements with similar sets of facts.

Supporters of LWEC systems point to the parties' ability to settle familiar types of cases within narrow bounds of estimates as a virtue of this approach. They contend that subjective assessments need not result in protracted and costly disputes. However, opponents of this approach suggest that when LWEC operates in this way, individual justice is being replaced by average justice, which is little different from an impairment basis for setting benefits. But this criticism may not be appropriate: Settlements can and often do take into account individual features of claims. A more appropriate criticism is that settlements may be unrelated to either past or future actual wage losses, reflecting only consistency over time.

In practice LWEC appears to be prone to disputes. The subjective assessment of future employability and earnings for the claimant is no simple matter at best, and in a contentious environment in which either side materially gains or loses, disputes often result. Because the claimant's argument that future earnings loss will be great gains weight if the post-injury experience has been unfavorable, LWEC is also criticized on grounds that it discourages prompt return to work.

The greatest strength of the LWEC is that it allows all possible factors bearing on future earnings loss to be considered. Thus, the worker's age, education, training, experience, the local labor market, and the impairment can all be elements in the rating of disability. However, the general accuracy of these projections of future earnings loss is not known, and, case by case, ratings are not likely to correlate with actual wages lost

Wage Loss. A small number of states rely on an approach to PPD known as wage loss (WL). This method compensates workers with permanent partial disabilities *based on their actual loss of wages*, not on the forecast of their earnings loss (LWEC).

In a typical WL state, compensation benefits are paid so long as the worker is unable to return either to work or to the pre-injury level of earnings. Even when the person does return to employment at or above the pre-injury earnings level, a subsequent drop in earnings can cause compensation benefits to be renewed.

The primary strength of a working WL approach is that it can compensate workers for the economic consequences of their work injury or illness. This is a reasonable objective for any social insurance program, and it appears to have been the intent of those who created workers' compensation. The WL approach shares with the LWEC method of compensation the advantage of giving employers an incentive to rehire their disabled employees if an employer's insurance costs are sensitive to actual experience. Moreover, both the WL and LWEC seem to provide a standard for assessing their performance--i.e., they can be judged by the extent to which either serves to actually replace lost earnings.

The major difficulty with the WL approach is the challenge of administrating it well. Actual wage loss--the target for benefits and the standard for judging success of administration--is, in practice, almost impossible to determine. Is the permanent impairment the source of some temporary or long-term decline in a worker's earnings, subsequent to having reached maximum medical improvement? Or is the job loss or reduced wage rate or lower average hours of work a product of labor market conditions and independent of the workplace injury or disease? And to what extent does a WL approach provide a disincentive to a worker to restore his or her actual wage earnings?

In its pure form, a WL approach would provide no PPD benefit to a worker who sustains even a very serious impairment if that condition causes no earnings loss to the worker. A shortcoming of the approach is the apparent public value that it is unfair for a seriously impaired worker to receive no compensation for a PPD simply because the worker has had the personal strength to return to employment at earnings comparable to the pre-injury level.

Some systems deal with the practical problems of a WL approach by not confronting them. Rather than estimating actual wage losses in each case, parties quickly close cases through compromise. The result is to convert a WL approach to one that is an implicit LWEC scheme.

Hybrids

No two states have exactly the same system for compensating PPD. Often states hybridize their approach to paying these benefits. Three types of hybrids are common.

- A state may employ an alternative system for different types of injuries. For example, a state system might use a schedule of benefits (impairment) for injuries to certain parts of the body and use a LWEC or WL benefit for other, unscheduled injuries. Oregon is such a state.

- Some states pay both an impairment benefit *and* a LWEC or WL benefit for the same form of injury. Massachusetts has used this method for its PPD cases. Florida and Texas use another variant basing payments on impairment only, with additional payments made for WL in very limited cases after impairment benefits have ended.

- The same injury may lead to either an impairment-only benefit *or* a wage-loss-only benefit. Until very recently, Minnesota used this approach. Some prefer to term this a bifurcated approach.

Where states have mixed methods for paying PPD benefits, they have sought to avoid some of the problems attached to a particular approach. However, their success in fine-tuning such hybrids is arguable. The state-specific discussion that follows provides a more detailed consideration of these issues.

PPD EXPERIENCE IN TEXAS, COLORADO, MINNESOTA, WASHINGTON, AND OREGON

We now turn to a more detailed discussion of the PPD system in selected states. We begin by describing the PPD systems in Texas, Colorado, Minnesota, Washington, and Oregon. These five are not a representative sample of all states; rather, they were selected because their experiences with their PPD systems--problems, reforms, and outcomes--hold potential lessons for the assessment of California's PPD system. Specifically,

- Colorado and Texas made very significant changes in their laws within the past 5-6 years. Though these modifications are relatively recent, we can draw some conclusions about the development of their new programs.
- Oregon has made some major changes in its workers' compensation program since 1990. In some structural respects, Oregon's approach to PPD is more like California's than is any other state's. Oregon's PPD scheme is being reshaped by both legislative and court-imposed decisions.
- Washington's permanent partial disability program shares several unusual features with California's: Quantitative impairment ratings are not done by doctors, although ratings are made by a process that draws on medical evaluations. Another key similarity to California before the 1993 statutory changes is that medical evaluations are rarely done by treating doctors.
- Minnesota represents an approach somewhat different from that found in most states. It once used a bifurcated approach to PPD benefits with the basis for setting benefits depending on whether or not the worker had returned to work. However,

Minnesota recently abandoned the bifurcated approach and replaced it with a uniform approach.

Unfortunately, the information available about the outcomes of the PPD systems in these states--both earlier systems and those resulting from recent changes--is uneven. Thus the profiles presented here are not always consistent.

Texas

Introduction. During the 1980s, Texas typified those states whose workers' compensation programs were regarded as troubled. System costs rose rapidly, along with expressions of employer discontent. One very large domestic insurer was on the verge of insolvency (and subsequently was forced out of business), and other insurance carriers were unwilling to underwrite much business in the state. Because Texas is almost unique in not having a mandatory system, increasing numbers of employers chose (legally) not to have their employees covered by workers' compensation insurance. The permanent partial disability scheme was only one of many system features that was perceived to be responsible for the state's problems.

In several respects, Texas's approach to PPD was a conventional one. Certain "specific" injuries (essentially to extremities and the eyes) appeared in a schedule. The loss of an extremity provided the employee with 66-2/3 percent of the worker's average weekly wage, subject to a weekly minimum and maximum, for the number of weeks listed for that injury in the statute. The loss of or loss of use of a hand paid the weekly benefit for 150 weeks.

However, if an injury resulted in the *partial* loss (or partial loss of use) of a member, the criteria for assessing the extent of the loss were no longer purely impairment-based. Instead, the statute required that the compensation be determined by taking into account the physical injury (impairment) *and* the age and occupation of the employee. (These variables were not factored in according to any mechanistic or quantitative formula.) Thus, a "specific" injury resulting in a *partial* loss was compensated according to some hybrid of impairment and lost wage earning capacity. The duration of compensation specified for the loss of the entire member served as the upper bound for the duration of benefits in cases involving a partial loss.

"General" injuries, those not on the schedule and that resulted in a permanent partial disability, were to be compensated in the amount that was 66-2/3 percent of the difference between the worker's average weekly wage at the time of injury and the person's wage earning capacity at the time of permanent partial incapacity. Wage earning capacity meant "ability and fitness to work in gainful employment for any type of remuneration, . . . whether or not the person is actually employed. It does not necessarily mean the actual wages, income, or other benefits received during the period inquired about."[2] The subjectivity of this formulation invited contention. Moreover, because compensation for "general" injuries could be stretched to result in larger awards than for a "specific" injury, gifted attorneys found ways to turn a specific injury into one that was general.

The Current Law. In 1989 the Texas law was changed, effective 1/1/91. The basis for awarding compensation for a permanent partial disability was completely revised. PPD benefits are now based solely on the degree of permanent impairment, with one notable exception.

If an employee is left with a permanent impairment at the time that temporary income benefits (TTD) end, the worker is entitled to receive an impairment income benefit (IIB). This benefit is set at 70 percent of the worker's average weekly wage. The worker is entitled to receive 3 weeks of benefits for every point of rated impairment, i.e., a 10 percent impairment rating qualifies the worker to receive 30 weeks of benefits. By statute the impairment is to be rated on the basis of the *AMA Guides*, 3rd edition, 2nd printing.

There is no adjustment made for the worker's age, education, occupation, etc. Weekly benefits are a function solely of the worker's average weekly wage, subject to the statutory maximum. No adjustment is made to raise or lower the amount of the weekly benefit if impairment rates are higher or lower. The only variable is the number of weeks

---

[2]Texas Pattern Jury Charges, 1970.

these payments are made, i.e., three weeks for every percentage point of impairment.

The Texas law recognizes that a benefit based strictly on an impairment rating could do serious harm to some workers who suffer substantial earnings loss from their injury or disease. To open the door for such workers, under certain circumstances a worker may draw a supplemental income benefit (SIB) when the IIB expires. The SIB is set at 80 percent of the difference between 80 percent of the worker's pre-injury wages and the worker's weekly earnings over the reporting period. A SIB may not exceed 70 percent of the state's average weekly wage. The maximum entitlement to weekly benefits (including temporary, impairment, and supplemental) is 401 weeks from the date of injury--unless the worker is permanently and totally disabled.

To constrain the applicability of SIBs, only workers with serious impairments, 15 percent or higher, are eligible. Moreover, while an eligible worker must have made a good faith effort to obtain employment commensurate with his or her ability to work, he or she cannot have returned to work or, if returned, can earn no more than 79 percent of pre-injury earnings. In addition, the worker cannot have taken the impairment income benefit as a lump sum. Workers awarded a SIB must be reevaluated every 3 months.

Estimating Impairment. The Texas law seeks to provide PPD benefits based on uniform and objective standards and to minimize disputes and litigation. Clearly, any impairment-based approach to PPD benefits must anticipate that the primary source of disputes will be the impairment rating, though other issues may also be disputed. In Texas, the worker is able to choose the treating physician. The initial impairment rating is made by the treating doctor, either when the worker has reached maximum medical improvement (MMI) or when 104 weeks of benefits have accrued. The rating must be made in accordance with the *AMA Guides*, 3rd edition. The insurer may also designate the doctor who will rate the worker. The worker and the insurer have up to 90 days to dispute the initial rating.

In the event that either party disputes the rating, the Texas Workers' Compensation Commission issues a written order assigning a "designated doctor." The insurer and the employee have 10 days to agree to substitute a designated doctor. However, in most instances the Commission's selection is utilized. If the designated doctor is selected by agreement of the parties, that doctor's impairment rating is binding. If the designated doctor is one selected by the Commission, the doctor's rating is given "presumptive weight." Though presumptive weight is not as conclusive in law as a binding determination, the former has rarely been successfully challenged and overturned.

Designated Doctors. To be a designated doctor, the individual must have completed a Commission-approved training course in the use of the *AMA Guides* and passed a written examination on the rating of impairment. Designated doctors must also take additional training at least once every two years. (Treating doctors, who may also rate, have no such requirements.) The designated doctor must have been regularly treating patients over the previous three years. Doctors can be removed from the list for a variety of causes including four refusals to examine a worker within 90 days, unnecessary referrals to other doctors, or submitting an impairment rating that is subsequently overturned. Approximately 1,000 designated doctors are on the Commission's list.

The designated doctor is paid by the insurer according to a maximum fee schedule established by the Commission. For example, the maximum fee is $300 for the designated doctor to rate one body area and $150 for up to two other body areas.

Evaluating the Texas Approach. An evaluation of the Texas system and its changes highlights limits in assessing permanent partial disability systems. First, major changes in compensating PPD cases occurred as part of a total system reform. Although other states made broad changes in workers' compensation systems at this same time, the 1989 Texas reform may have been more sweeping than any other. The former state agency, the Industrial Accident Board (IAB), one of the nation's weakest state agencies, was replaced by the Texas Workers' Compensation Commission (TWCC), one that is highly proactive. The former system was highly litigious while the new one is not. A survey of workers with injury dates from 1/1/91 to 6/30/94 revealed that 5 percent were involved in a dispute and 8 percent hired an attorney, compared to over 50 percent under the old law.[3] Of those reporting that there was some dispute in their case, 42 percent had an attorney, 35 percent had no attorney and did not attempt to hire one, and 23 percent had no attorney and were unsuccessful in an attempt to hire one. The near absence of attorneys in Texas who take workers' compensation cases for claimants suggests that the environment there is quite different than that in most other jurisdictions. In short, major changes in PPD compensation grew out of dissatisfaction with the workers' compensation system as a whole. As a consequence, it is problematic to credit or blame outcome changes solely to the new approach to PPD.

An evaluation of the Texas PPD approach under its new workers' compensation system must focus on three central issues: (1) the impairment rating system, (2) the benefits provided to workers with permanent impairments, and (3) the effect on return to work.

Impairment Rating System. As noted above, the initial impairment rating is made by the treating doctor, though in about 17 percent of cases a doctor to whom the worker was referred, typically a specialist, conducted the initial rating.[4] For indemnity claims with injury dates from 7/1/94 to 11/7/96, an insurer's doctor also conducted an impairment rating after the initial evaluation in about 8 percent of the cases and a designated doctor was used in approximately 18 percent of the claims. In some instances the designated doctor became involved because the worker was dissatisfied with the initial rating.

A notable feature of the Texas system is that the treating doctor need not have been trained in rating impairment or in the use of the *AMA Guides*. Also of interest is that the designated doctor is provided with the rating assigned by the initial rater and, if applicable, the rating assessed by the insurance company doctor. A recent study completed by the Research and Oversight Council on Workers' Compensation in Texas concludes that "there are marked differences in the impairment ratings being assigned by treating, insurance, and designated doctors."

---

[3] "Attorney Representation of Injured Workers Is Low Following 1989 Reforms," *Texas Monitor*, Vol. 1, No. 1, Spring 1996, p. 11.

[4] "Discrepancies in Impairment Ratings by Types of Doctors," *Texas Monitor*, Vol. 1, No. 4, Winter 1996, p. 7.

Treating and insurance doctors show the biggest discrepancy with a mean
difference of 6 rating points; treating and designated doctors are quite
close, on average just 1.6 points apart. Both the treating physician
and designated doctors consistently give higher ratings than those given
by insurance doctors.[5]

Initially the designated doctor scheme created some delay in
resolving medical disputes. Regulations now provide for early
scheduling of examinations and for prompt reporting by examiners.
Compared with many other states, most disputes in Texas are resolved
with relatively little delay.[6]

A problem with the designated doctors approach is the difficulty of
finding specialists, especially in rural areas. For example, a thinly
populated county may not have a designated doctor in a certain
specialty, or the designated doctor may have treated the injured worker,
and is therefore ineligible to serve. A designated doctor from another
specialty may then be asked to do the rating. In some jurisdictions,
workers may be sent elsewhere for an examination or a doctor may be
brought in from another locale to do the rating. The problem is not
unique to Texas but may be more severe because the population is so
dispersed and the state so large.

Benefits Provided to Workers with Permanent Impairments

Developing a full picture of the new Texas worker's compensation
system will take many years. Even for injury year 1991, the complete
picture is still emerging. For example, though an injury may have
occurred in 1991, a compensable claim may not develop for several years.
Once compensation begins, the employee may receive TTD benefits for up
to two years. If the claim results in permanent impairment, PPD
benefits can be payable for several years (for three weeks per point of
impairment). Under special circumstances SIBs may be paid over an
additional period.

---

[5]"Discrepancies," p. 8.
[6]Barth and Eccelston (1995), p. 60.

For injury year 1991, TTD benefits were paid to 113,200 employees.[7]
Another 37,972 workers received impairment income benefits, with the
average weekly benefit of $225 paid for 34 weeks.[8] As of 12/31/95,
1,640 workers had received SIB benefits with an average weekly payment
of $252, and 6,928 injury cases from accident year 1991 had been
classified as potential SIB cases.[9] Of this potential number, 18
percent had received at least one SIB payment, 8 percent were still
receiving IIBs, 58 percent had gone 13 months or more beyond their last
IIB and were no longer eligible for a SIB, and 15 percent had completed
their IIBs within the past 12 months. According to the state's Research
and Oversight Council on Workers' Compensation, new SIB claims are
likely to be in the range of 1,500 to 2,300 new cases annually.[10]

SIB cases tend to be disproportionately contentious, in part
because the entitlement to a SIB must be renewed every three months.
Thus, there is a potential for four disputes per year over the size of
benefit payments and whether any payments are warranted. It is too
early to assess fully the level of disputes over SIBs.

A critical issue regarding Texas's approach is the unavailability
of SIBs for workers with impairment ratings below 15 percent. The Texas
approach can create economic difficulty for workers whose impairments
are rated below 15 percent, but who suffer continuing injury-related
earnings loss after the impairment income benefit ends. A 1996 survey
of persons with 1993 work injuries who received final impairment ratings
between 8 and 14 percent examined the significance of this issue.[11] Of
these, 34 percent reported that they were not working at the time of
interview due to their work injury. One half of these (17 percent of
the cohort) had no single calendar quarter since their injury where
their earnings were at least two-thirds of their pre-injury average

[7]"An Early Look at Supplemental Income Benefits," *Texas Monitor*,
Vol. 1, No. 2, Summer 1996, p. 2.
[8]Texas Workers' Compensation Commission (1997).
[9]At least one impairment income benefit had been paid, and the
impairment rating was 15 percent or higher.
[10]Research and Oversight Council on Workers' Compensation (1996a),
p. 8.
[11]"Return-to-Work Patterns for Permanently Impaired Workers," *Texas
Monitor*, Vol. 1, No. 4, Winter 1996, pp. 1-3.

weekly wage. The other 17 percent who were not employed had at least one calendar quarter in which post-injury earnings were equal to or greater than two-thirds of their previous earnings. (Excluded from these estimates are another 11 percent who were not employed, but for reasons not related to their work injury.)

Return to Work. An important criterion in evaluating the new law as it relates to PPD is its effect on the promptness of return to work. A study of return to work patterns under the old law (1989) and the new law (1991) was conducted by the University of Texas for the Texas Workers' Compensation Research Center.[12] The study concluded that the new law has resulted in quicker return to work and a smaller decline in gross earnings. For example, under the old law, 30 percent of the injured workers were employed in both calendar quarters after the quarter when injury occurred, compared with 40 percent under the new law.

It is not possible to say whether the reform law has caused coverage to expand under workers' compensation in Texas. Precise estimates of non-coverage did not exist under the old system. It is widely believed, however, that as insurance costs have fallen for workers' compensation with the new law, fewer employers are opting out of the system. In 1995, 44 percent of employers were non-subscribers; in 1996, that number had fallen to 39 percent.[13] Over the same time period, the number of uncovered employees in the state fell from 21 percent to 20 percent.

If the rate of non-subscription has fallen as a result of the reform law, the cause of the decline would be attributable to many aspects of the law, not solely to changes in the PPD system.

Colorado

Introduction. Until 1991, Colorado relied on a traditional, bifurcated approach to PPD benefits. A schedule listed benefits for the loss of extremities. For determining the extent of a nonscheduled permanent disability, the statute defined the criteria as ". . . taking

---

[12]King, Pavone, and Marshall (1993).
[13]Research and Oversight Council on Workers' Compensation (1996b).

into consideration not only the manifest weight of the evidence but also the general physical condition and mental training, ability, former employment and education of the claimant."[14] In practice, "manifest weight" was applied by taking into account the worker's age, employment, and anticipated wage loss. The maximum benefit available for a permanent partial disability under the old law was $37,560.

The enactment of SB 218, effective in 1991, sought to change the nature of the workers' compensation program in Colorado. Its goal was to curb or reduce employer costs by taking aim at a variety of perceived causes of difficulty: relatively frequent findings that an injured worker was permanently and totally disabled, escalating medical costs, substantial litigation, and disputes about permanent partial disability.

Senate Bill 218. The 1991 law made sweeping changes in Colorado's system. The permanent partial disability system, though still bifurcated, was changed to an impairment standard. A scheduled benefit is paid at a flat rate of $150 for the number of weeks shown in the schedule. For example, a worker who has lost (the use of) an arm is entitled to 208 weeks of benefits, at $150/week ($31,200) in addition to any temporary total disability benefits. No adjustments are made to take account of the worker's age or pre-injury earnings level.

Nonscheduled benefits are based on a medically determined impairment rating utilizing the *AMA Guides*, 3rd edition. The benefit is calculated according to the following formula:

TTD rate x impairment rating x age factor x 400 weeks

Actual weekly payments are subject to a maximum of 50 percent of the state's average weekly wage, but not less than $150 week. A maximum benefit of $60,000 from both TTD and PPD benefits applies for any impairment rated 25 percent or less. For an impairment rated above 25 percent, the combined TTD and PPD benefit ceiling is $120,000.

The age factor has a sizable effect on benefits. It is noteworthy because it is at odds with other jurisdictions that explicitly or

---

[14]C. R. S. # 8-422-110(b).

implicitly take age into account. Colorado's age factor *causes the size of a PPD benefit to fall as age increases*. For an injury to a worker 20 years of age or younger, the age factor is 1.80, dropping in increments of .02 for each additional year. Thus the age factor falls to 1.20 for a 50-year-old and to 1.00 for a worker age 60 or older.

Several other features of the Colorado scheme warrant notice. While a worker's wage does not affect the size of a scheduled benefit, it is a basis for a nonscheduled benefit. In most cases, the amount of benefits potentially payable is considerably higher in the case of a nonscheduled injury. Also, for purposes of the $60,000 or $120,000 ceilings just discussed, any TTD benefits are combined with the PPD award; however, no such linkage occurs in scheduled injuries. The large difference in ceilings for nonscheduled injuries rated over 25 percent creates an important target for workers to exceed and a likely source of dispute. The potentially large difference between scheduled and nonscheduled impairments creates incentives for workers to escape the schedule and another source of dispute.

The 1991 law provided low benefits for serious scheduled injuries, both in absolute terms and relative to unscheduled benefits. In 1992, House Bill 1365 sought to remedy this by removing from the schedule any injury that resulted in the *total* loss or *total* loss of use of an arm, hand, foot, leg, or eye. The schedule still applies to injuries that result in the partial loss of or partial loss of use of one of these members.

Rating Impairment. The importance of the medical impairment rating as a tool for improving the PPD system was evident to those who shaped SB 218. The statute provides that the rating be done, where possible, by the treating doctor, with some provision for resolving disputes over the rating.

A two-tier accreditation system was created for health care providers. Persons accredited at Level I (based on a training session and an examination) are able to bill for primary care to employees whose work injuries cause them to lose 3 or more days of work.[15] Medical

---

[15]Rules of Procedure XIV, L, Colorado Division of Workers' Compensation (as of April 1997).

doctors or doctors of osteopathy need not be accredited at Level I in order to provide such services, but only physicians accredited at Level II can rate impairment. Level II accreditation requires state-mandated training and passage of an appropriate test. Chiropractors and psychologists cannot become Level II accredited.

Treating doctors provide an initial rating. If the treating physician is not Level II accredited, he or she will recommend another physician to rate the worker. The insurer may have the worker rated as well.

Any party to a claim may request that an impairment rating be conducted by a Division Independent Medical Examiner (IME), a physician who is Level II accredited and has at least 384 hours per year of direct patient care, or certification by the American Board of Independent Medical Examiners or the American Academy of Disability Evaluation Physicians. The IME may be selected by the agreement of the two parties--this rarely happens--in which case the IME's findings are binding. Where no such agreement occurs, the Division submits the names of three potential IMEs, with each side able to strike one name. An IME's finding in these cases can be overturned only by clear and convincing evidence. In practice the treating doctor's rating can carry considerable weight.

The Division has a panel of approximately 250 Level II IMEs. Currently, about 700 physicians are Level II accredited.

Special Conditions. SB 218 contained specific provisions that limit claims for mental stress. Permanent partial disability benefits will not be awarded for mental stress arising from certain circumstances, e.g., as result of a personnel action. However, no special constraints are placed on PPD benefits for mental stress claims arising from injuries for victims of crime or violence or in cases commonly known as physical-mental, i.e., a mental impairment that is a consequence of a compensable physical injury. For other compensable mental injuries, PPD benefits are limited to 12 weeks of benefits.

Certain repetitive strain injuries including carpal tunnel syndrome are compensable as a scheduled impairment. Other repetitive injuries are considered nonscheduled.

The Colorado Supreme Court recently handed down a series of decisions related to impairment.[16] In one case, an injured worker sustained both a scheduled and nonscheduled permanent impairment. At issue was whether or not the total of the two impairments could be added and compensated as a nonscheduled impairment. The court found that the aggregated rating could be compensated as an unscheduled disability, entitling the claimant to a larger award. The real significance of this decision flows from the sizable difference between unscheduled and scheduled impairments. If the decision is left intact, a worker with a scheduled impairment may claim a mental injury (physical-mental) that would then allow the claimant to leave the schedule. It may also push the worker's rating above the important 25 percent threshold.

This outcome may be short-lived. A bill has been recently passed to undercut the Supreme Court's position but was vetoed by the Governor.[17]

Evaluating the Experience Under SB 218 and Its Amendments. Since 1993, Colorado has had an actuarial firm conduct annual closed claim surveys to analyze how its system is functioning. The 1997 study examines a sample of 1,693 claims involving permanent benefits. The claims, arising from injuries suffered in 1991, were closed some time in the period between October 1991 and August 1996.[18] Data are provided by insurance carriers.

The study has important limitations. Because it tracks the experience of claims beginning in 1991, it contains almost no information that permits comparison of pre-1991 and post-SB 218 experience. In addition, because it looks at closed claims, it does not include the small number of cases that remained open in late 1996, some of which involve very serious (expensive) claims and cases in litigation.

Despite these limitations, the study indicates that a very sizable reduction has occurred in the average costs of permanent disability

---

[16]See *Mountain City Meat Co. v. Emiliano Oqueda*, Colorado No. 95 SC 246, 4/24/96.
[17]Colorado Senate Bill 97-139, Sixty-First General Assembly.
[18]Millimann & Robertson, Inc. (1997).

claims under SB 218. Some of the reduction must be attributed to the 1991 law change that reduced the number of permanent and total disability cases.

Unfortunately, for more than 90 percent of the claims, no impairment/disability rating was indicated. Thus it is not possible to learn from available data whether many claims are clustered at or near the all-important 25 percent threshold. The data do show that for every unscheduled impairment case closed, there were 1.18 scheduled cases closed.

A 1996 study has data from the Colorado Division of Workers' Compensation on impairment ratings for claims arising after 7/1/91 and closed by 1995.[19] These data (see Table 3.1) may have a skewed distribution because of the nature of cases remaining open. Unfortunately, no other data on the distribution of impairment ratings are available at this time.

Table 3.1

**The Distribution of Claims
by Impairment Rating**

Impairment Ratings Percentage	Percentage of All Ratings
1-5	23
6-10	26
11-15	26
16-20	17
21-25	7
26 or above	5
Mean rating = 12%	

Minnesota

Introduction. For at least a decade or more, the workers' compensation system in Minnesota has been considered problem-ridden. As a result, workers' compensation laws have been changed frequently. In 1995, a major set of modifications were legislated, some of which

---

[19]Telles and Fox (1996), p. 33.

fundamentally restructured the PPD program. In certain respects, however, other portions of the state's PPD scheme were left unaltered.

The 1984 Change in PPD Compensation. Prior to legislation that became effective on January 1, 1984, PPD benefits were based on subjective disability ratings made by the treating doctor. The statute identified the maximum weeks of benefits associated with a given impairment, but there was no common or standardized method of evaluating anything less than a 100 percent loss to the body part involved. For example, back impairments were included in the schedule, but there was no guidance as to how to rate anything less than the full loss of the back.

The law was changed in 1984, and the Department of Labor and Industry was given responsibility for developing a new permanent rating schedule. The resulting schedule included an extensive list of disabling conditions along with the criteria for rating them. If a condition was not in the schedule, then PPD benefits could not be paid for it.

The 1984 law also created a new bifurcated approach to PPD benefits. An impairment compensation (IC) benefit was to be paid to a permanently disabled worker in line with the impairment rating taken from the state's schedule. A step function of benefits was provided that increased with the degree of impairment. For example, for an impairment rated at 0-25 percent, the worker would receive $750 per point of rating. For an impairment rated in the 26-30 percent range, the benefit would be $800 per point. If the worker had returned to work for 30 days or more, the IC benefit would be paid as a lump sum. If a job offer had been made but not accepted, the IC benefit would be paid out at the PPD rate until the award was exhausted.

As an alternative to the IC benefit, an Economic Recovery Compensation (ERC) benefit was to be paid to an employee who sustained a permanent impairment and had not been offered suitable employment within 90 days of having reached maximum medical improvement. Unlike the IC benefit, the ERC benefit was tied to the worker's pre-injury earnings level. Again, a stepwise formula linked the number of weeks of benefits to the severity of the impairment, as measured by the state rating schedule. The weekly benefit was set at the worker's TTD rate. As a result, higher paid workers received larger ERC benefits than did lower paid workers. ERC benefits were more generous than IC benefits. The minimum ERC benefit was 120 percent of the IC benefit. However, the ERC benefit was always paid out to the worker weekly, not as a lump sum.

The aim of the two track approach was to encourage employers to rehire their injured workers. However, it also created an incentive for workers not to return work. And the two different benefits encouraged either side to litigate over the issue so as to affect the type and size of the PPD benefit.

Under either IC or ERC benefits, the evaluation of the degree of impairment is central to determining the size of the award. Although Minnesota law does not prevent the use of neutral doctors, they are not used in PPD disputes. Without neutral doctors, hearing officers engaged in dispute resolution or adjudication must rely on their own judgment as to which impairment assessment is to be accepted.

By 1995, 35 percent of 1990 indemnity claims and 32 percent of 1991 indemnity claims resulted in a PPD benefit.[20] Over the years 1984 to 1991, the average (mean) disability rating for an IC case was typically in the 6-7 percent range. The mean ERC rating varied over the same time period and was in the range of 8-11 percent. As of 1995, ERC cases were 20 percent of PPD cases for injuries occurring between 1985 and 1990.

Among claims closed in 1995, including injury dates from 1984 through 1995, the average benefit in an IC claim was $5,200, about 37 percent of the average $14,000 benefit paid in an ERC claim.[21]

The 1995 Amendments. A 1995 statute fundamentally changed the state's PPD program, eliminating the ERC benefit which was seen as a source of litigation and cost.[22] Under the new law, Chapter 231, a worker who sustains a PPD can receive only an IC benefit, paid not as a

---

[20]Data supplied by the Research and Statistics Unit, Minnesota Department of Labor and Industry, 1997.

[21]Data supplied by the Research and Statistics Unit, Minnesota Department of Labor and Industry, 1997.

[22]Wisconsin has also experienced far higher litigation for its "Earning Capacity Benefits" claims (similar to Minnesota's ERCs) than for claims evaluated solely on degree of impairment. Boden (1988).

lump sum, but over time at the weekly TTD rate. In addition, a ceiling of 104 weeks has been set on TTD benefits. Minnesota followed other states that have simplified their PPD systems and limited the use of lump sum benefits.

The Minnesota Department of Labor and Industry estimates that the change in the PPD approach will reduce system costs in the long term by about 2 percent and that the overall effect of the 1995 amendments will be to reduce workers' compensation costs by approximately 11 percent.[23]

Washington State

Introduction. Washington State is one of six states that does not permit private insurers to sell workers' compensation insurance. As an exclusive ("monopolistic") state fund state, it has responsibilities both as the insurance carrier and as the agency that administers the state law. Self insurance is permitted in Washington.

The state's approach to permanent partial disability is of interest because it shares several elements with California. One of these is that physicians who do impairment examinations do not actually report a percentage of impairment but, instead, choose a category, e.g., "moderate," that directly or indirectly converts to a quantitative rating. And like California in the recent past, impairment exams are seldom done by the attending (treating) doctor.

PPD Benefits. Like Colorado, in Washington permanent disabilities are either specified or unspecified. Specified injuries are those that appear in a list or schedule in the statute, and for which specified sums are provided. For example, as of 7/1/96, the total loss, or loss of use, of an arm was set at $77,257. The benefit amount is subject to annual change in line with the Consumer Price Index. The benefit is paid in addition to temporary disability benefits. An injury that results in the partial loss, or loss of use, of a specified member is to be compensated proportionate to the degree of loss. Thus, if a worker is found to have lost 50 percent of the use of an arm, the PPD benefit is set at $38,628 (50 percent x 77,257).

---

[23]Minnesota Department of Labor and Industry (1995), p. 36.

Unspecified permanent partial disability is also compensated solely based on the degree of medical impairment. Benefits for an unspecified disability (backs, internal organs, etc.) are based on the degree of impairment multiplied by the whole amount set by statute for body impairment. As of 7/1/96, total body impairment in Washington was valued at $128,762, subject again to adjustment by the Consumer Price Index. Thus, a worker with a 30 percent impairment rating could receive $38,629 (30 percent x $128,762) for an unspecified permanent disability.

Benefits for a permanent partial disability are paid to the worker at the same rate as for a temporary total disability. That rate will vary depending upon the worker's marital status and the number of children in the household. A ceiling on temporary total disability (or PPD) monthly benefits is set at 120 percent of the state's average monthly wage. A worker with a permanent partial disability may apply to the state agency to have the monthly benefit payment converted to a lump sum.

Determining the Degree of Impairment. Impairment is rated according to the type of disability. Specified loss, that is, an impairment associated with any loss of vision or hearing, an amputation, or the loss of function of extremities, is evaluated based on the most recent edition (4th) of the *AMA Guides*. An unspecified disability, for example, a permanent impairment of the spine or internal organs or a psychiatric disorder, is rated according to the state's own Category Rating System.[24] The system aims to provide consistent bases for rating and to make them relatively simple to apply. For example, a dorso-lumbar and lumbo-sacral impairment would be rated based on 5 sets of variables:

- Muscle weakness and either atrophy or EMG abnormalities
- Reflex loss (asymmetric)
- Imaging and x-ray findings
- Other findings, including decreased range of motion
- Any surgery (with or without fusion)

---

[24]Department of Labor and Industries (1996a), p. 16.

The first four factors are essentially evaluated as being "none," "mild," "moderate," or "marked," with numerical ratings for each category. Criteria are given in the Category Rating Guides to facilitate consistent choices. A simple arithmetic formula averages these, though the final score is not the impairment rating. Thus, though the impairment evaluator derives a quantitative assessment, that number is ultimately (and simply) converted to an impairment rating by someone other than the evaluator. It would take no effort for the impairment evaluator to learn how to transform that rating to an impairment percentage, and it is likely that experienced evaluators know this.

Impairment rating examinations can be conducted by one of three types of persons: (1) attending doctors if they are doctors of medicine, osteopathy, podiatry, or dentistry or are chiropractors on an approved list; (2) referral doctors (consultants-specialists) drawn from these same categories, or (3) doctors who have been approved by the Department to conduct independent medical examinations and who may work as individuals or as members of panels. The latter, physicians who can do impairment ratings and other independent medical examinations even if they are the attending doctor, must be certified by the Department upon meeting two of three criteria: They must be Board-certified, in full- or part-time active practice, and/or meet a geographic need. Approved examiners are not obligated to accept referrals.

Independent Medical Examinations. In most states, medical examinations conducted by "neutral" doctors typically occur as a consequence of a dispute. However, this is not the case in Washington. Although attending physicians are encouraged by the agency to do impairment evaluations of their patients, they seldom do so.[25] In cases where the attending physician does not evaluate, a claims examiner for the State Fund will usually ask that an IME be selected to do so. If the attending doctor completes an evaluation, the State Fund or the worker may ask that an IME be appointed to do another evaluation.

_____
[25]Department of Labor and Industries (1996b), p. 52.

The independent medical examination may be conducted by an individual examiner or by a doctor who belongs to a panel. A panel is an organization or group of doctors who provide examinations.[26] In 1995, 19 percent of IME examinations were conducted by single examiners not on a panel, 72 percent by panel doctors, and about 9 percent by attending physicians.

About 32,000 independent medical examinations were conducted in 1995, at a total cost of $14.4 million.[27] The fee paid to a physician to conduct an examination varies from $156 (for a limited IME, single examiner), or $228 (a standard examination), to $258 (a complex examination, single examiner). A psychiatrist receives $448 for an independent medical examination. The same fee schedule applies to examinations done by the attending or consulting physician or an appointed IME.

The Department has encouraged attending doctors to do more independent medical examinations.[28] In 1995, the Department began two pilot programs on long-term disability prevention and has used these to communicate to local disability physicians the utility of their conducting evaluations of their own patients.[29] Apparently, there has been some increase in attending physician independent medical examinations in these communities since 1995.

Other. The category rating scheme developed by the Department of Labor and Industries has been designed for simple application. It is intended to raise the level of consistency across raters, thereby reducing the likelihood of disputes. Washington's approach provides an interesting alternative to the *AMA Guides* as a method of evaluating and rating impairments. Surprisingly, given the simplicity of this scheme, few attending physicians evaluate impairment in Washington. The reasons for this may be a combination of custom, of the fee paid for such examinations, and/or of the reluctance of the attending physician to become embroiled in a legal controversy.

---

[26]Department of Labor and Industries (1996a), p. 18.
[27]Department of Labor and Industries (1996a), p. 18.
[28]Department of Labor and Industries (1995), p. 1.
[29]Department of Labor and Industries (1996c).

One other feature of Washington's approach to PPD warrants future attention. Unlike many states in the 1990s, Washington significantly raised the benefits that are available for a permanent partial disability. Because that change became effective on 7/1/93, it is too soon to determine its effect. However, the increase was sizable and it is likely that it will affect behavior by claimants, their representatives, employers, and the Department of Labor and Industries.

Oregon

Introduction. A well-publicized legislative reform of Oregon's workers' compensation program occurred in 1990 with the enactment of SB 1197. The effect of this change has been substantial. However, it is difficult to assess the full importance of SB 1197 because it was one of a series of important changes in the Oregon approach, beginning with reform in 1987 (HB 2900) and continuing in 1991 (SB 732) along with several other modifications in 1991 and subsequently.

Dissatisfaction with the Oregon approach prior to 1991 centered on the combination of very high costs to employers and low benefit levels to workers, at least as measured by several conventional standards. Overall, aggregate benefits paid for permanent partial disability per employee in the state were well above the national average. Oregon appeared to have the worst of both worlds.

The legislative changes in 1987 and 1990 did not deal directly with the *structure* of PPD benefits, though benefit levels were changed. However, other system changes brought about by the series of reforms did affect the PPD scheme in Oregon.

The PPD Approach in Oregon. Like Washington and Colorado, Oregon uses two parallel methods for determining PPD benefits. Scheduled disabilities for impairments to extremities or to vision are based solely on the degree of functional impairment. Each listed body part is valued in terms of degrees. Any partial loss, or loss of use, of an extremity is rated in proportion to the extent of the full loss of the body part, in accordance with the *AMA Guides* (3rd edition). For every degree of scheduled disability, the worker is entitled to $420. For example, the loss of a hand, valued as 150 degrees, entitles the worker to $63,000, to be paid in monthly installments of 4.35 times the weekly TTD rate, which increases with pre-injury wage levels. Scheduled disabilities of 64 degrees or less ($26,880 or less) are paid in a lump sum. The result of this approach is that a worker's total benefit for a PPD does not vary with his/her wage level, but the payout period for a lower-paid worker with a more serious impairment (above 64 degrees) will be longer.

The approach for unscheduled disabilities is not as straightforward. The amount of compensation for an unscheduled disability such as impairment of the back or internal organs or mental impairment may or may not be based exclusively on impairment. In June 1995, the Governor signed SB 369, effective immediately. As a result of this legislation, a worker with an unscheduled PPD who has returned, or has been released to return, to regular work will be compensated solely on the basis of the impairment sustained. For an unscheduled PPD where the worker has not been released to return to regular work, the PPD benefit will depend on a number of variables. These are:

- Degrees of impairment, based on the Department of Consumer and Business Services (DCBS) impairment rating method
- Age
- Education
- Adaptability factor

The formula that ties these together is:

Degrees of disability = ((age + education) x adaptability factor) + impairment rating.

If the worker is 40 years old or older, the age variable is 1. If the worker is less than 40 years, the age variable is 0.

The education variable is based on the worker's highest level of educational attainment, and on specific vocational preparation. This variable can be valued from 0 to 6.

The adaptability factor is evaluated by comparing the worker's "base functional capacity" to the residual, post-injury capacity. The former is measured through the utilization of the *Dictionary of Occupational Titles*, presumably to assess the physical needs of the pre-injury employment. This variable can range from 0 to 7. The product of the adaptability factor and the sum of the age and education values is the measure of the loss of earning capacity. This loss, measured in degrees, is added to the impairment rating to derive the disability rating.

Prior to 1992, an unscheduled disability was compensated at the flat rate of $100 per degree of disability. Thus, the maximum benefit that a worker could receive for an unscheduled PPD was $32,000, based on the maximum disability of 320 degrees. Thereafter, a tiered approach was employed to reflect the legislature's goal of providing relatively more generous benefits to the more seriously disabled workers. At the present time, the benefits are paid according to the schedule shown in Table 3.2.

Table 3.2

Benefit Payment Schedule

Degree of Disability	Benefit per Degree
0-64	$130
64.1-160	230
160.1-320	625

For example, a worker with a 75 degree permanent partial unscheduled disability is entitled to $10,850 ([64 x $130] + [11 x $230]).

Oregon explicitly seeks to compensate for the loss of wage earning capacity, at least in unscheduled cases and where release to or return to regular work has not occurred. In most other states, the loss of wage earning capacity is vague and subjective, increasing the likelihood that the matter will be litigated. Oregon has sought to use objective or mechanical (if arbitrary) measures of lost earning capacity (age, education, and physical impairment rating) to reduce the likelihood of litigation.

The level of impairment is still central in setting the value of the PPD benefit. The impairment measure is typically more important than the loss of wage earning capacity in valuing an unscheduled disability. Moreover, impairment, or at least a variant of it, plays a role in establishing the adaptability factor.

Evaluating Impairment. When an injured employee's condition becomes "medically stationary" (MMI) or the person has returned to work, the insurer may determine that a Notice of Closure may be filed. The Notice includes the insurer's finding of the degree, if any, of permanent disability. The insurer's calculations can be based, at least in part, on the attending doctor's impairment rating. Impairment ratings are based on measurement techniques drawn from the *AMA Guides*, with the values then converted to Oregon's rating scheme. The attending doctor need not have any special training or certification in order to do an impairment rating. The insurer may also choose a doctor to carry out an impairment examination.

If the worker is dissatisfied with the rating in the Notice of Closure, he or she may request a "reconsideration" by the Department's Appellate Unit. This action represents the first level in Oregon's dispute resolution process. If there has been a disagreement over an impairment rating, or if the Department finds that the medical information is not sufficient for its purposes, the Department will refer the issue to a "medical arbiter." If either party so requests, it will be referred to a panel of 3 arbiters. The arbiter or the panel is selected from a list that the Department maintains of about 400 doctors previously selected by the Department in consultation with the state's Board of Medical Examiners. The cost of the medical examination is borne by the insurer.

The findings of the arbiter or the panel are submitted to the Department for reconsideration. After the reconsideration has been completed, and an order has been issued by the Department, no subsequent medical evidence is admissible before the Department, the Workers' Compensation Board, or the courts for purposes of making findings of impairment. An appeal of the reconsideration order leads to a formal hearing before an administrative law judge of the Workers' Compensation Board.

In 1996, the Appellate Unit received almost 5,900 requests for reconsideration and over 6,299 reconsideration orders were issued.[30] About 77 percent of 1996 requests were postponed, mostly for referral to a medical arbiter. The most common issue in reconsideration orders was the extent of scheduled disability followed by unscheduled disability controversy. PPD was at issue in 85 percent of orders. In 41 percent of orders, PPD benefits were granted or increased, while in 11 percent of orders, PPD awards were reduced.

In cases in which a change was made in a PPD award, 32 percent involved a back injury. Overall the average net increase in PPD benefits through reconsideration was $2,476 or 11 degrees.

In 1996, the Hearings Division reported the lowest percentage on record of requests for hearings for determination of permanent disability (the equivalent of filing a notice of readiness in California). Moreover, both the percentage and the absolute number of requests for hearing regarding the extent of PPD had fallen for the sixth consecutive year. Several factors account for the decline. First, since 1990 there has been a decline annually in the number of accepted disability claims. Second, changes in claims procedures brought about by SB 1190 probably contributed to this decline in requests for a hearing. These include the required use of more informal dispute resolution (i.e., the reconsideration process), the use of the medical arbiter or panel, limitations on the introduction of new evidence at hearings, more objective standards in unscheduled PPD cases, and the ability to use "claim disposition agreements" (C&Rs in the California idiom). Some number of potential disputes have been eliminated by limiting the unscheduled PPD determination strictly to impairment where the worker has been released to return to regular work.

Mental and Repetitive Stress Cases. Oregon does not appear to have a severe problem with certain types of mental stress cases that have been difficult for other states. In 1987 (HB 2271), Oregon restricted

---

[30]Oregon Department of Consumer and Business Services (1997).

mental stress claims to those arising out of real and objective
employment conditions not generally found in every working situation.
Additionally, it required that there be clear and convincing evidence
that the mental disorder arose out of and in the course of employment.

Repetitive stress injuries are also not a very significant problem
in Oregon. In 1995, of 30,100 claims closed, 1,145 (slightly less than
4 percent) involved carpal tunnel syndrome with an average cost per case
of $10,900 (including medical, time loss, and any PPD benefits).[31]

System Costs. The Insurance Commissioner approved a reduction in
insurance premium rates for 1995, the fifth year in a row that rates
fell. Of course self-insurers do not buy insurance. To estimate the
cost of insurance for them, Oregon "simulates" what they would be paying
for workers' compensation insurance, were they to buy it. This
represents a simulated premium, net of dividends, had they purchased
insurance in the open market and allows for some cost comparisons. In
1995, the simulated net premium for self-insurers fell 7.3 percent, to a
level that represented 1.63 percent per $100/payroll.[32]

Florida

Introduction. Finally, it is useful to include a brief description
about noteworthy changes in Florida, which borrowed heavily from the
Texas reforms when it modified its law in 1993. In 1979, Florida had
enacted a major revision of its permanent disability benefits approach.
With very considerable national attention, Florida altered its law to
move into line with what some regarded to be the original intent of
permanent disability compensation. Workers with permanent impairment
were to receive compensation, subsequent to temporary disability
benefits, based on any loss of earnings due to the condition. Only in
the case of amputations, serious head or facial impairments, or loss of
use of 80 percent of vision in an eye would an impairment income benefit
be paid. These workers and others with permanent impairments were also
eligible to receive up to 350 weeks of benefits (originally) for any

---

[31]Data provided by the Oregon Department of Consumer and Business
Services, Research and Analysis Section, March 1997.

[32]Department of Consumer and Business Services (1997).

actual wage loss due to the disability. Benefits for wage loss were set at 90 percent of the difference between (1) the greater of (a) actual post-injury earnings or (b) what the worker could earn, and (2) 85 percent of pre-injury earnings.

In 1990 benefits were scaled back and in 1993 the system was scrapped in response to the view that it had become too costly, litigious, and difficult to administer. The redirection was also prompted by a sense that reform was needed in order to remove the disincentives to return to work that the wage loss approach had fostered.

1993 Changes. In many respects Florida's law is patterned on the new Texas scheme. Temporary benefits are limited to 104 weeks (considerably shorter than under the previous law). At 104 weeks, or at the time of MMI if earlier, the worker is rated for impairment, using an impairment schedule based on the Minnesota formulation. For each percentage point of impairment the worker is entitled to 3 weeks of benefits, set at 50 percent of the worker's temporary total disability compensation rate. A Supplemental Benefit can be paid to a worker once the impairment income benefit has been exhausted, where the worker is earning less than 80 percent of the pre-injury wage. However, only workers with an impairment rated at 20 percent or above are potentially eligible to receive a Supplemental Benefit. Unless a worker is found to be permanently and totally disabled, benefits for temporary impairment and supplemental benefits cannot exceed 401 weeks. Clearly, it is too early to determine how many workers will receive a Supplemental Benefit.

The movement by Florida away from the almost pure wage-loss approach to one based almost entirely on impairment meant that the incentive to return to work had been shifted more to the worker. To keep some pressure on the employer, the state has mounted an aggressive set of incentives for the employer. These include both carrots and sticks. A Preferred Worker Program provides an employer an insurance premium reimbursement for up to 3 years as a bonus for hiring workers who have been certificated by the Division of Workers' Compensation as previously having had a compensable injury with some permanent impairment. Further, employers with 50 or more employees must rehire their previously injured workers within 30 days of MMI or face penalties for non-compliance. Also, the Division can tap the Workers' Compensation Administrative Trust Fund to facilitate re-employment assistance for a worker. Insurance carriers are required to implement re-employment status reviews or refer workers to qualified rehabilitation providers.

PPD SYSTEMS: EMERGING THEMES

This description of a handful of states illustrates the rich variety of practices in permanent partial disability compensation. However, despite the many differences, certain generalizations can be drawn that may assist persons responsible for setting California's future course.

Type of Setting

In recent years a number of states have made dramatic changes in their approach to PPD compensation. The common thread appears to be a movement to, or in the direction of, an *impairment-based approach*. Texas shifted from its LWEC approach to an impairment system, except in the limited instances where a supplemental income benefit (a wage loss approach) could be paid. Colorado does not have a counterpart to the Texas SIB and has an even purer form of an impairment-based benefit. The age adjustment factor in Colorado, itself an oddity in its application, does not weaken the characterization of the state's movement toward an impairment-based system. Minnesota did not alter its impairment-based benefit but extended its applicability by eliminating its wage loss alternative.

The Oregon program for unscheduled disabilities is the one that most closely resembles California's, at least in broad terms. Both states are, and have been, LWEC states. Both base benefits on some anticipated future effect on earnings of a permanent impairment. Yet both Oregon and California are unlike many of the other LWEC states. In most states that compensate based on LWEC, future earnings losses are projected on an individually determined basis. This "individualized justice" can be subjective, leading to contention and high friction costs.

California and Oregon have sought to avoid contention by mechanically applying a formula to a small number of objective variables to determine future earnings losses. This avoids the attempt to project wage loss on a case-by-case basis, instead projecting it upon typical wage loss expected for workers with certain characteristics and particular levels of impairment (in California, specific types of injuries). In California, it is the worker's age and occupation that modify the measure of the worker's impairment assessment. In Oregon, for an unscheduled injury, the objective modifiers are age and education, which are then applied to the "degrees" of medical impairment and the adaptability factor, a variable related to occupation that is not completely objective in its measurement. (The adaptability factor is somewhat like California's "work capacity guidelines," which are used to rate impairment for a specified class of disabilities.) Thus, Oregon (for unscheduled injuries) and California dispense "average justice" in their PPD approach to determine the worker's loss of earning capacity.

Oregon and California differ somewhat in their treatment of scheduled injuries. Oregon's approach is more conventional and is strictly an impairment approach. California's schedule assesses the degree of impairment, then modifies this factor based on the worker's age and an occupational adjustment that considers both the age and the type of injury.

Washington can be described as a strict impairment state both for scheduled (specified) and unscheduled (unspecified) injuries. It shares a common feature with California in that it uses what Washington calls a Category Rating System. Impairment raters identify the extent of a condition in terms such as "mild," "marked," "moderate," or "none," which can be readily converted to a quantitative impairment rating, just as in California. This approach is limited to unspecified disabilities in Washington, parallel to California's application in similar cases.

Rating Impairment

With the exception of the states that rely on the wage-loss approach, determination of the amount of PPD benefits begins with the rating of the extent of the worker's permanent impairment. This is true

even in those states that utilize the LWEC approach, since the
impairment rating is one of the factors that is used to determine the
extent of the loss of a worker's earning capacity.

Because the degree or extent of impairment is so critical, the
method used to evaluate impairment can be central to the operation of
the PPD system. States have turned increasingly in recent years to
using some type of standardized rating method. Sometimes the
standardized schemes are mandatory; in other cases they are optional,
but strongly encouraged by the state agency or by adjudicators. The
most commonly used standard is the *AMA Guides to the Evaluation of
Permanent Impairment.*

In 1995, 25 states and the District of Columbia had mandated that
the *Guides* be used to rate impairment. In two other states, the *Guides*
were mandated for certain injuries while another guide was required for
other injuries. The *AMA Guides* were used, with greater or lesser
encouragement by the state's authorities, but not mandated, in eight
additional states. In three states, the *AMA Guides* were used in
addition to the *Orthopedic Surgeon's Manual.* Seven states, including
Minnesota, Oregon, Washington, and Florida, required the use of the
state's own guides.[33]

Some have criticized the use of the *Guides* in assessing *disability.*
In fact, those who believe that *disability* cannot be measured by a guide
measuring *impairment* are probably attacking the impairment-based method
of compensating permanent partial disabilities, and not the *Guides* per
se. The *AMA Guides* have been criticized[34] (e.g., *Harvard Law Review*)
and may or may not be qualitatively strong for purposes of measuring
impairment. Most of the critics point to their relevance, or lack of
it, as a standard on which to base the disability determination.

Of course, it is not solely the use of the *AMA Guides* or of any
other rating guides that causes PPD benefits to be generous or tight-
fisted. The dollar value of any impairment rating depends upon the size

---

[33]Usage of the *AMA Guides* reaches even abroad. Victoria State in
Australia relies heavily on the *Guides* and has mandated their use in
determining eligibility for use of the common law remedy in work injury
cases.

[34]See, e.g., Stone (1988), and Pryor (1990).

of any weekly benefits and the length of time over which these are to be paid. Either of these can be modified so as to expand, contract, or leave unchanged the size of a PPD program. Advocates for guides believe they have a rational basis and provide more consistency in ratings. However, states that are considering adopting a guide should understand that using such standards will not eliminate all variations in impairment ratings. Even when guides are used by conscientious and objective raters, differences in ratings can occur.

A more specific criticism of the *Guides* comes from those who note that a number of jurisdictions use older editions of the *Guides* rather than the most current versions. Among the reasons states give for using an older edition is that a state's constitution might not permit a legislature to require ex ante that new *Guides* be adopted as they become available.

Other critics focus on areas of the *Guides* that they perceive to be weak or where the *Guides* are mute. In most instances where jurisdictions have developed their own guides, they have relied on some sections of the *AMA Guides* and then supplemented them as desired. Florida's impairment guide is largely patterned after Minnesota's. British Columbia has its own guide, one that draws heavily upon the *AMA Guides*.

In most states, impairment ratings are made by the treating doctor. Typically, the treating doctor will provide a quantitative assessment of the degree of impairment rather than preparing a report or comment in prose form that is then translated by a disability evaluator into a numerical measure. Variations on this theme exist as were noted above in the multi-state description. Colorado requires certification of raters. Washington State is eager to have treating doctors do ratings but has to overcome a history where treaters did not do ratings. No special training or certification is required for treating doctors to rate impairment in Oregon or Texas.

Rating impairment requires certain skills. Some states offer training to their physicians to acquaint them with the use of rating guides. Since preparing a proper rating takes time, treating doctors expect to be remunerated in line with their effort. Further, some treating doctors are reluctant to rate impairment because they fear it will mire them down in subsequent litigation. An alternative is to turn over the impairment rating to forensic doctors who might specialize in making such ratings. In a third option, found in many states including California, the treating doctor makes the initial rating; the forensic doctor becomes involved only if a dispute arises over the rating.

In several ways, California has set itself apart from other jurisdictions with regard to the role of various doctors in evaluating impairment. California's procedural distinction in the case of represented or unrepresented applicants may be unique. California's use of agreed medical examiners (available only where the applicant is represented and not commonly employed) is not unusual. California is unusual, however, in its use of Qualified Medical Examiners. Unlike the QME approach in California where each side selects its own rater, other jurisdictions may use only a single rater beyond the treating doctor, and that rater is not selected freely by one or the other party.

Return to Work

Little research has been completed on the relationship between PPD programs and return to work practices. Some of the early evidence from Texas is consistent with better return to work rates where an impairment-based scheme eliminated prior incentives for remaining out of work--incentives that are not present in California. Minnesota's new law suggests that its former scheme under ERC did not succeed in hastening return to work. In theory, an impairment rating based on objective standards should not vary because of the length of time for which the worker had been disabled. California's impairment is somewhat more subjective than others. Conceivably, a physician's rating may be influenced by the period of disability prior to the condition becoming permanent and stationary. If so, or if perceived to be so, this may induce persons to delay return to work in order to receive a rating that will yield a greater benefit.

CONCLUSION

Permanent partial disability is a central feature of a workers' compensation program. However, it is only one component of a complex system. If the system tends to be contentious and to carry high transaction costs, and if it demonstrates and reinforces socially unacceptable practices, it is likely that PPD compensation will be so characterized. How can it be otherwise? On the other hand, if a state seeks to reform its workers' compensation system, it cannot succeed unless it improves its treatment of permanent partial disability.

4. UNDERSTANDING PROCESS ISSUES, PARTICIPANT VALUES, AND THE OUTCOMES ASSOCIATED WITH RECENT REFORMS

Our interviews with knowledgeable participants in the workers' compensation system served several important research functions. First, the interviews provided us with a means to understand quickly how this complex system really operates. Second, given the politically divided views and interests regarding workers' compensation, they helped us to understand and to take into account the beliefs, values, and desires of various participant groups, a critical need. Even for issues that could be addressed by our quantitative analyses, the interviews provided important political and system insights that could not be gleaned solely from the data. Third, participants told us how the 1989 and 1993 policy reforms affected practices of the workers' compensation system. Finally, the interviews provided the most current window on operations of the workers' compensation system. Time lags in the administrative data (WCIRB, DEU, and WCAB) prevent up-to-date quantitative assessments of workers' compensation and effects from recent major reforms.

The qualitative interviews helped us focus and direct our quantitative analyses, identified policy problems, and guided our proposals for policy reforms.

At an initial meeting, members of the advisory committee formed by the Commission on Health and Safety and Workers' Compensation to support our work (the member list is included in Appendix A) expressed concern that regional variations in processes were leading to erratic and potentially inequitable outcomes, as well as to system inefficiencies. In an attempt to address this issue we decided to complete the qualitative interviews in two matched sets, one in the northern part of the state and one in the south. Both sets of interviews included representatives of the following stakeholder groups: (1) treating physicians, (2) forensic physicians, (3) applicants' attorneys, (4) defense attorneys, (5) DEU staff, (6) IMC staff, (7) DWC staff, (8) insurers, (9) third party administrators (TPAs), (10) insured employers, (11) self-insured employers, (12) SCIF staff, and (13) labor representatives. Although we interviewed participants in 13 separate participant groups, for simplicity of analysis and for reporting results we collapsed the interviews into six major categories: (1) applicant attorneys; (2) defense attorneys; (3) members of the medical community; (4) insurers (including SCIF), insured employers, and TPAs handling insured claimants; (5) self-insured employers and TPAs handling self-insured claimants; and (6) staff members of the DWC (including persons who work for the DEU, the IMC, and the WCAB).

In this study we report the results of all of the interviews we completed with system participants, but do not report our interviews with state service providers (DWC staff). Our DWC interviews were completed so that our interviews with system participants would be informed by a detailed understanding of the way the various sections of the state system structure work, and so that we could make a better assessment of what kinds of policy reform efforts would be supported by these state employees. Standard interview protocols were not used in the interviews with DWC staff. Consequently, individual DWC staff descriptions of the functioning of their particular unit did not lend themselves to the summary analysis used with the other interview categories. Insights gathered in these interviews guided the development of the interview protocols used for all of the other interview categories and played an important role in informing our policy recommendation decisions.

Because of financial and time constraints, sample sizes in each category were small (on average 3-5 people per category). Sharp differences in the makeup of each of the groups required us to develop separate selection criteria for each group. However, our overall goal was to interview a reasonable cross section of individuals in each group.

With only one or two exceptions, the qualitative interviews were performed at the participant's place of work. The interviews were completed one-on-one, although in a small number of cases we accommodated requests to include small groups of participants from the same firm or practice. We completed all of the interviews in person.

Interviews relied on a semi-structured interview format, with most lasting approximately two hours. Our interview protocols were standard for each participant group, and varied considerably across different groups. For simplicity of analysis the interview results will be presented thematically, covering the following major topics: (1) effects of the 1989 and 1993 reforms; (2) areas in which further reform is desired; (3) the claims process including paperwork requirements, changes in caseload, time to closure, and litigation rates; (4) the court system; (5) the rating system including use of and support for the DEU, the current rating schedule, and the *American Medical Association (AMA) Guides*; and (6) the medical process including the role of the treating physician, issues related to medical evaluations, the presumption of correctness, the QME process, and the IMC.

We guaranteed confidentiality to all persons who agreed to be interviewed. All references to specific interviews will be made by identifying the participant group to which the interviewee belongs--no additional identifiers will be provided. We completed follow-up interviews by phone with many of the interview participants. These follow-up contacts were used to clarify issues raised in the original interviews, and to discuss a number of possible policy reforms.

The participants' interviews were completed in September and October of 1996, well in advance of the quantitative analyses. In June and July of 1997, we conducted a second set of interviews--this time focusing on a small set of stakeholders--representatives of critical interest groups. With these interviews we moved beyond issues of process and system structure, focusing primarily on possible policy reform proposals and the preliminary conclusions of our research. Feedback from these interviews led us to carry out a number of additional research efforts prior to completing this report and helped us to fine-tune our policy reform proposals.

In July of 1997 we held a second meeting for the advisory group to the Commission. That meeting focused on this study's findings, and the suggested policy reform proposals, and provided an additional forum for participant/stakeholder input into the draft report.

RESULTS OF THE QUALITATIVE PARTICIPANT INTERVIEWS

As stated above, the qualitative interview results are reported thematically beginning with issues related to the 1989 and 1993 reforms, and continuing on through questioning on the following topics: areas in which further reform is desired, the claims process, the court system, the rating system, and the medical process. Each of the six participant groups are reported separately if their answers to particular questions were dissimilar. In areas in which two or more groups held very similar views about a particular question, their answers are reported together. For example, in some areas the applicant and defense attorneys do not see the world in the same way. In such cases their responses are reported separately. However, in other areas, they hold quite similar views. In these cases these two participant categories are collapsed into one, and their responses are reported together.

Effects of the 1989 and 1993 Reforms

Because the 1989 and 1993 reforms made so many changes to the workers' compensation system in California, and because many of these changes are not yet reflected in available quantitative databases, we relied heavily on the qualitative interviews for insights into how these reforms affected the various parts of the permanent partial disability system. We asked questions about pre- and post-reform periods and ways these periods differed (for better or for worse) from each other. In addition, we addressed issues specific to each reform cycle. For example, we asked questions about the effect of fee schedules on both medical providers and on claimants; we discussed how the presumption of correctness for treating physicians had affected attorneys, medical providers, insurers, employers, and claimants. We asked questions about system complexity and whether it had improved or worsened following the reform cycle, and about the success or failure of anti-fraud efforts mandated by the reforms. Given the open-ended nature of our interview format, many of the interviews flowed in the directions of interviewees' greatest knowledge and concerns, reaching issues that went well beyond our formal interview protocols. Responses to formal questions, and issues raised by the interviewees themselves, are both reported below.

Applicant Attorneys. The applicant attorneys interviewed argued that the reforms in 1989 and 1993 increased, rather than decreased, the complexity of the workers' compensation system. They believe that it has become more difficult for claimants without counsel to maneuver through the system. However, most believe that the increased complexity generally works to the attorneys' advantage. The complexities particularly burden insurance adjusters. Increased competition in the insurance industry has led to ever-increasing claims loads for the average insurance claims adjuster (see the subsection on insurers) which, even in the best circumstances, increases the likelihood that a claims adjuster will make errors in complying with required procedures or deadlines. The statutory changes increased these requirements and also produced three distinct sets of requirements depending upon when a claim was filed. This increased complexity inevitably leads to adjuster errors which applicant attorneys can use to their client's advantage.

The increased complexity of the workers' compensation system has led all but one interviewed applicant attorney to significantly reduce caseloads. Average caseloads in the 1980s were reported to be in the range of 550-600 per attorney. Current caseloads are reported to be between 400-500. The one attorney who asserted that his caseload has remained stable stated that increasing computer automation has compensated for increasing system complexity and increasing paperwork demands.

Applicant attorneys based in both Northern and Southern California believe that fraud has been substantially reduced in recent years. All admitted that the late 1980s and early 1990s were years in which fraud played a significant role in the California workers' compensation system and that the applicant's bar was not immune from the problem. One described the years 1985-1992 as "the dark period" in the California applicant's bar.

Under provisions of the statute, applicants can now select the WCAB court in which a claim will be filed and heard. This switch to venue selection by the applicant has been a very favorable change in the eyes of all applicant attorneys included in our interviews. For most it has meant an increase in productivity because they have been able to consolidate their practices to one or two boards--eliminating a great deal of travel to and from geographically disparate board locations.

Defense Attorneys. Caseloads are also down in the defense community, both as a result of the increasing complexity of the system, and because of competition and consolidation in the insurance industry. According to defense attorneys, more insurers are using in-house counsel and hearing representatives to handle litigation. This trend, combined with the overall reduction in total claim filings has led to a significant reduction in the demand for defense attorneys across the state. Defense attorneys agree with the applicant's bar asserting that the 1989 and 1993 reforms largely succeeded in making the workers' compensation system more complicated, particularly for claimants without representation. All of the defense attorneys interviewed stated a concern that increased complexity in the system is adversely affecting the quality of law practiced in the industry. It was a universal concern that there are defense attorneys (as well as applicant attorneys) practicing workers' compensation law who do not understand all of the complexities of the post-reform period and so make procedural errors that adversely affect their clients.

Defense attorneys in both the north and south report a significant decline in fraud in the last five years and largely attribute this reduction to the 1989 and 1993 reforms. They note in particular that the new limits on the compensability of stress and post-termination claims closed out a lot of questionable doctors and lawyers. The workers' compensation defense bar clearly sees the reduction of claims abuse as one of its principal contributions. All of the defense attorneys interviewed see a continued need for vigilance in the area of fraud prevention and prosecution. All agreed that although the system is much improved there are still legal and medical mills functioning in both Northern and Southern California. Some report that a number of the worst offending lawyers and doctors moved to Northern California in response to the greatly increased attention to fraud in the south.

The Medical Community. All interviewed doctors were heavily affected by the 1989 and 1993 reductions in fee schedules, by the restrictions on the number of compensable medical evaluations, and,

among psychiatrists and psychologists, on the reductions in
compensability of stress claims. All interviewed forensic doctors (both
those working for applicants and those working for the defense) stated
that their practices had to be restructured away from more detailed
assessments towards a simpler, higher volume approach to business. This
area of practice has contracted a great deal in the last five years, as
shown by sharp reductions reported both by the WCIRB and the University
of California, in number of claims, number of medical evaluations per
claim, and costs of medical evaluations particularly in the period 1992-
1993. Doctors working as treaters, defense and applicant evaluators,
and as Agreed Medical Examiners (AMEs) have all cut back their
practices, retired, or taken on other kinds of medicine (non-industrial,
or personal injury primarily).

The doctors we interviewed agreed that fee schedules are a
necessary tool in the workers' compensation system, admitting that pre-
reform fees charged by many doctors were excessive. However, most
believe that the existing fee schedule has gone too far in the direction
of cutting costs and restricting the compensability of medical
evaluations. All complained that the current fee schedule does not
fairly or adequately compensate doctors for their services, but some
said that their old fees were lower than the current schedule. Also,
many noted that the new fee schedule had imposed perverse incentives on
doctors' billing practices. For example, some of the new fee schedules
for evaluations cut costs by relying on reduced hourly fees--giving
doctors a disincentive to complete evaluations efficiently.

With only one exception the psychologists and psychiatrists we
interviewed (all of whom have had mixed practices working as treaters
and evaluators for defense attorneys, applicant attorneys, and as AMEs)
agreed that limits were needed on the compensability of psychiatric
injuries, but that the current rules are too restrictive. The 1993
statute tightened requirements for filing claims based on stress or
mental health problems. Under this statute, work-related stress must
amount to over 50 percent of the cause of a psychiatric injury in order
for it to be classified as compensable. They all agreed that the 50
percent apportionment threshold before a psychiatric claim can be

considered compensable is too high a mark. The 1993 reforms also
eliminated coverage for stress claims resulting from "good faith"
terminations. There was also considerable concern that business
decisions (such as restructuring and layoffs) have real psychological
costs for which employers should be held responsible, whereas current
law absolves them of responsibility unless it can be proven that they
acted in bad faith. One psychologist differed from the rest (the only
medical practitioner interviewed who left the field of industrial
medicine after the 1993 reforms) asserting that the "collapse" of the
stress claim industry was a wholly positive outcome for the workers'
compensation system. He went on to argue that the same sort of "clean-
up" was necessary in orthopedic practice.

Again, members of the medical community all agreed that medical
fraud was a significant problem in the late 1980s and early 1990s. All
support the state's effort to put unethical medical practitioners (both
treaters and forensic doctors) out of business and all agreed that the
efforts to reign in fraud have met with a great deal of success. Most
concluded that the fee schedules helped drive fraudulent doctors out of
the system--there simply isn't enough "easy" money to be made in the
post-reform era. Doctors who largely complete work for the defense
community assert that there are still a number of medical mills in
business (particularly in Southern California). All of the doctors
interviewed, regardless of their training or role in the workers'
compensation system, support continued efforts to identify and prosecute
doctors involved in unethical medical practices.

The doctors we interviewed were universally dissatisfied with the
increased complexity of the workers' compensation system resulting from
the 1989 and 1993 reforms. Paperwork demands in the workers'
compensation system have taken an ever-increasing toll on their
practices. Many noted that the increased complexity appears to be
linked with a parallel issue, which is an increase in the adversarial
nature of their relationships with patients. The doctors we
interviewed, both in Northern and Southern California, in a variety of
specialties, all agreed that claimants today are much more apt to be
hostile towards their medical provider (either during treatment, or

during evaluation). Most believe that increased system complexity has left claimants confused and angry and that this anger plays itself out not just against employers and insurers, but also in their relationships with treating and evaluating physicians.

The Insured Community. As a result of the 1993 statute, California went to an open insurance market, eliminating state-imposed minimum rates. As a result, insurance premiums plummeted. All of the insurers interviewed expressed concern that premiums are now below what they must be to be sustainable over the longer term. Carriers had to cut premiums in response to the shift to open rating. Those we interviewed foresaw likely adjustments increasing premiums as the industry stabilizes in the new environment. None of the insurers we interviewed reported major changes in retention of business in the shift from regulated to open rating. Most stated that current customer losses are not clients who are shifting to self-insurance, but rather clients who are shifting to other insurers currently offering even lower premium rates. The insurers we interviewed believe that even for large companies in the state, premiums are now so competitive that it is cheaper to insure rather than self-insure. All of the insurers we interviewed stated that they have changed the nature of their sales efforts for new business in the new open rating environment--either abandoning pursuit of new California business entirely or focusing on multi-state or national firms with business in California.

The Self-Insured Community. None of the self-insured firms included in our study changed their status in or out of the self-insured market as a result of the switch to open rating in the insurance sector. All of these firms looked at the available insurance program offers and decided that self-insurance was still the most favorable option, both financially and in terms of control over claims management. Even with the availability of significantly reduced premiums being offered by many insurance carriers, the self-insured firms were adamant that self-insurance is still an obvious financial choice for all of them (one described the financial part of the self-insurance choice as a "slam dunk").

The Insured and Self-Insured Community. The insurance and self-insurance communities echoed the complaints of the medical community and of attorneys, stating that the 1989 and 1993 reforms made an already complex system even more difficult to manage. According to insurers and self-insured firms, increased system complexity resulting from the two reform efforts, increasing paperwork demands generated by the DWC in the same period, and system instability as a result of ongoing procedural changes have been in large part responsible for (1) increased time to closure for many claims, (2) increased transaction costs, (3) the need for reduced caseloads for adjusters, (4) inevitable inconsistencies in claim handling procedures, and (5) inadvertent adjuster errors in paperwork filings.

According to members of the insurance and self-insured community, the anti-fraud statutes, the medical-legal fee schedules, and the reductions in the compensability of post-termination and psychiatric claims enacted with the 1989 and 1993 reforms helped to put a lot of medical and legal mills out of business, contributing to an overall reduction in claim volume and in total claim-related costs. In addition to the effect of the reforms, a number of insurers and self-insured firms stated that some of the more fraudulent medical and legal mills looked largely in pools of unemployed workers to find people willing to file fraudulent claims. As the state moved out of its recession, it was hypothesized that it became harder for fraudulent doctors and lawyers to find willing co-conspirators.

Medical fee schedules, limits on the compensability of post-termination and psychiatric claims, limits on the number of compensable medical-legal reports per claim, and the cap on vocational rehabilitation payments are all supported by the insurance and self-insured community. Most insurers and self-insured firms felt that medical, medical-legal, and vocational rehabilitation expenses in the pre-reform era were excessive and difficult to predict and control. The 1989 and 1993 reforms not only limited some of these expenses, but they brought significant increases in the predictability of these costs.

Areas in Which Further Reform Is Desired

Beyond the immediate and ongoing results of the 1989 and 1993 reform efforts, we were very interested in policy areas in which system participants saw room for new reforms. We provided no starting point for this forward-looking discussion, but rather encouraged each person interviewed to think about policy areas that would best be left alone, and areas that they believed needed new policy reform attention.

Applicant Attorneys. Many of the applicant attorneys interviewed stated that rather than implementing any further reforms they would prefer a guaranteed period of stability in which policymakers and the DWC promise to leave the system alone. Many went so far as to argue that if they were going to change anything they would revoke the reforms and return to the system as it was prior to 1989.

One change the applicant attorneys interviewed would support is an increase in the fines applicable to insurance companies who pay late or inadequate indemnity payments and who delay in making required medical payments. The applicant attorneys interviewed believe that the current fine levels are not high enough to dissuade insurance companies from engaging in "bad behavior."

Defense Attorneys. Much like the applicant attorneys, the majority of the defense attorneys included in this study worry about continued changes in the California workers' compensation system. Fearing increased rather than decreased complexity, tired of instability and the need to apply one set of rules to certain claims, and entirely different rules to other claims depending on whether they were filed before this or that policy change--the defense attorneys expressed their desire to have the state clarify and enforce existing rules rather than adopt new ones.

One area in which defense attorneys support a policy shift concerns the presumption of correctness for the treating physician. All of the defense attorneys would like to see the period of employer control over the treating physician extended, or at least switched to joint control after the first 30 days. The presumption of correctness for the treating physician would be much more palatable in the defense community if control over physician choice was shared between the insurance company/employer and the employee. The majority view was that treating physicians are largely unprepared for the role thrust on them with the presumption. Further, the Southern California defense attorneys assert that there are still a large number of unethical doctors functioning within the system--noting that in the post-reform era questionable medical opinions generated by unethical doctors can hold a great deal of weight in the court system.

The Medical Community. Interviewed doctors reported a significant increase in unpaid medical bills and therefore in medical liens. All would favor policy reforms aimed at resolving the lien issue, such as increased fines on insurers or self-insured employers for failure to make payment, or DWC pressure on referees to force settlement of medical issues that are currently left unresolved. One doctor asserted that only 20 percent of his bills are paid on time, 5 percent of his defense or AME exams are never paid for, and nearly 20 percent of applicant evaluation bills are never paid. All assert that in recent years they have had to become much more careful about which patients they agree to treat or evaluate. They avoid claimants covered by certain insurance companies and employers who always pay late, or fail to pay at all. Also many have learned to avoid referrals from particular attorneys because these attorneys consistently fail to get medical bills paid. A number of the doctors we interviewed stated that the worst offender for late and inadequate medical bill payments is the State Compensation Insurance Fund (SCIF).

All doctors urged additional efforts to reform the fee schedules. All believe that these schedules need fine-tuning, that the current schedules are too restrictive and have gone too far in the effort to reign in medical costs. One specific repeated suggestion was that the current fee schedule fails to recognize that applicant evaluations typically take considerably less time to complete than do defense exams.

The Insured and Self-Insured Community. One issue both the insurance and self-insured community focused on in our interviews was their desire for predictability in claim costs. For example, in the area of vocational rehabilitation, the issue for insurers and self-insured firms is not so much where the cap on costs is placed, but that there is a cap at any level. Caps on expenditures set clear boundaries for adjusters. The insurance and self-insured companies we interviewed stated their desire for future reforms that focus on improving the predictability of claim costs.

Both insurance companies and self-insured firms we interviewed repeatedly questioned why compromise and release (C&R) claims agreed to between an adjuster and a represented worker should still be required to go before a WCAB referee for approval. There is strong support in these communities for eliminating this requirement.

Insurance companies and self-insured firms are largely unsatisfied with the current rating schedule used to determine permanent partial disability payments in California (for a complete discussion of this issue, see the subsection titled The Rating System). They would strongly support further reform efforts aimed at simplifying the current schedule, increasing its objectivity, and reducing its reliance on and recognition of subjective measures of disability and/or impairment.

The insurance industry and self-insured firms remain quite dissatisfied with the level of complexity currently found in the California workers' compensation system. Efforts to streamline paperwork and other claims processing requirements would be strongly supported by both groups.

Representatives of the insurance industry and of self-insured firms would strongly support increased efforts to enforce already existing rules against procedural variation within the WCAB system (see the complete discussion of the insurance and self-insured industry view of the WCAB system in the subsection titled The Court System).

Both self-insured firms and insurance company representatives are unhappy with the existing system governing employer control over physician choice, tied with the current presumption of correctness for the treating physician. All of the insurers and self-insured firms interviewed (with the sole exception of one self-insured firm) would support an increase in the period of time during which employers control physician choice.

The insurers included in this study hold mixed views about the presumption of correctness for treating physicians. Insurers are

concerned about the ability of treating physicians to complete adequate
and unbiased evaluations of their patients. Much like the defense
community, the insurance industry would find the presumption of
correctness far more palatable if it was tied to a longer period of
employer control over choice of treating physician. Representatives of
the self-insurance community we interviewed were of one mind about the
presumption of correctness for the treating physician--they believe it
is a terrible idea. All of the self-insureds questioned the ability of
treating physicians to adequately evaluate claimants. The self-insureds
argued that treating physicians are far too frequently ignorant of the
language of industrial medicine--causing them to submit medical
evaluations that are inappropriate and misleading and, in the current
system, binding.

All of the participant groups had opinions about the need for
future reforms of the disability rating schedule. Those views are
summarized in the subsection titled The Rating System.

The Claims Process

The data available to us for quantitative research had limited
information on the claims process. Consequently, we had to rely heavily
on qualitative interviews in order to develop an understanding of the
central issues at play in this area. Most of the responses we report
are from the insured and self-insured communities because other
participant groups (such as attorneys and medical providers) have only a
second-hand view of these processes. Questions elicited comparisons
between pre- and post-reform cycle paperwork requirements, caseloads,
time to claim closure, and litigation rates.

The Insured Community. All of the insurance industry
representatives complained about rapidly increasing paperwork
requirements in claims management. They assert that these requirements
are less a direct result of the 1989 and 1993 reforms, but rather have
been driven by demands generated by the DWC. All of the insurers
expressed frustration that these demands are not only excessive but
often elusive as well. They complained that the DWC does not notify
them about changing reporting requirements. Most insurers stated that

they rely on the California Workers' Compensation Institute (CWCI) for current information about such changes. Many admitted that they often find out about new paperwork requirements only after they have failed to file something properly--not before.

Claims processing was also heavily affected by the 1989 and 1993 reforms. All of the insurers we interviewed described ongoing struggles to keep their adjusters apprised of new statutory requirements. Foremost on their minds is the difficulty in managing claims that now fall into three distinct categories: (1) claims filed before the 1989 reforms, (2) claims filed in the "window period," between the 1989 and 1993 reforms, and (3) claims filed after the 1993 reform date. Each category of claims has separate and quite different rules and paperwork requirements. Each insurance company has wrestled with the most efficient way to manage this claim treatment diversity, and none were fully satisfied with their solution. In response to the increased complexity of claims processing, insurers have had to reduce average caseloads for claims adjusters. All insurance companies we included in our sample have dropped caseloads for their adjusters from pre-reform levels of between 200-400 claims to caseloads today of between 150-180 claims.

Litigation rates were down at all of the insurance companies included in our sample. Reasons for the decline were stated to be (1) declining plant closures and statutory changes in the compensability of post-termination claims (according to insurers, most post-termination claims were litigated), (2) anti-fraud measures included in the 1989 and 1993 reforms, and (3) increased vigilance on the part of adjusters. For those insurance companies willing to report approximate litigation rates (not all were), current rates are in the range of 30-55 percent of all lost-time claims. All of the insurers asserted that there is still a significant disparity in litigation rates between Northern and Southern California--with rates in the south still significantly higher than in the north. Although all of the insurance companies interviewed have increased their use of hearing representatives as a way to manage legal issues, none were comfortable with relying on them exclusively, particularly for more complex legal issues.

A minority of insurance companies interviewed have begun to use nurse case managers as a way to improve control over medical treatment and medical expenditures.

The Self-Insured Community. Self-insured firms choose to self-insure both because they believe that it is the most cost-effective way to provide insurance to their employees, and because they believe there are other benefits, beyond reduced costs, to controlling workers' compensation insurance internally. The self-insured firms we interviewed described this desire for direct control over insurance matters as being a part of the management culture of their firms, a management culture they believe is quite different from that seen at insured firms. A number of claims management practices differentiate self-insured firms from insured firms. Self-insured firms consistently report their interest in and active development of integrated return to work programs, which they believe reduce overall costs associated with workers' compensation and improve employer/employee relations (programs that are relatively rare in the insured sector). Self-insured firms report lower rates of unrepresented or represented workers switching from employer-selected treating physicians to doctors of their own choosing than do insurance companies. The self-insured firms we interviewed report remarkably low litigation rates (for lost-time claims) compared to those reported by insurance companies. Self-insured firms in our sample report litigation rates as low as 4 percent, with the most common range being between 8-12 percent. Self-insured firms widely report the use of nurse case managers as a way to more directly manage medical issues on a per claim basis. As stated above, only a very small minority of insurance companies have begun trial nurse case-manager programs.

The self-insured firms echo the insurance industry's complaints about excessive paperwork requirements and increasing overall system complexity, both as a result of the two major statutory reforms, and as a result of ongoing procedural changes emanating from the DWC. They complain about the difficulty in keeping up-to-date with changing requirements and with the complexity brought on by having to manage claims with three separate sets of statutory requirements. Much like the insurance companies, they have tried a number of different ways of dealing with claim management complexities, and none are completely satisfied with the system they are currently using. Increasing paperwork demands and overall system instability has been in large part responsible for significant reductions in claims' adjuster caseloads. Pre-reform caseloads were in the range of 200-250 claims per adjuster; current caseloads have fallen to between 125-180 claims each.

The self-insured firms noted a number of claims management paperwork requirements that they believe are unnecessary and/or ill-conceived. First, they contend that the requirement to deny claims within 90 days is too tight a time limit. They argue that specific injury claims can be sorted out in that time frame, but more complex cases involving repetitive stress or cumulative trauma injuries are not well-developed enough at the 90-day mark for them to make an accurate assessment of whether or not the claim should be denied. All of the self-insureds argue that too many forms are required for an employee to waive his or her right to choose a treating physician after the window of employer control has ended.

The Insured and Self-Insured Communities. All of the insurance companies and self-insured companies we interviewed try to C&R claims if the employee has left the employment of the insured firm. They do not favor using C&Rs for employees still employed at the same firm, preferring instead to use a Stip (Stipulated Agreement) as the method of claim settlement in such cases. Stips make it possible for them to provide additional medical treatment for prior claims, rather than opening new claims--with the risk that additional indemnity payments will be required. For claimants no longer in the employment of the insured firm, or in their own employment for self-insured firms, both communities would also like the option of settling vocational rehabilitation payments under a C&R agreement. Vocational rehabilitation payments take several months to pay out, adding processing requirements and transaction costs that could be avoided if the payment was made in a lump sum as a part of an overall C&R agreement.

The Medical Community. The medical community asserted that they are seeing more claims with disputes over AOE/COE (arising out of employment, in the course of employment) issues in the post-reform period than they did in the period before the reforms. AOE/COE refers to whether or not the injury or illness is really industrial in nature, and if only partially so, what percentage of the responsibility for the injury or illness is apportioned to the employer. They hypothesized that cumulative trauma cases are on the rise and that apportionment is more often an issue in such cases than it was in cases involving specific trauma.

The Court System

Our interview questions concerning the court system focused on three main issues. First, we discussed the overall functioning of the courts including the quality of referees, the quality of judicial decisionmaking, and the speed of the courts. Second, we addressed issues of regional variability, both in terms of outcomes and in terms of rules and procedures. And third, we discussed the effect of the recent reforms, and whether continued change is either necessary or desirable.

Applicant Attorneys. All of the applicant attorneys interviewed believe that the WCAB is understaffed, and most assert that the quality of the referees is suspect and at best inconsistent.

Defense Attorneys. The defense attorneys interviewed held mixed views about the quality of the referees currently practicing in the WCAB system. A majority expressed the view that referees are on the whole underpaid, and that consequently lawyers attracted to the board tend to be less motivated--attracted to the board by their interest in predictable, nine-to-five work. The majority asserted that referees are too hesitant to adjudicate and that widespread reticence to decide cases has contributed to increasing delays in the court system. The minority position in the defense community was that the court system is functioning well enough, that referees are competent, and that referees bear little blame for the broader ills of the workers' compensation system.

The Insured and Self-Insured Communities. The insurance and self-insurance company representatives interviewed have little positive to say about the WCAB system. One of their principal concerns was a general frustration with regional variation in court requirements and procedures. It was asserted that although the DWC has attempted to enforce rules against such regional variation, these efforts have largely failed. Insurers and self-insurers report that many referees have their own ways of doing business, including idiosyncratic paperwork requirements--which has only served to make an already complex system even more so. The self-insured firms complain that not only is there a great deal of variability between the boards in terms of required paperwork and procedures, but that it is extremely difficult for even the most "right" minded adjuster to consistently identify what "right" is. As a consequence, these firms argue that their adjusters can make mistakes that should in large part be blamed on poor communication from the boards, rather than on adjuster negligence.

A second complaint that was made by both insurance firms and self-insured firms is that WCAB referees are too hesitant to adjudicate. These two groups both assert that this unwillingness to make decisions plays a significant role in delays in claim closures. If referees were willing to make difficult decisions, insurance companies and self-insured firms believe that their adjusters would be able to process claims much more efficiently.

Finally, both the insurers and self-insured firms included in our study argue that the WCAB has become increasingly overburdened with cases and that they are not meeting state-set guidelines concerning how long it should take to calendar mandatory dispute resolution conferences, trials, or other board-related activities. WCAB-generated delays are aggravating the overall difficulty in closing claims in a timely manner.

The Rating System

Our questioning about the rating system focuses on three central issues. First, we discussed the nature of the rating tool participants believe should be used to determine indemnity payment outcomes. Second, we discussed who should best use that tool; should it be doctors (treating or forensic), adjusters, independent raters, state raters, or otherwise? And third, we discussed how much weight the favored rating tool should play in the overall determination of benefits for an injured worker. We also asked adjusters (insured or self-insured), and attorneys, to tell us who currently completes their ratings (if they use the DEU or rely on internal or outside independent raters). Finally, we asked all of the interviewees to discuss their impressions of the DEU, and to assess their support, or lack thereof, for its continued participation in the rating process.

Applicant and Defense Attorneys. None of the applicant or defense attorneys interviewed favor a shift to use of the *AMA Guides*. All favor a flexible schedule that allows attorneys and referees to better tailor outcomes to the needs of individual applicants. Many asserted that the rating system is rarely the cause of litigation. These attorneys asserted that cases are largely litigated over procedural issues and apportionment, not because of disputes over ratings. All fear that a move to the *AMA Guides* will necessarily come with a shift towards "average" rather than individual justice.

Many of the attorneys interviewed rely on outside raters or rate cases themselves, rather than using the DEU. Most stated that although the DEU is more unimpeachable than a rating completed by an outside rater, DEU raters are too slow and are inadequately trained. All of the attorneys (both applicant and defense) asserted that they are just as capable of rating cases as any of the DEU staff. Defense attorneys also avoid the DEU because it is their sense that the DEU has a consistent pro-applicant bias. They believe that they get much more objective ratings from outside raters. Particularly in Southern California, lawyers avoid AMEs because the AME effectively becomes the judge for the claim. Lawyers in Northern California reported greater use of and better experiences with AMEs.

The Medical Community. None of the doctors we interviewed actively support a move to using the *AMA Guides*. Many stated their concern that neither treating nor forensic doctors in California have the training needed to use the *Guides* adequately. Most noted that there is little evidence that the *Guides* are either a valid or reliable tool for assessing impairment or disability. The majority of doctors we interviewed would support a change in the type of schedule used in California to one that is more objective and more rigid--but expressed hope that a better system could be devised than that currently used by the AMA. A number commented that the existing California schedule could be adjusted such that less weight is placed on subjective rating factors, and more weight is placed on objective ones, rather than wholly abandoning the existing California schedule.

The doctors interviewed support the use of AMEs. All noted that serving as an AME requires that both sides (applicant and defense) respect a doctor's work and ability to complete a balanced evaluation of a claimant. These doctors believe AME evaluations can and do play an important role in dispute resolution.

The doctors interviewed held mixed views concerning the question of who is the appropriate person to evaluate and rate a case. Half of the doctors interviewed (covering a range of specialties) believe that doctors should not rate cases, but rather that independent raters (DEU or otherwise) are in the best position to complete ratings. The other half of the doctors were split between those who think that doctors can be trained to complete ratings and should play that role once trained and another set who are indifferent on this question. Few doctors see any benefit in having attorneys complete ratings.

The Insured and Self-Insured Community. The representatives of the insurance and self-insurance industries included in our interviews have favorable views of the *AMA Guides*. Most believe that doctors would provide more consistent evaluations using the *Guides* than they do using the present California system. A number of the insurers noted that switching to the *Guides* would be looked at favorably by companies thinking about doing business in California. A number of adjusters, working for both insurance companies and for self-insured firms, noted that in order to use the *Guides* in California, an adjustment mechanism would be needed so that they address issues related to disability, not simply impairment.

All of the insurance companies and self-insured firms interviewed stated that adjusters complete their own ratings. Many adjusters use the computer program "Top Rate," generally as a check on the rating they came to without the program. Cases are generally sent to the DEU for a rating if the case is unrepresented. Represented cases are sent much less frequently. All of the insurers and self-insured firms interviewed believe that the DEU has a pro-applicant bias, and that DEU raters are using the new upper extremity protocols, even though they were officially left out of the January 1997 schedule revision. All of the insurance company and self-insured firm representatives expressed their support for efforts aimed at improving inter-rater reliability within the DEU, including efforts to norm the raters by randomly assigning a subset of claims to multiple raters, and through increased rater training. All expressed the firm belief that the DEU continues to be plagued by backlogs and inconsistent outcomes. Most asserted that if consistency and speed could be improved they would support the continued use of DEU raters, particularly in unrepresented cases.

The Medical Process

Questions posed about the medical process focused on the role of the treating physician; the quality of medical evaluations, and what kind of doctor should complete them; the presumption of correctness; the QME process; and the role and success or failure of the IMC.

Applicant and Defense Attorneys. All of the applicant attorneys interviewed expressed concern about applicants trading away their right to future medical payments in an effort to boost their near-term cash intake. The applicant attorneys interviewed asserted that they nearly always advise their clients against settling future medical, but that many claimants feel they have no other choice.

Both applicant and defense attorneys are concerned about the general level of training in the treating physician pool. Most argued that the QME exam does little to keep poorly trained doctors out of the workers' compensation system. All of the attorneys interviewed favor more extensive training and examination requirements for doctors serving as QMEs. All of the applicant attorneys opposed the current limit of one compensable medical-legal report, stating that many of their clients have multiple medical issues at stake and require the forensic attention of more than one medical specialty.

As stated above, defense attorneys oppose the presumption of correctness for the treating physician on the grounds that treating physicians are largely unprepared and untrained for this role. Further, many are concerned that treating physicians often carry a bias in favor of the applicant in that they have developed relationships with their patients and feel responsibility towards them.

The Medical Community. All of the doctors we interviewed oppose the presumption of correctness for the treating physician, both doctors who serve primarily as treaters, and those who generally serve as forensic evaluators. They agreed universally that treating physicians generally lack the skills necessary to fill this role. There was consensus that on most cases the doctor most experienced with industrial medicine is the one completing the evaluation, not the one providing treatment and, if anything, the evaluator's opinion should be given more weight. Interviewed doctors, including treating physicians, also expressed concern that patients can manipulate their relationship with their treating physician in order to affect the report the treater will file on them. They believed that it is more difficult for claimants to manipulate a forensic doctor since claimants generally see forensic doctors only once or twice. In addition, many were concerned that it is difficult for them individually to complete unbiased evaluations of patients they are currently treating, and all shared a concern that other doctors, besides themselves, must struggle with this issue as well. For all of these reasons they believe that resting the presumption with the treater is at best highly problematic.

All but one of the doctors interviewed support the concept of the QME system in theory, but have reservations about how it has been implemented in practice. This group of doctors believes that the QME exam is not rigorous enough, which has allowed suspect doctors to pass the exam and take on the legitimacy and business referrals associated with the QME designation. In addition, a number of the doctors interviewed noted that the QME exam does not test medical skills or

honesty, only paper knowledge of the industrial medical system. A
number of the doctors who support the QME system in concept, rather than
in practice, would support using a QME system for both represented and
unrepresented claimants if the exam and training processes could be
improved to address their general concerns. The single exception was a
doctor who views the QME system as "a total sham" which has not served
to ensure medical quality or fair medical treatment for unrepresented
claimants.

      The Insured and Self-Insured Community. Representatives of both
the insured and self-insured communities focused considerable attention
during our interviews on the low quality of medical evaluations being
submitted by both treating and forensic physicians. There was consensus
that the IMC has failed to provide enough guidance and training to the
average treating physician to ensure that proper medical information is
being provided to raters. Much like the attorneys, there was support
for a QME system in theory, but a strong belief that in practice the
actual QME system has failed. It is widely believed that unethical, and
incompetent doctors were able to get through the examination process and
are now practicing medicine in the system with a QME stamp of approval.
Most disliked the presumption of correctness, believing that treating
doctors are not capable of providing informed, unbiased evaluations that
are needed for resolving workers' compensation claims. In particular,
they reported that treating doctors did not routinely obtain the medical
histories needed to address issues of causation in AOE/COE disputes.

CORE OBSERVATIONS FROM THE QUALITATIVE INTERVIEWS

      Below we summarize the core observations generated by the
qualitative interviews.

- The workers' compensation system is overwhelmed, with both
  claims and complicated paperwork. Participating groups
  complain that it is difficult to give individual cases fair
  attention. It was asserted that mistakes in procedures and in
  paperwork filing often occur out of misunderstanding, not
  malice.

- The current system for rating disability in California is suspect to many participating groups. Concern was expressed about the consistency, predictability, and validity of the rating schedule and rating process. There is no consensus for moving to use of the *AMA Guides* in place of the current rating schedule.

- Claims are difficult to process and close. Delays within the WCAB, procedural variation between different boards, complex paperwork requirements, lengthy medical treatment, rating backlogs, system instability, and heavy caseloads were all identified as contributing to the sluggishness of the claims process.

- Transaction costs associated with processing claims are still high, particularly compared to benefits paid. Reducing the transaction costs attributed to litigation and to required paperwork are of highest priority to the insured, self-insured, and medical communities.

- Geographic differences between Northern and Southern California are less significant than in years past.

- The 1989 and 1993 reforms did a great deal to limit fraud. Continued attention to this issue is still needed.

- Many groups are dissatisfied with the general quality of medical reports generated in the workers' compensation system, and with the presumption of correctness for the treating physician.

- The switch to open rating substantially lowered premiums in the state. Insurers expressed concerns that some of these low premiums are below levels that can be sustained over the long term.

- System instability and the current situation with three claim tracks (pre-1989 reforms, the "window period", and post-1993 reforms) make an already complex system even more difficult to manage.

- Delays in the payment of medical liens have substantially increased in the post-reform period.

5. BENEFITS, WAGE LOSS, AND BENEFIT ADEQUACY

Under California's workers' compensation statute, workers are entitled to several different kinds of benefits. These include indemnity benefits, vocational rehabilitation, and medical care.[1] In this section, we will describe the various benefits to which workers with permanent partial disabilities are entitled, and the ways in which the benefits are calculated. Focusing on indemnity benefits, and using a unique database of workers' compensation claims data linked to wage data, we will then examine the adequacy of indemnity benefits. We will also discuss the amount of other benefits received under workers' compensation and some issues related to adequacy of these benefits.

To estimate the adequacy of indemnity benefits, we estimate the lost earnings of PPD claimants over the 4-5 years following the injury and estimate the fraction of this earnings loss that is replaced by workers' compensation benefits. Our analysis compares the post-injury earnings of PPD claimants to the earnings of an innovatively constructed "control group." We selected as controls workers who were working at the same firm as the injured worker when the latter was injured, making approximately the same wage. We then followed the injured worker and the control for up to five years after the accident, measuring earnings loss by comparing the quarterly earnings of the injured to the control.

To analyze the workers' compensation system empirically, we used data collected by the Workers' Compensation Insurance Rating Bureau (WCIRB). While these data were not intended for research, they offer a rich source of information on claims, benefits, and process. To compare benefits paid to lost earnings, we matched the claims data to data used for the administration of the unemployment insurance system. PPD claims for injuries occurring during 1991-1994 were matched to wages for claimants from the fourth quarter of 1989 through the second quarter of 1996. As a result, we have up to five years of pre- and post-injury wages for every claimant.

---

[1]Death benefits are also available for dependents.

In the next subsection, we describe the benefits available to workers with permanent partial disabilities in California and provide some descriptive information on benefits paid. The third subsection provides our evaluation of the adequacy of indemnity benefits. This subsection includes a detailed discussion of our conceptual model and our estimation approach, and then describes the data and reports the results. This section concludes with a discussion of the adequacy of medical and vocational rehabilitation benefits.

OVERVIEW OF WORKERS' COMPENSATION BENEFITS

Types of Benefits Available and the Calculation of Payments

A worker with a permanent partial disability in California is entitled to three kinds of benefits:

1. Indemnity: Injured workers are entitled to *temporary disability* (TD) to replace lost income while the worker recovers, and *permanent partial disability* (PPD) after recovery to compensate for residual disability.[2]

2. Medical: All medical care necessary to cure or relieve the injury or illness acquired at work is paid for.

3. Vocational rehabilitation: Workers who, as a result of the injury, cannot return to the occupation in which they were employed are entitled to training for another occupation and a *vocational rehabilitation maintenance allowance* (VRMA) to support them while receiving rehabilitation.

Injured workers are eligible to receive temporary total disability (TTD) if temporarily unable to work as a result of the injury. They can receive TTD until they return to work (or until a doctor certifies that they can return to work), or when they are deemed "permanent and stationary" and are eligible for PPD benefits. Until July 1994, the temporary disability benefit was set at two-thirds of the average weekly wage received at the time of the injury, with a maximum benefit of $336.

---

[2]A totally disabled worker who will not be able to return to work is eligible for permanent total disability (PTD) benefits.

As a result of the 1993 reforms, the maximum was increased three times and since July 1996, the maximum has been $490.[3]

Using the 1991-1993 WCIRB data, we found that the mean duration of temporary benefits is 22 weeks. For ratings less than 25, the mean duration is 16 weeks, and for ratings greater than 25 it is 41 weeks.

We found that the fraction of PPD claimants with the maximum benefit was 28 percent. While we do not have the WCIRB data for claims occurring in 1996, we calculated the fraction of workers in 1991-1993 who would have received the higher maximum of $490, and found it to be 9 percent. Therefore, approximately 20 percent of injured workers would have received a benefit increase under the new maximum.

Permanent partial disability benefits are intended to compensate workers for any permanent disability that results from a workplace injury. The weekly benefit is two-thirds of the pre-injury average weekly wage subject to a maximum that depends upon the disability rating. The maximum benefit was raised in 1991 for workers with disability ratings of 25 percent or higher to $148, while workers with disability ratings below 25 percent remained at $140. To address a perceived inadequacy of benefits for higher disability ratings, the maximum benefit increased several times as a result of the 1993 reforms. Currently, the maximum benefit is $160 for ratings between 15 and 24.75, $170 for 25-69.75, and $230 for 70 percent and over. The weekly benefit remains at $140 for ratings of 15 percent and below.

The disability rating also determines the number of weeks the worker receives benefits. Each disability rating point translates into a certain number of weeks, and as the rating increases above certain thresholds, the marginal number of weeks per disability rating point increases.[4] The calculation leads to, for example, 15 weeks of benefits for a rating of 5 percent, 30.25 weeks of benefits for a rating of 10

---

[3]Workers are also eligible to receive temporary partial benefits (TPD) if a doctor certifies that they can work, but only at a reduced number of hours, or if the employer says that only part-time work is available given the worker's temporary disability. The benefit is set at two-thirds of the difference between the old wage and the new wage.

[4]The thresholds were lowered and another added to increase benefits for high-rated claims as part of the 1989 reforms.

percent, 70.5 weeks for 20, 241 weeks for 50, and 606.5 weeks for 90.[5] We will discuss the distribution of benefits received as reported in the WCIRB in detail below.

After PPD benefits are exhausted, workers with disability ratings greater than or equal to 70 are entitled to a *life pension*. To calculate the life pension, the pre-injury average weekly wage, subject to a maximum, is multiplied by a number that depends upon the disability rating.[6] Until July 1994, this maximum was $107.69. In the 1991-1993 WCIRB data, the average life pension for workers with disability ratings greater than 70 was $33.09. As part of the program to increase benefits for the highest disability ratings, the maximum was increased in July 1996 to $257.69. Recalculating the life pension for the 1991-1993 WCIRB under the new maximum benefit leads to an increase in the average life pension to $76.15.

The medical coverage of workers' compensation is extensive. All medically necessary treatment and medication is covered, without a deductible. The worker is even entitled to reimbursement for travel to and from doctor's appointments or to the pharmacy, currently at the rate of $.24 per mile (Ball, 1995). The right to future medical coverage is not limited. In practice, however, most claimants accept a lump sum cash settlement in exchange for forgoing the right to coverage for future medical care.

Finally, vocational rehabilitation is available for workers when their doctor determines they cannot perform the functions of their previous job or cannot return to their previous job without causing further injury. An individualized rehabilitation plan, including counseling, training and education, and job placement, is designed to facilitate finding employment in another occupation. Workers who are permanent and stationary while receiving rehabilitation are eligible to receive a vocational rehabilitation maintenance allowance.[7] VRMA pays two-thirds of the average weekly pre-injury wage up to a maximum of

---

[5]For more detail see, for instance, Barth and Telles (1992) or Ball (1995).

[6]To calculate the multiplier, the rating less 60 is divided by 100 and multiplied by 1.5.

[7]Otherwise, they are still eligible to receive TTD.

$246, which is less than TTD but more than PPD. Concerned with the high cost of vocational rehabilitation, the 1993 reforms limited VRMA to 52 weeks, and limited the cost of the entire vocational rehabilitation plan to $16,000.

Descriptive Information on Benefits Paid

Table 5.1 summarizes all three types of benefits--indemnity, medical and vocational rehabilitation--for workers who had accidents that led to permanent partial disability claims. The data are from the Uniform Statistical Reporting Plan (USR) database from the WCIRB, a private entity responsible for regulating workers' compensation insurance premiums. All claims for permanent partial disability in insured firms in California are reported to the WCIRB. They supplied RAND with data for claims that occurred on policies that opened from 1989 to 1994.[8] The data from the WCIRB provide detailed information about the characteristics of claims and injuries, benefits and expenses as they were incurred and paid, and some information about how claims were processed. These data are provided only for claims submitted against employers who are covered by workers' compensation insurance carriers, approximately 70 percent of the PPD claims within California. There is no comparable source of claims-level data for workers' compensation claims filed against self-insured employers.

The data in Table 5.1 are closed claims for 1993 accidents.[9] The table shows the median (50th percentile) benefit--the one most representative or typical of claims within each group. There is considerable heterogeneity among claims in the system, so the data are reported broken down along several dimensions. They are reported separately for five disability rating categories 1-10, 11-20, 21-40, 41-70, and 71-100.[10] Due to a perception that the workers' compensation

---

[8]Policies reopen every year, and therefore all policies with claims are included.

[9]Several of the variables in the table were first required to be reported in 1993 policy year, which covers 1993 and 1994 accidents. We have reported closed claims because we have found that paid amounts are unreliable on claims that are still open.

[10]The first two rating categories constitute the bulk of the claims in the system. See Section 7 for an extensive discussion.

Table 5.1

PPD Benefits: Median Indemnity Benefits, 1993 Accident, Closed Claims

Closing Report Level	Disability Rating at Last Report									
	1-10		11-20		21-40		41-70		71-100	
	Not Rep	Rep	Not Rep	Rep	Not Rep	Rep	Not Rep	Rep	Not Rep	Rep
Medical										
1	1,311	2,918	2,205	4,785	6,488	6,838	12,042	7,269	(b)	2,127[a]
2	3,108	3,945	5,919	6,981	9,384	10,225	13,506	14,996	18,307	26,581
3	3,358	4,300	7,686	7,717	11,450	11,199	16,284	15,655	24,597	28,862
Temporary Disability Indemnity										
1	625	504	1,410	1,734	2,530	3,012	3,222	3,265	(b)	2,867[a]
2	990	908	3,030	3,024	5,775	6,138	8,880	9,499	10,000	12,769
3	672	804	2,870	3,318	5,556	6,496	8,262	10,094	9,477	5,913
Permanent Partial Disability Indemnity										
1	1,656	2,100	5,915	6,000	13,020	14,019	31,949	33,456	67,814a	65,756[a]
2	2,000	2,500	7,035	7,035	15,059	15,500	34,188	34,034	66,527	69,838
3	2,000	2,640	7,035	7,500	15,586	16,130	35,483	37,000	66,939	78,677
% Receiving Vocational Rehabilitation										
1	5	4	12	13	23	32	33	29	20[a]	25[a]
2	8	11	28	38	53	67	67	76	56	71
3	8	13	30	44	57	70	71	77	69	62
VRMA										
1	500	1,132	2,500	2,621	4,744	3,543	7,691	3,317[a]	(b)	(b)
2	2,855	4,182	5,000	5,783	6,396	7,000	8,275	7,841	9,700	10,000
3	3,909	4,347	5,994	6,117	6,888	7,312	8,000	8,000	9,467	8,000
Rehabilitation Plan										
1	500	500	1,500	599	1,825	2,000	10,874	846	(b)	(b)
2	475	622	1,500	2,995	8,395	12,364	14,000	15,807	10,000	16,916
3	475	807	1,500	4,780	10,000	12,871	15,000	15,000	16,000	10,548

[a]Based on at most 7 cases.

[b]1 to 3 cases, too few for meaningful reporting.

system is different depending upon whether the claimant has attorney representation within each of these categories, data are presented separately for represented and unrepresented claimants. The WCIRB requires up to 5 reports on every claim, and the data are broken down by report level at which the claim closed. The first report is 18 months after the policy opens. Reports occur annually after the first report. Therefore, claims that closed at the first report level closed in fewer than 18 months. Second report level claims closed between 18 and 30 months, and the third report level closed between 30 and 42 months.

In addition to separately reporting TTD and PPD, three types of data are reported for rehabilitation: (1) the percentage of claimants within each of these groups who obtain rehabilitation benefits, (2) the median amount of VRMA paid, and (3) the amount of money paid to the rehabilitation program for injured workers' participation. The latter two types of rehabilitation payments are reported as the median among those applicants who participate in the rehabilitation program. For example, only 5 percent of applicants with ratings of 10 or less who were not represented and who closed their claims within the first report level receive rehabilitation benefits, and among these the average indemnity payment as well as the average payment for a rehabilitation plan is $500. Since only 5 percent of applicants participate in rehabilitation, the median across all applicants within this category would, of course, be zero, i.e., 95 percent of claimants have no payments and no plans. In general, the average cost for rehabilitation for these claimants is very modest, perhaps one-twentieth (i.e., 5 percent) of $500 for indemnity and one-twentieth of $500 for rehabilitation or $10 on average for each.

Among the cash benefits, PPD is the most significant. It is larger than TTD in every case and larger than VRMA in general. For those applicants whose PPD ratings are 20 or less, indemnity payments during rehabilitation programs can represent a significant component of overall benefits. Only a small minority of claimants with PPD ratings of 10 or below receive rehabilitation, but among those who do, the indemnity benefits exceed both PPD and temporary benefits combined. Among workers with disabilities rated between 11 and 20, a somewhat larger proportion of applicants receive rehabilitation benefits and the percentage increases from the first to the third report level. When workers with disability ratings between 11 and 20 receive indemnity payments for participation in rehabilitation programs, the payments are almost as much as what they receive for permanent partial disability indemnity.

However, medical treatment is the primary benefit to most PPD applicants and perhaps the primary cost to employers. The medical benefits are substantial for all categories of disability ratings. But for applicants with ratings between 1 and 10 and between 11 and 20--the vast majority of the claims--medical benefits are equivalent to or greater any other type of benefit. For claims in the category of ratings between 11 and 20, medical benefits are approximately equal to the indemnity benefits paid to PPD claimants. For those applicants with lower-rated disabilities, 10 or less, the amount of medical benefits are approximately equal to all other categories of indemnity--temporary plus permanent partial disability, plus payments made for rehabilitation. PPD benefits exceed medical benefits for workers with disability ratings of 20 and above.

It is impossible to draw causal implications from the differences between represented and unrepresented claimants. However, the largest difference in indemnity occurs for rehabilitation benefits. Particularly among workers with disability ratings between 11 and 20 and for those with somewhat more severe injuries--disability ratings between 21 and 40--represented applicants are substantially more likely to receive rehabilitation benefits. In contrast, there is relatively little difference in medical benefits, temporary disability benefits, or permanent partial disability benefits.

WAGE LOSS AND THE ADEQUACY OF INDEMNITY BENEFITS

In this subsection, we will evaluate the adequacy of the three types of cash income received by workers with permanent partial disability claims, TD, PPD, and VRMA. Our measure of adequacy is the fraction of lost wages replaced by indemnity payments.

Measuring adequacy of TD and VRMA by comparing to wage loss requires no justification, since these benefits are intended to replace income, but permanent partial disability indemnity is intended to compensate the worker for a permanent disability. Disability is a multidimensional concept, encompassing all the social limitations that result from an impairment, from lost earnings capacity to lost quality of life. There is considerable controversy over what disability is intended to be compensated by the workers' compensation system. The least controversial target of compensation is the "loss of the ability to compete in an open labor market," and we use lost earnings as a

measure of lost ability to compete.[11]   This approach is consistent with
two previous evaluations of PPD benefits in California using data from
the 1960s and 1970s, CWCI (1984) and Berkowitz and Burton (1987).   Our
results from the 1990s can be compared to theirs.

Wages and Wage Loss

A permanent disability reduces the wages that a worker is able to
receive for his or her labor.   The difference between what the worker
would have received had he or she not been injured and what the worker
is able to receive constitutes *wage loss*.   To estimate wage loss and to
correct for missing wages during time out of work, we compare the wages
of the injured worker to the wages of a control group.   The control
group is selected to match the characteristics of the injured worker.
In this subsection, we describe the problem of estimating wage loss and
the control group methodology we adopt to deal with it.

There are many reasons why an injured worker suffers wage loss
associated with the injury.   The first and most obvious reason is
impairment: Certain tasks may become difficult or impossible to
complete.   In addition to impairment, if recovery and return to work
require a significant amount of time, there can be a disruption in
working habits.   If a worker cannot return to his or her previous
employer, there is an associated loss in skills that are specific to the
employer and loss in the benefits of tenure or seniority.   A workplace
injury can lead to a disruption in one's career, even when working for
the same employer; this can have long-lasting economic consequences.[12]

In Figure 5.1, the wages of a hypothetical worker who experiences a
workplace injury and then returns to regular employment are plotted over
time together with the wage the worker would have received had he or she

_____

[11] In terms of the typology in Section 3, California is a LWEC
state. Our analysis uses actual post-injury wage loss as a measure of
the loss of wage earning capacity.

[12] A reasonable comparison can be made to "displaced workers"--
workers who lose their jobs due to downsizing. Recent literature has
discovered large long-term wage losses for such workers, even though
there is no disability associated with the displacement. See, for
instance, Jacobson, Lalonde, and Sullivan (1993) and Schoeni and Dardia
(1996).

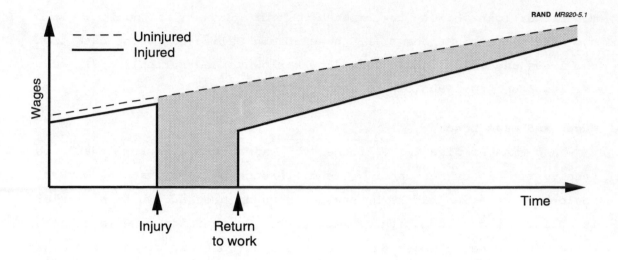

Figure 5.1--The Hypothetical Effect on Wages of a Workplace Injury

not been injured. We will refer to the former wage as the *observed injured wage* and the latter wage as the *latent uninjured wage*. The observed injured wage is represented in Figure 5.1 by the dark solid line, and we will denote it by w_{it} where the subscript t is also added to denote time from the injury. The latent uninjured wage is represented by the dashed line and is denoted by w_{ut}. The shaded area represents *wage loss*. It is the total amount of wages that the worker would have received if uninjured minus the total amount the worker actually received after the injury. Symbolically, the wage loss between the time of injury, which we will denote $t = 0$, and some future date, T, is

$$\text{wage loss} = \sum_{t=0}^{T} (w_{ut} - w_{it}) \qquad (1)$$

In Figure 5.1, after the injury, w_{it} is zero until the worker returns to work. This is the period during which the worker would receive TTD. After returning to work, the observed wage increases and eventually exceeds the pre-injury wage. However, a worker experiences wage loss until the observed wage equals the latent uninjured wage and in Figure 5.1, the worker continues to experience wage loss at the end of the period of observation. While w_{it} increases, w_{ut} increases over time also, representing accumulated experience in the labor force and tenure at a firm. Even when the observed injured wage equals the pre-injury wage, it may continue to be less than the latent uninjured wage.

If we could observe the wages in Figure 5.1 for every injured worker, estimating wage loss would be straightforward and given by Eq. (1) above. However, w_{ut} cannot be observed, and an estimate, $\hat{w}_{ut}$, must be constructed. As already noted, the pre-injury wage would not be a suitable choice as an estimator for w_{ut} because even when the observed injured wage equals the pre-injury wage, the worker may experience significant wage loss. Particularly if a worker takes a long time to recover to w_{ut}, it is likely that the worker's career is considerably behind what it would have been without the injury.

For the methodology to estimate the unobservable latent uninjured wage, we draw our inspiration from the training program evaluation literature. In that literature, to estimate the effect of a training program, the wages of the worker after training must be compared to the wage the worker would have received without the training. In the ideal case, a training evaluation would use the scientific method and randomly assign some workers to training and other workers to a *control group*. Because assignment is random, the controls and the trainees will be very similar to each other on average. Random assignment is very expensive and not always feasible. Therefore, nonexperimental methods have been developed to evaluate training programs. Recent literature has found that when an experiment is not possible, matching the trainees to other workers who have similar characteristics can, under certain circumstances, yield results that are comparable to those achieved by random assignment (Heckman, Ichimura, and Todd, 1997).

Our approach to estimating the latent uninjured wage is to match the PPD claimants prior to the injury to workers with similar characteristics. If PPD claims were randomly assigned to workers, a matching control group would be a random sample of workers in California. However, for several reasons, PPD claims are not randomly assigned. First, some industries are more likely to have injuries than others. Second, within an industry, there are differences among firms in injuries and in claiming. For instance, unionized firms have more claims than nonunionized firms (Hirsch, MacPherson, and Dumond, 1997). In addition, some firms may have in place procedures that minimize injuries or claims, such as safety awards for supervisors. Third, within a firm, there are differences among employees in the probability of an accident and in the probability of making a PPD claim given that an accident occurs. There are also differences over time in the probability of making claims depending upon, for instance, local economic conditions faced by the worker at the firm at the time of the injury.

For these reasons, we match the PPD claimant to another worker who is working in the same industry in which the injured worker worked in the quarter of injury. We require that the matched worker be working at the same firm as well, and also that he or she be working during the injured worker's quarter of injury. These conditions assure that the firm and industry conditions are held constant, and that the local economic conditions facing the control and the injured worker are also the same. Within the firm, we require that the control have wages that are similar to the wages received by the injured worker prior to injury.

It is possible that among workers in the same firm making the same wage, workers who make PPD claims will be systematically different from those who do not. Since the data from which the controls are drawn do not have any demographic variables that can be used in matching, differences in gender, tenure, age, and education, among other things, may remain between a particular worker and that worker's control. However, to the degree that gender, tenure, age, education or other things do not affect the probability of injuries or PPD claims after conditioning on industry, firm, and wage, the sample of controls should have the same characteristics as the sample of injured workers. Below, we compare the contemporaneous wages of the injured workers and their controls before the injured worker's quarter of injury as a check on the quality of the controls.

After the injury, in each quarter, the wages of the injured workers, w_i, are compared to the wages of their controls, $\hat{w}_u$, to estimate wage loss. An estimate of cumulative wage loss is calculated by summing over time for every worker the wage loss in every quarter, discounted to the quarter of injury. We then calculate cumulative *proportional wage loss*, which divides cumulative wage loss by the total wages received by the control over the period.

While the statistical problem is the same, namely, estimating the latent uninjured wage, our methodology and data differ from those used by CWCI (1984) and Berkowitz and Burton (1987). Both reports projected pre-injury wages into the post-injury period.[13] Our approach has several advantages. First, like Berkowitz and Burton, but unlike CWCI, our approach incorporates economic changes during the post-injury period. This may be particularly important in California, since many of the workers in the sample were injured during a recession and recovered simultaneously with California's economic recovery. Second, our methodological assumption, that an injured worker would have done as well as a comparable worker at the same firm, is not dependent upon arbitrary functional form and distributional assumptions. Third, the control group can provide a comparison not only for wages but also for time out of work. As a result, the effect of workplace injuries can be broken down into effect on wages and effect on time out of work, providing a more complete analysis of wage loss.

Disability and Labor Force Participation

Return to work after a workplace injury is often regarded as synonymous with recovery. However, if permanently disabled workers are more likely to have difficulty retaining employment, we may also observe

---

[13]CWCI, using claims from 1975-1976, estimated the latent uninjured wage by calculating an average pre-injury quarterly earnings and multiplying it by 16 (the number of quarters in the four years after the injury over which they observe benefits). They then compared this amount to actual earnings over the four years following the accident to determine gross earnings loss. This methodology ignores, as they note in the report, any raises or promotions that would have occurred in the years after the accident, an omission that would be more significant for young workers. After some adjustments to gross earnings loss, they then projected the loss to age 65 to obtain a lifetime measure. Berkowitz and Burton, using claims from 1968, calculated the latent uninjured wage by multiplying pre-injury wages by an expected growth ratio (EGR) calculated using the observed post-injury growth rate of workers who received a 1-5 percent disability rating. They then subtracted actual post-injury earnings from the estimated post-injury earnings.

a reduction in labor force attachment for injured workers after the initial return to work.[14] Indeed, economic theory predicts that workers who have suffered a loss in ability to compete in the labor market are more likely to choose not to work. Working may have a higher cost for the injured worker--for instance, the worker may be in pain at work. At the same time, the benefits from work, for instance, the wage the worker is able to receive, may be lower. Since the costs are higher and the benefits lower, other activities such as raising children or retirement may be preferred to working disabled.

Calculating wage loss by comparing the wages of individuals who work to the wages of their controls does not take into account this additional time out of work. There are two reasons why labor force attachment after the injury should be accounted for in calculating wage loss. First, if the typical injured worker works fewer quarters after the injury than the typical control, even if both make the same wage when they are working, the total wages over time will be higher for the controls than for the injured workers. This ought to be counted as wage loss. Second, even if the typical injured worker worked the same number of quarters as the typical control, if the workers with the most severe disabilities are more likely to be unable to work, then failing to include the workers without wages effectively excludes the largest wage losses and therefore the estimated wage loss is too low.

However, there are many reasons why individuals may choose not to work. They might have become unemployed, or they might have chosen to spend time raising a child or going to school even if they had not been injured. An additional problem is data-related: In the administrative wage data used in this analysis, if an individual moves out of state and

_____

[14]Evidence that employment retention after initial return to work is problematic for injured workers is provided by Butler, Johnson, and Baldwin (1995). Using a sample of 1,850 workers injured between 1974 and 1986 in Ontario who initially returned to work, they found that 40 percent were not working at the interview date (during 1989-1990) due to their work injury. Since their sample was drawn from workers still visiting their workers' compensation doctor in 1989-1990, we expect that the employment retention of our sample will be higher than theirs. As discussed in Section 3, see also "Return to Work Patterns for Permanent Impaired Workers," *Texas Monitor*, Vol. 1, No. 4, Winter 1996, pp. 1-3.

works in another state, their wages are missing. We do not want to attribute all missing wages to wage loss.[15]

In this report, we approach the problem of missing wages in two ways. The first way assumes that only the initial period of missing wages following the injury is wage loss. After initial return to work, any subsequent quarters out of work are treated as random and ignored even when the control is working. Wage loss and cumulative wage loss are calculated using only the wages observed when both the control and the injured worker are working. The second way assumes that all time out of work over and above what the controls experience is injury-related. This approach assumes that the controls capture the time out of work that would have happened had the injured worker not been injured.

The first approach, referred to as Method I, is illustrated in Figure 5.2. The figure plots the wages over time of a hypothetical injured worker and the control. The solid line represents the injured worker's wage, and the dashed line represents the control worker's wage. As in Figure 5.1, the injured worker spends some time out of work after the injury but then returns to work. Figure 5.2 differs from Figure 5.1 in that the injured worker experiences additional time out of work after the injury beginning at time A. The injured worker has a second return to work at time B, and eventually both the injured worker and the control retire (at the same time) and the injured worker experiences no further wage loss. As before, the shaded area represents wage loss. This approach does not count as wage loss the wages received by the control while the injured worker is out of work the second time, between times A and B.

---

[15]This problem is noted by CWCI (1984) as well. They calculated injury-related earnings loss by adjusting the gross amount downward using survey responses for a sample of claimants and the judgment of the analysts. One rule they adopted is that any earnings loss that occurred after the claimant's physician provided an unrestricted medical release to return to regular employment is ignored. Other rules were applied on a case-by-case basis. The difficulty with this approach is that it is impossible to judge whether the rules adopted were appropriate. It is also impossible to replicate.

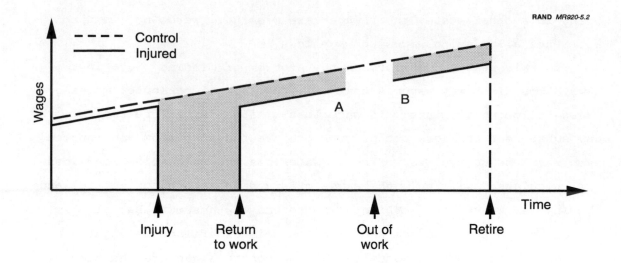

Figure 5.2--Calculation of Wage Loss During Quarters When Both Are Working

The second approach, referred to as Method II, is illustrated for the same hypothetical worker and control in Figure 5.3. In this case, at all times when the injured worker is out of work and the control is still working both during the period after injury and between times A and B, the injured worker is assigned zero wages, and the wages of the control are counted as wage loss for the injured worker. However, after retirement, since the control is not working either, no further wage loss is counted for the injured worker. In Figure 5.3, the shaded area is larger than the shaded area in Figure 5.2--there is more wage loss under the second approach than under the first. But this is not necessarily so, if the control is out of work. Although not illustrated in Figure 5.3, in the second approach, if the control had been out of work but the injured worker had not, then the control would have been assigned wages of zero, and the injured worker would have experienced wage *gain*. Total wage loss will be larger in the second approach only if injured workers spend more time out of work than their controls. We do observe greater wage loss observed in the second approach, indicating that workplace injuries lead to additional periods of time out of work even after first return to work.

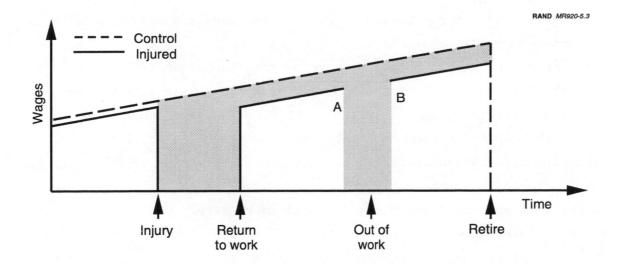

Figure 5.3--Calculation of Wage Loss Including Quarters of Nonwork

We report both estimates because the first approach may be regarded as a lower bound on wage loss and the second approach as an upper bound. If the target of PPD is to replace earnings loss, as it is for TTD or VRMA, then it is straightforward to see that the first approach is an underestimate: Workplace injuries lead to lower labor force attachment and resulting lost earnings that are not counted in the first approach. The second approach is an unbiased estimate of lost earnings, but may still be an overestimate of losses due to disability. Time out of work may be affected by the PPD payments as well as the injury. A large literature in labor economics has shown that higher amounts of nonlabor income increase the probability that an individual will choose not to work. Workers' compensation benefits increase the nonlabor income of PPD claimants and therefore increase the probability they will not work.[16] This benefit-induced increase in time out of work, if it

_____

[16]There are likely to be different effects from TTD benefits and PPD benefits. A large literature has shown that TTD benefits increase the time it takes to return to work. For example, Meyer, Viscusi, and Durbin (1995) estimate the effect of temporary disability benefits on injury duration using a "natural experiment" provided by the increase in the maximum weekly benefit in Kentucky in 1980 and Michigan in 1982. Their estimates suggest a 3 to 4 percent increase in injury duration resulting from a 10 percent increase in the benefit level. PPD benefits will have a smaller effect than TTD benefits because TTD benefits are not paid when an individual returns to work, leading to a disincentive

exists, should not be counted as part of the wage loss that needs to be compensated by PPD indemnity.

It may be that a better measure of the loss of ability to compete is not earnings loss, but the amount that would have been lost had the injured worker returned to work. If this is the case, the first approach is still an underestimate, and the second is still an overestimate. The wage that nonworkers could have made if still working is likely to be smaller than the actual wages for the workers who are working (since the greater the wage, the more likely you will choose to work). In other words, consider two workers who each made $20 before an injury. After both are injured, one can now make only $5, and the other can make $15. After the injury, both would have chosen to work at $15, and both would have chosen not to at $5. Therefore, one is working, and one is not. Our first approach to estimating wage loss, since it does not count workers not working, estimates the average loss as $5. Our second approach counts $20 for the nonworker and $5 for the worker, making the average loss $12.50. The true loss of ability to compete would be $5 for the worker and $15 for the nonworker leading to an average loss of $10. The first approach, therefore, is an underestimate of the true loss, and the second approach an overestimate of the true loss.

Wage Loss Replacement

Since workers' compensation benefits are intended to replace wages lost (TTD and VRMA), and to compensate for lost ability to compete in the labor market (PPD) (by our proxy, wage loss), an evaluation of the adequacy of workers' compensation is provided by determining what fraction of wage loss is replaced by benefits for the average PPD claimant.

---

to return to work, whereas PPD benefits are paid while the individual works, and are not reduced when wages increase. The effect on employment is an example of what economists refer to as "income" and "substitution" effect. TTD leads to lower employment because TTD is a substitute for employment. PPD is not a substitute, but it still may lead to lower employment because it has an "income effect:" The need to work will be lower so the worker may choose not to work.

The measure that we will focus on to evaluate adequacy is the
fraction of wage loss that is replaced by workers' compensation
benefits, or the *replacement rate*:

$$\text{replacement rate} = \frac{\text{benefits}}{\text{wage loss}}$$

The estimates of the replacement rate reported below are calculated
by (1) aggregating the wage loss across the workers in the category
being analyzed (e.g., all PPD claimants or claimants with a particular
disability rating range), (2) aggregating benefits within the category,
and then (3) dividing the aggregate benefits by the aggregate wage
loss.[17]

In California and many other states, the statutory wage replacement
goal for temporary total disability benefits and for permanent total
benefits is two-thirds of pre-injury wages. By extension, we assume
that the test for adequacy for permanent partial benefits is two-thirds
as well.[18] This is also the test for adequacy employed by Berkowitz and
Burton (1987) and CWCI (1984).

Data

Our analysis of the adequacy of workers' compensation indemnity
linked the WCIRB data (described above) to wage data from the State of
California Employment Development Department (EDD). Every quarter,
employers covered by Unemployment Insurance (UI) in California are
required to report the quarterly earnings of every employee to the EDD.

---

[17]This approach is adopted because for any particular worker, the
estimate of wage loss calculated using the control methodology may not
provide a good estimate of the lost wages for that worker. For
instance, an injured worker may be matched to a control who moves out of
state two quarters after the injured worker is injured, even though the
injured worker would not have moved. On average, however, for large
enough sample sizes, the control methodology provides a good measure of
wage loss since some injured workers are matched to controls that
understate wage loss, while others are matched to controls that lead to
overstated wage loss.

[18]The most direct comparison is TPD in California, which, as noted
above, compensates the worker with two-thirds of the difference between
what he or she made before and what he or she currently is making in
modified work.

These reports are stored in the Base Wage file. The industries covered
by UI are virtually identical to the industries covered by workers'
compensation[19] and therefore a worker injured at a firm for which he or
she can make a workers' compensation claim should also have a record for
that quarter in the Base Wage file. With greater than 90 percent of
employees in California covered by the UI system, the matched WCIRB-EDD
data provide a substantially complete and accurate California quarterly
earnings history for PPD claimants. We linked claims data[20] from
injuries occurring in 1991-1994 to wage data for every claimant from the
fourth quarter of 1989 through the second quarter of 1996.[21]

As noted above, the WCIRB data do not include workers injured at
self-insured firms. This is likely to lead to a sample of workers drawn
from firms that are on average smaller than the average firm in
California. We believe that if this biases our results, the direction
of bias is toward overstating the amount of wage loss. Larger firms are
generally more able to place disabled employees in modified work, so the
claimants excluded from our sample may be more likely to return to their
employer. This exclusion is likely to artifactually increase our

----

[19]In both systems, federal civilian and military employees, U.S.
postal service workers, railroad employees, and the self-employed are
excluded.

[20]We do not restrict our analysis to closed claims. Closed claims
may be an unrepresentative sample of claims. We also do not use paid
dollar amounts, but instead use incurred dollar amounts. When claims
close, the incurred is equal to the paid amount. We have found that the
incurred amounts are good predictors of the future paid amounts when
closed.

[21]To link the WCIRB data to the EDD data, the Social Security
Number (SSN) of the claimant on the WCIRB was sent to EDD, and an
extract from the Base Wage file was returned to RAND. To match claims
to wages, the record on the WCIRB had to have an SSN. In 1991 and
1992, less than half of the claims have SSNs (41 percent in 1992 and 32
percent in 1991). The primary reason for this is that the WCIRB did not
require reporting of SSN until 1993. Only if a claim is still open at
the time of the 1993 report level can it have an SSN (i.e., claims that
closed at the first report level for 1992 cannot have SSNs, or 15
percent of 1992 claims, and claims that closed by the second report
level for 1991 cannot have SSNs, or 27 percent of claims). Even if the
claim is open by the 1993 report level, while many reported SSNs, it was
not required. The results using 1991 and 1992 data are biased toward
later closing claims, but the implications of this for wage loss are
unclear.

estimate of time out of work following injury, and may also artifactually decrease our estimate of the wage received upon initial return to work.

There are also several limitations to the EDD data. First, taxes paid by workers are not subtracted from the quarterly earnings reported to the EDD.[22] Since workers' compensation benefits are untaxed, and earnings are taxed, wage loss calculated from the EDD is before-tax, while benefits received are essentially after-tax. Therefore, the fraction of after-tax income replaced will be higher than the fraction of before-tax income replaced. We examine the sensitivity of our results to this limitation of the data at the end of this section.[23] Another limitation of the data is that information on a maximum of only five years of post-injury earnings is available. If earnings losses are sustained beyond five years after the injury, our measure of earnings loss will be understated, and the fraction of wage loss replaced correspondingly overstated. We also examine the sensitivity of our results to this limitation of the data at the close of this section.

Another limitation of the EDD data is the level of wages reported, which is quarterly. With quarterly wages, if two workers make the same weekly wage and one works only half of the quarter, the latter worker will have a lower quarterly wage. This implies that our first approach for estimating wage loss includes some time out of work.

_____

[22]Employer-provided fringe benefits are not reported to EDD. If loss of employment is a large component of wage loss, then the loss of fringe benefits such as health insurance should also be counted as wage loss. Even for workers who do not lose their jobs, fringe benefits increase with income, an effect that is attributed to the relationship between income and productivity which leads to greater bargaining power for higher income workers (see, for instance, Benedict and Shaw, 1995). If disabled workers experience a decrease in fringe benefits along with the decrease in income, then the wage loss results even for those still working are understated.

[23]Another limitation of the EDD data is that they do not report earnings in the uncovered sector, or, more importantly, earnings in another state. However, the control methodology provides a way to correct for this problem. Only if the injured worker is more likely than the control to receive earnings in the uncovered sector or out of state will this bias the result.

Due to data limitations, we had to simulate the benefits paid from the WCIRB data for our comparison with the wage loss calculated using the EDD data. We assume that TTD benefits commence during the quarter of injury, followed by VRMA benefits.[24] When both VRMA and TTD are exhausted, we assume that the payment of permanent partial disability benefits begins. We use the WCIRB disability rating[25] and the WCIRB average weekly wage to derive the weekly benefits paid and the number of weeks of benefits using the benefit schedule.[26]

We do not subtract lawyer's fees from the benefits paid to the claimant, although in practice, benefits for represented claimants are reduced by 12 percent to pay the attorney. Data on attorney representation and applicant lawyer's fees are reliably available only for closed claims in the WCIRB, but our analysis is not restricted to closed claims. Our replacement rates will therefore overstate the fraction of wage loss actually replaced by indemnity.

Our approach to calculating benefits may be regarded as an evaluation of the system as it is supposed to work. It has the considerable additional advantage of allowing for simulation of alternative benefit schedules. For example, we later report our

---

[24]The WCIRB data do not report the duration of either temporary total benefits or vocational rehabilitation benefits. We calculate a weekly benefit for each using the average weekly wage reported in the WCIRB data. We derive the number of weeks of benefits of TD from the weekly benefit and the total TD benefits incurred. Similarly, we calculate the number of weeks of benefits of VRMA from the average wage and the total VRMA incurred.

[25]We use the last rating observed in the WCIRB data.

[26]In practice, a large fraction of PPD benefits are paid in a lump sum upon compromise and release. Our method spreads the payment out over time, using the manner in which it would be paid if the case were not settled by compromise and release. The reported disability rating in the WCIRB is set to justify the indemnity amount paid, so the two methods should yield the same final amount. However, our method will understate the total benefits paid for workers with very large disability ratings (a very small fraction of claimants) who have received their future benefits in a lump sum, since payments continue to be made after five years and the simulation will capture only the first five years of benefits. On the other hand, these workers are likely to continue to experience significant wage loss beyond the window of time in which we observe them. Therefore, our benefit calculation undercounts their benefits, but our wage loss calculation undercounts their wage loss.

simulation of the 1993 reform benefit increases on the injured workers
in our data.

The match rate between the WCIRB and the EDD data was very high.
Out of 343,576 claims for accidents from 1991-1994 with valid Social
Security Numbers[27] on the WCIRB data, only 5 percent were not found on
the Base Wage file. We used a number of steps to arrive at a
considerably smaller final analysis sample of injured workers matched to
controls. Among those claims with wage data, 3 percent of claims were
later deleted because no wages were found prior to the quarter of
injury.[28] From the remaining claims, we drew a 20 percent random sample
and selected controls. As discussed above, we selected controls by
choosing another employee at the firm where the injured worker was
injured. Like the injured worker, we require that the control worker
have wages in the quarter of injury and in at least one quarter prior.
We also require that the injured worker and the control receive very
similar wages. [29] We selected up to 10 controls per worker.

---

[27]We eliminated claims with SSNs that appeared multiple times in
the WCIRB data, and had three or more names and three or more
birthdates. This eliminated less than 1 percent of the claims. After
matching, an additional 0.7 percent of claims with more than 2 names in
the quarter of injury on the EDD file were deemed invalid and deleted.

[28]If wages were not found in the quarter of injury, the quarter of
injury is reassigned to the last quarter with wages prior to the injury,
up to one year. If no wages are found before the quarter of injury at
all, the worker was not used in the analysis because it was not possible
to match to a control using a pre-injury wage.

[29]Specifically, we average the wages for the injured worker in the
four quarters prior to injury to obtain an average quarterly wage. Once
a potential control worker is found working at the same firm, that
individual can be a control for the injured worker only if the log of
the average quarterly wage of the potential control worker is equal to
the injured worker's log average quarterly wage plus or minus 10 percent
of the standard deviation of the log average quarterly wage of the
population of PPD claimants for injuries in that quarter. For example,
for a worker with an average quarterly wage of $3,000, the log average
quarterly wage is 3.48. If the injury occurred in first quarter 1993,
the standard deviation of the log average quarterly wage is .80.
Therefore, the log of the average quarterly wage of the control must be
between 3.40 and 3.56. This implies a range in dollars between $2,512
and $3,631. The average for the control is taken over the five quarters
prior to and including the injured worker's quarter of injury. For both
the worker and the controls, if wages are not found in a quarter prior
to the injury quarter, the missing quarter is not included in the

Approximately 65 percent of SSNs were matched to controls.[30] Finally, among those with controls, only workers with disability ratings greater than or equal to 1 (i.e., only those that receive permanent partial disability benefits) and without missing disability rating, total temporary disability benefits paid, and preinjury average wage were included in the final analyses.

Many of the injured workers have multiple controls. We use all controls in the analysis and weight each control. For a worker with n controls, the weight is given by $1/n$. This increases the reliability of the estimates. With multiple controls, the injured worker is being compared to the average of the outcomes for workers at the same firm making the same wage. Table 5.2 reports the number of observations and the number of corresponding controls by year and disability rating. The total number of controls is 102,526, and the total number of injured workers is 29,322.

RESULTS

In this section, we report the results of the wage loss analyses conducted so far. The first set of results characterizes the adequacy of the California workers' compensation system for permanently disabled workers. We find that an important component of wage loss is time out of work after the initial return to work. The second set of results describes time out of work of California PPD claimants over the 4-5 years after the injury. Finally, we describe the proportional wage loss and the replacement rate by disability rating categories and assess the equity of the system.

---

average. Both the injured worker and the control worked at least one quarter prior to the injury.

[30] In addition to making the same average total wage as the injured worker over the four quarters prior to the injury, the control also was required to receive this wage during at least one quarter at the firm at which the injured worker was injured. This additional condition was added to reduce the data extraction complexity for EDD. We expect that this reduced the match rate considerably, but do not expect that it has any effect on the results. In future work, we hope to eliminate this condition.

Table 5.2

Final Sample Sizes by Injury Year and Rating Category, PPD Claimants and Controls

Injury Year	Disability Rating Category	Number of PPD Claimants	Number of Controls
1991		6,289	21,344
	1-5	1,348	4,440
	6-10	1,165	3,889
	11-20	1,660	5,541
	21-35	1,279	4,485
	36-99	837	2,989
1992		5,779	20,183
	1-5	1,200	4,024
	6-10	1,074	3,602
	11-20	1,567	5,510
	21-35	1,260	4,548
	36-99	678	2,499
1993		8,107	28,862
	1-5	1,522	5,360
	6-10	1,543	5,482
	11-20	2,339	8,361
	21-35	1,791	6,444
	36-99	912	3,195
1994		9,147	32,137
	1-5	1,848	6,198
	6-10	1,931	6,861
	11-20	2,883	10,068
	21-35	1,798	6,382
	36-99	687	2,628

Wage Loss and the Adequacy of Workers' Compensation

In Table 5.3, we report the cumulative wage loss, proportional wage loss, and replacement rate for accident years 1991-1993. All dollar amounts are before-tax, and expressed in 1997 dollars using the Southwest Regional CPI. The cumulative wage loss is the discounted sum over all quarters of the difference in before-tax quarterly wages between the injured worker and the control worker in the years after the injury.[31] This represents our estimate of how much injured workers lost in wages for the period of 3 to 5 years. The proportional wage loss divides the cumulative wage loss by the total amount of before-tax

---

[31]An annual rate of 2.3 percent is used to discount future earnings. This is the same real discount rate used in research by the Social Security Administration.

Table 5.3

Cumulative Wage Loss, Proportional Wage Loss and Replacement Rate, 1991-1993

Year of Injury	Years from Injury	Method I. Only Quarters with Injured and Control Working				Method II. Including Injury-Related Time Out of Work			
		Cumul. Wage Loss	Bene-fits	Prop. Wage Loss	Repl. Rate	Cumul. Wage Loss	Bene-fits	Prop. Wage Loss	Repl. Rate
91	5	23,692	11,426	19.9	48.2	46,677	17,684	39.9	37.9
91-92	4	20,844	11,232	20.9	53.9	37,829	16,070	39.3	42.5
91-93	3	15,939	10,613	19.9	66.6	29,201	14,722	38.2	50.4
91	5	23,692	11,426	19.9	48.2	46,677	17,684	39.9	37.9
91	4	21,705	11,092	21.8	51.1	38,743	16,043	40.1	41.4
91	3	18,182	10,458	23.0	57.5	31,960	14,682	41.8	45.9
92	4	19,121	11,513	19.0	60.2	36,016	16,123	37.6	44.8
92	3	14,761	10,867	18.6	73.6	27,122	14,764	36.1	54.4
93	3	14,258	10,458	17.3	73.4	27,990	14,721	35.7	52.6

dollars earned by the controls. This estimates the proportion of income that a worker would have earned but has lost due to the injury. The replacement rate divides the total amount of benefits paid by the cumulative wage loss. This estimates what portion of the total wage loss was compensated by workers' compensation indemnity benefits.[32]

Results are reported for three, four, and five years after the injury for pairs of workers-controls who were still present. We do not include missing data in the calculation of cumulative wage loss. During quarters where wages are missing, we do not count the benefit received either. The results are also reported for each year separately for as many years after the accident as are available for that accident year.

Method I reports the results calculated using only quarters where both the injured worker and the control are working, the method illustrated in Figure 5.2 above that provides a lower bound (underestimate) of wage loss. Using Method I, the results in the first

[32]As noted above, the after-tax replacement rate will be higher than the before-tax replacement rate reported in the table. This is because workers' compensation benefits are not taxable. We report all estimates in before-tax dollars because we do not have data on taxes paid. We report the sensitivity of the estimates to taxes and other data limitations later in this section.

row of Table 5.3 indicate that over the five years after the injury, PPD claimants earn $23,692 less than their controls. This represents a 19.9 percent proportional wage loss. The fourth column in each panel reports the replacement rate. Using Method I, the replacement rate in the five years following the injury is only 48.2 percent. In addition, the replacement rate falls with additional years after the injury, from a 66.6 percent replacement rate after three years. Since most PPD recipients no longer receive benefits after five years, this suggests that wage loss is severe and growing after five years. The results show an increase in cumulative wage loss between the fourth and fifth year of approximately $3,000.

Method II reports the results adjusting for injury-related time out of work, the method illustrated in Figure 5.3 above that provides an upper bound (overestimate) of disability-related wage loss. We expect that if injured workers have lower labor force attachment, experiencing more time out of work than their controls after the initial return to work, then the Method II results will show greater wage loss. Indeed, significantly greater wage loss is observed in Method II. When we add to wage loss the periods when injured workers drop out of work (after their initial lost time with the injury), cumulative wage loss doubles. PPD claimants earn $46,677 less than their controls over the five years following the accident. This represents a proportional wage loss of almost 40 percent. After five years, only 37.9 percent of this loss is replaced by workers' compensation benefits. Even after three years, the replacement rate is only 50.4 percent when injury-related time out of work is included.

The only year for which five years of post-injury earnings are available is 1991. Therefore, the five-year replacement rates for the 1991-1993 pooled sample are determined by 1991 data only. It is necessary to compare the 1991 data to the later years to determine whether the five-year results are generalizable. In addition, when comparing the third, fourth, and fifth years in the pooled sample, the comparison is not only among workers injured in the same year over time, but also among workers injured at different times. For instance, in the pooled sample the increase in lost earnings between the fourth and fifth year could represent an increase in lost earnings for 1991 workers, but it can also represent a decrease between 1991 and 1992 in the effect of the injury. We therefore report the results disaggregated by year in the table.

The three-year wage loss results are available for all three injury years. In Row 6, the replacement rate for workers injured in 1991 using the conservative Method I is 57.5 percent. By comparison, the three-year Method I measure of wage loss for 1992 (in Row 8) and 1993 (in Row 9) is almost three-quarters. This indicates that the five-year replacement for 1992 and 1993 is likely to be higher than the results in Row 1 suggest.

The Method II wage loss results--which include injury-related time out of work, indicate once again that workers injured in 1991 suffered more severe wage loss and lower wage replacement than workers injured in 1992 and 1993. This may be because more of the recovery period for injured workers in 1991 occurred during California's recession. It may also be because the 1991 data over-represent late-closing claims. A third explanation may be that beginning January 1, 1992, the number of weeks of benefits for workers with disability ratings above 25 was increased. Nonetheless, the Method II replacement rates are less than 55 percent in every injury year, even when only three years of wage loss have accumulated. The differences across years are not as large as for the Method I results.

The wage loss results are represented graphically in Figures 5.4 and 5.5. These figures plot the mean quarterly before-tax wages of the injured workers and the controls over time, in the same manner as was presented hypothetically in Figures 5.1-5.3. The horizontal axis measures quarters before and after the injury, with 0 representing the quarter of injury. The vertical axis measures quarterly wages and benefits. The solid lines represent before-tax wages, while the dashed line represents the sum of before-tax wages and workers' compensation benefits of the injured worker. The thin dotted lines represent two standard deviations above and below the means. The sample contains 1991-1993 data, the years for which a minimum of four years of post-

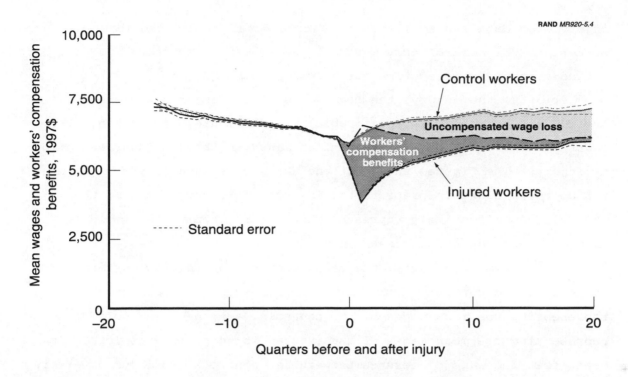

Figure 5.4--Mean Quarterly Wages and Benefits for Workers Injured Between 1991 and 1993 and Controls, Including Only Quarters When Both Are Working

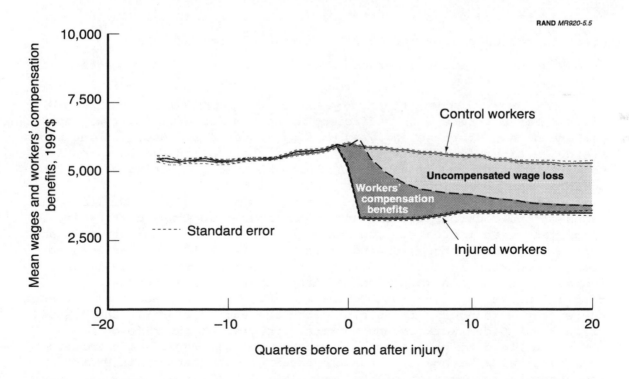

Figure 5.5--Mean Quarterly Wages and Benefits for Workers Injured Between 1991-1993 and Controls, Including Injury-Related Time Out of Work

injury wage data are available.[33] Figure 5.4 includes the injured
worker and the control only when both are working, Method I. Figure 5.5
includes injury-related time out of work, Method II.

Prior to the injury, the mean wages of the injured workers and
their controls are indistinguishable in both Figure 5.4 and 5.5. The
controls were selected to have similar wages in the four quarters prior
to injury. The figures show that the two groups have very similar wages
for up to 10 quarters prior to the injury. This suggests that the
controls can effectively represent what the injured worker would have
made if he or she had not been injured.

At the time of injury, the mean wages of the injured workers and
the controls diverge.[34] The area between the upper solid line,
representing the mean wages of the controls, and the lower solid line,
representing the mean wages of the injured workers, is wage loss. It is
clear that the wage difference between the controls and injured workers
is statistically significant. When only working quarters are included,
the proportional wage loss is 20 percent over 4-5 years. When injury-
related time out of work is included in the wage loss calculation, the
proportional wage loss increases to almost 40 percent. This is apparent
from Figures 5.4 and 5.5, as the area between the quarterly wages of the

---

[33]We have aggregated across years in the plots to increase sample
sizes. For quarters with sufficient numbers of observations, we have
performed many of these analyses on single quarters alone, and the plots
are not noticeably different, except that the smaller sample sizes lead
to more volatility. We also think that the averaged estimates have the
advantage of averaging across economic conditions.

[34]In all of the figures with working quarters only, Method I, the
wages of the controls decline until the injured workers' quarter of
injury and then increase. The reason for this is that the controls are
chosen from among those working in that quarter. If a worker is also
observed working 10 quarters prior, or 10 quarters post, this is an
indication that this worker has greater labor force attachment.
Marginal workers enter close to the quarter of injury, and drop out soon
thereafter. Younger workers also enter the sample close to the quarter
of injury. Older workers and workers with greater labor force
attachment tend to have higher wages than younger workers and workers
with marginal attachment. Thus the observed wage pattern is driven by
the changing composition of the controls. A similar effect will occur
for the average wages of the injured workers, and the control method
insures that the pattern does not lead to biased wage loss estimates.

controls and the injured workers is considerably larger in Figure 5.5 than in Figure 5.4.

The wage loss is divided into two areas. Below the dashed line is the fraction of lost wages replaced by workers' compensation indemnity benefits. This is larger in Figure 5.4 (54 percent replaced after four years and 49 percent after five) than in Figure 5.5 (43 percent replaced after four years and 38 percent after five).

In Figures 5.4 and 5.5, the replacement of lost earnings is concentrated in the period immediately after the injury. In the initial four quarters, the replacement rate appears to be high. This suggests that temporary disability benefits adequately compensate for much of the lost earnings associated with the time out of work immediately following the injury. Given that, as noted earlier, fewer than 30 percent of the injured workers are receiving the weekly benefit maximum ($336), it is not surprising that a large fraction of initial earnings losses are compensated. The fraction of lost earnings replaced declines as the time from the injury increases. If a worker is still out of work and receiving VRMA, the maximum benefit for VRMA ($246) is lower than for TD. If the worker is still out of work and receiving PPD, the maximum benefit is lower still. This would lead to a declining replacement rate for workers still out of work.

If the worker has returned to work, and is now receiving PPD benefits, the replacement rate may be high while they are still receiving benefits, but the benefits are of short duration relative to the duration of wage loss. In neither Figure 5.4 nor 5.5 is there much evidence of recovery since the post-injury difference between the mean wage of the injured workers and of the controls does not diminish with time after the injury.[35] Therefore, the fraction of wage loss replaced

_____

[35]The lack of wage recovery is not driven by workers who do not ever return to work. The results do not change if the fewer than 10 percent of workers who never return to work after the quarter of injury are excluded. Approximately one-half of this is "injury-related" since 5 percent of controls do not return after the injured workers' quarter of injury, which is the quarter in which they are selected. Of those who return to work, 74 percent of claimants return to work within one quarter. Ninety-five percent have returned at least once by two years.

diminishes rapidly as an increasing number of injured workers exhaust their PPD benefits.

Further evidence on the quality of the controls is offered by Figure 5.6, which shows the average quarterly before-tax wages and benefits of workers injured in 1994 and their controls. Since the data are available from fourth quarter 1989, it is possible to construct a five-year (20 quarter) pre-injury wage history. As is apparent from Figure 5.6, even five years before the injury, the match between the controls and the injured workers is of very high quality.

The large increase in proportional wage loss when injury-related time out of work is included in the wage loss calculation requires some further investigation. Figure 5.7 reports the number of workers injured in 1991-1993 and the number of their controls working in each quarter, i.e., with wage observations in the EDD Base Wage file. The number of workers is highest in the quarter of injury, the only quarter where we are certain that the workers are observed. Progressively, prior to the injury, the sample size increases as workers enter the sample. The decline in the number of controls working after quarter 0 reflects the natural attrition from the California labor force as (for instance) workers retire or move out of state. This occurs for both controls and injured workers. By comparison, however, the decline in labor force participation for the injured workers is dramatic. Initially, approximately one-third of the injured workers experience an injury-related absence. This decreases to one-quarter by the end of the period.[36] We have found that after initial return to work, the injured workers are more likely than controls to be absent in any given quarter. They are also more likely to disappear from the sample in any given quarter.

---

[36]The figure is truncated at 10 quarters because the fourth-quarter 1993 injured workers are not observed beyond 10 quarters after the quarter of injury. This would lead to a rapid decline in the sample size that is driven only by the data limitations and not by the working decisions of the members of the sample. Lower labor force participation after the injury continues out five years using the 1991 data. See Figure 5.8.

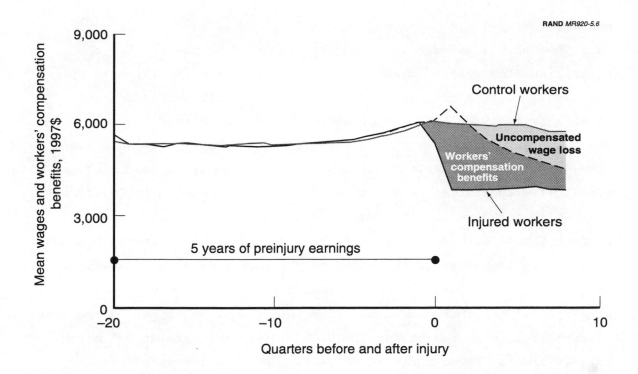

Figure 5.6--Mean Quarterly Wages and Benefits for Workers Injured in 1994 and Controls, Including Injury-Related Time Out of Work

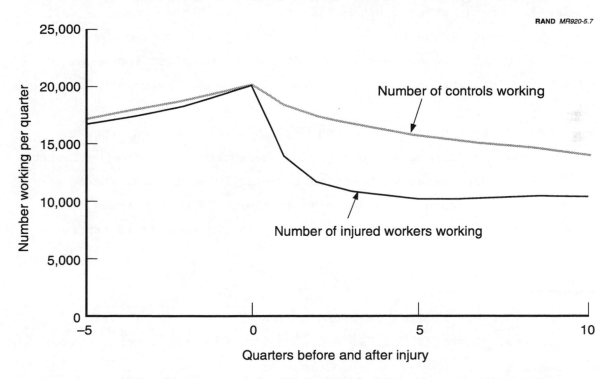

Figure 5.7--Number Working in Each Quarter, Workers Injured Between 1991 and 1993 and Controls

Summary

The results on wage loss suggest that by four years after the injury, half or less of disability-related wage loss is replaced by California workers' compensation benefits. If injury-related time out of work is included in the wage loss calculation, Method II, approximately half of wages are replaced after three years, and less than 40 percent are replaced after five. This suggests that time out of work following initial return to work is a large problem in California.

While not directly comparable, because the estimates are from a different time period and use different methods, our estimates are equal to or below the previous estimates of the wage replacement rate in California. Using data on PPD claimants from 1968, Berkowitz and Burton (1987) concluded that during the five years after an injury, 47 percent of lost wages were replaced. The CWCI (1984) wage loss study, using 1975-1976 data, found that the 49 percent of lifetime wage loss is compensated (a lifetime wage replacement that seems implausibly high based on our present analysis). Our conservative estimate of the replacement rate, which counts only wage loss while working, is 48.2 percent after five years. However, if injury-related time out of work is included, the replacement rates after five years are approximately 38 percent, which is much lower than that found by Berkowitz and Burton and CWCI.

By the standard of two-thirds wage loss replaced, our results suggest that California's benefits are inadequate.[37] However, given the difficulties associated with estimating wage loss, the robustness of this conclusion needs to be explored further. We will examine the sensitivity of our estimates to various data limitations in the next subsection.

ROBUSTNESS OF RESULTS

Our data are limited in various ways that may affect our conclusions. First, EDD data do not report after-tax income. Since

---

[37]Berkowitz and Burton (1987) were also able to calculate the fraction of wage loss replaced in Florida and Wisconsin. Florida replaced 59 percent of wage loss, and Wisconsin replaced 75 percent of wage loss. This suggests that the test for adequacy is attainable.

workers' compensation benefits are not subject to income taxes, the wage replacement rate of after-tax income will be higher than the estimates in the previous subsection. A second concern is the limited time horizon over which we measure wage loss. It is beyond the ability of our data to determine whether a permanent disability is indeed "permanent" or a worker's wages fully recovered after five years. But it is clear that wage losses are still significant after five years. Since only very high-rated disabilities continue to receive benefits after five years, this suggests that wage replacement rates of before-tax income after 10 years will be lower than the estimates in the previous subsection. Finally, recent reforms in California increased benefits and the results in the previous subsection are largely for injuries that occurred prior to the benefit increases. At the current benefit levels, wage replacement rates will be higher than the estimates in the previous subsection. In this subsection, we will analyze each of these three issues in turn.

Taxes

Because the EDD data do not report after-tax income, we must estimate the taxes paid by workers. However, we cannot construct direct estimates of the taxes paid by each worker without information on other matters that determine tax rates, such as other income, marital status, and number of dependents. Instead, we built a model using the tax rate on income for families in the middle of the California income distribution (i.e., between the 40th and 60th percentile), and used the model to adjust the aggregate numbers in Table 5.3.

The median family in California, according to Citizens for Tax Justice (1996), pays 8.8 percent of income in federal income tax, 10.5 percent for Social Security taxes, and 1.7 percent for state income tax. This implies a tax rate of 21 percent.[38] As Table 5.4 shows, the

---

[38]Overall tax rates, usually calculated by dividing total tax revenue by gross domestic product, are higher in California. However, various taxes, including sales tax, property tax, corporate income taxes, and excise taxes are not included because they are not subtracted from income and would therefore need to be paid from benefits as well as labor income. Note also that the state income tax rate reflects the

- 118 -

Table 5.4

Robustness of Wage Loss Results to Data Limitations

	Year of Injury	Years from Injury	Method I. Only Quarters with Injured and Control Working				Method II. Including Injury-Related Time Out of Work			
			Cumul. Wage Loss	Bene-fits	Prop. Wage Loss	Repl. Rate	Cumul. Wage Loss	Bene-fits	Prop. Wage Loss	Repl. Rate
					i. After-Tax Income					
1	91	5	18,717	11,426	19.9	61.0	36,875	17,684	39.9	48.0
2	91-92	4	16,467	11,232	20.9	68.2	29,885	16,070	39.3	54.0
3	91-93	3	12,592	10,613	19.9	84.3	23,069	14,722	38.2	64.0
				ii. Simulation of Wage Loss to 10 Years						
4	91-93	10	42,534	12,471	16.2	29.3	72,645	16,070	33.4	24.8
5	91-93	7.5	32,977	12,318	16.5	37.3	57,640	17,684	33.9	30.7
				iii. Simulation of Effect of 1993 Benefit Increases						
6	91	5	23,692	12,643	19.9	53.4	46,677	19,586	39.9	42.0
7	91-92	4	20,844	12,357	20.9	59.3	37,829	17,689	39.3	46.7
8	91-93	3	15,939	11,695	19.9	73.4	29,201	16,172	38.2	55.4
				iv. The Combined Effect						
9	91-93	10	33,601	14,033	16.2	41.8	57,390	20,324	33.4	35.4
10	91-93	7.5	26,051	13,802	16.5	53.0	45,536	19,840	33.9	43.6

cumulative losses that we report in Table 5.3 are reduced by 21 percent to yield an after-tax cumulative loss. This adjustment increases the replacement rate significantly, so that when time out of work is not counted, the replacement rate approaches two-thirds even after five years. When time out of work is included in the calculation, the tax adjustment increases the replacement rate to almost one-half.

Ten Years of Wage Loss

Estimating the wage replacement rate beyond five years requires an assumption about long-term wage recovery from workplace injuries. On the one hand, it is possible that with time in the labor force, workers continue to adjust to their limitations causing the marginal wage loss to decline with age and time from the injury. Alternatively, it is also possible that, with age, injuries acquired when younger increasingly interfere with a worker's ability to function, leading to increasing marginal wage loss and eventual early retirement.

---

highly progressive state income tax schedule, which leads to relatively low state income taxes for the median family.

It is possible to extrapolate from the wage losses observed in the first five years. Figures 5.4 and 5.5 suggest that wage recovery is largely complete after 2-3 years. It appears as though in subsequent quarters, the distance between the average wage of the controls and the injured workers does not increase or decrease. Therefore, to simulate a longer period of analysis, we assume that all wage recovery that will occur is completed by the last period in which an individual can be observed in our data. We also assume that no further deterioration occurs, and therefore that marginal wage loss beyond the last period is constant. Under this assumption, we perform a simple microsimulation in which we fix the loss observed in the last period, and then accumulate losses to five additional years. We use all individuals injured in 1991-1993, so that for workers injured in 1993, we fix their losses after three years, and for workers injured in 1991, we use the loss observed in the last period after five years.[39] We also simulate the benefits received to 10 years including the life pension for those who are eligible. Given that the model for continued wage loss after the first five years is based only upon an extrapolation from the first five years, the results of this exercise should be viewed as an example of the possible implications of continued wage loss, rather than a prediction.

The results of this microsimulation are also reported in Rows 4 and 5 of Table 5.4. As expected, the losses increase significantly, but since most of the workers have exhausted their benefits, the benefits do not increase by much. This leads to a wage replacement rate for Method I of 29.3 percent after 10 years. The wage replacement rate for the sample that includes time out of work, Method II, is below 25 percent.

The 1993 Benefit Increases

California's 1993 statutory reforms phased in a package of benefit increases that raised the benefits of workers with higher disability ratings. As discussed at the beginning of the section, these included increases in TTD maximum rates, PPD benefits, and life pensions.

---

[39]For missing workers in the last period they can be observed, we do not count wage loss.

Unfortunately, the most recent WCIRB data we have is for injuries in policy year 1994. Even for these workers, we have too few years after the injury to estimate cumulative wage loss. Therefore, we evaluated the effect of the reforms by simulating the benefit increases using the 1991-1993 WCIRB data. This approach cannot capture other changes in the system since 1993, such as changes in the distribution of injuries or disability ratings, nor will it capture changes outside the system, such as the improved economy.

In Rows 6, 7, and 8 of Table 5.4, we report the results of this microsimulation. Using the higher benefit levels in place in late 1996, we recalculated the benefits paid to each worker injured in 1991-1993.[40] On average, as can be seen in the table, the 1993 reforms led to increases in benefits of approximately 10 percent. As a result, the wage replacement rates for our sample increased. For the estimates ignoring additional time out of work, Method I, the wage replacement rate increased to 53.4 percent after five years. For the estimates including time out of work, Method II, the wage replacement rate increased to 42 percent.

The Combined Effect

While the 1993 benefit increases improve the replacement rate, the after-tax income has the most significant effect upon the conclusion with regard to the adequacy of indemnity benefits, with an upper bound that approaches the two-thirds goal. However, the effect of the limited time horizon, based upon a more speculative simulation, reinforces the conclusion that benefits are inadequate.

As a final exercise, Rows 9 and 10 report the combination of all three effects. The benefits in the 10-year microsimulation are adjusted to reflect the 1996 benefit schedule, and then the cumulative wage loss is converted to after-tax dollars at a tax rate of 21 percent. After seven and one-half years, the replacement rate in after-tax dollars ranges between 44 and 53 percent, and by 10 years, the replacement rate

_____

[40]We also increased the number of weeks of PPD for injured workers in 1991 with disability ratings above 25, a change that was instituted in 1992. For workers with greater than 52 weeks of VRMA, we truncated their VRMA benefits at 52 weeks.

is between 35 and 42 percent. Therefore, even if the model had assumed some recovery over the second five years after the accident, it is likely that benefits would not meet the two-thirds standard for adequacy, even using after-tax dollars. Given that the condition of workers may deteriorate, this is a strong result.

Other possible data limitations, including a limited number of variables for matching to controls, and a lack of information on self-insureds, are harder to evaluate. Nonetheless, we have no reason to expect that our estimates are systematically biased, and therefore, given the results of the last subsection and the robustness checks in this subsection, we conclude that the evidence suggests that indemnity benefits inadequately compensate wage loss in California.

The Adequacy of Medical Benefits

Consideration of the adequacy of medical and vocational rehabilitation benefits was outside the scope of the project. Information on the adequacy (or effectiveness) of vocational rehabilitation benefits will be provided in research that the University of California at Berkeley is conducting for the Commission on Health and Safety and Workers' Compensation. This research will analyze how outcomes for workers qualifying for the rehabilitation benefit differ from those of workers who suffer impairments, but are able to return to their customary occupation.[41]

One issue that bears upon the adequacy of medical benefits is the frequency of settlement by compromise and release (C&Rs). As noted above, the first dollar coverage for medical care to which injured

---

[41]The additional compensation invested in counseling, education and training, placement, and maintenance allowance have been calculated and are available in a 1997 commission report. UCB has performed an extensive review of the current knowledge of the effect of modified and alternative work on the effort to return injured workers to work (see Krause, Dansinger, and Wiegand, 1997). While this research suggests that workers receiving modified work return to work more quickly, and are more likely to return at all, it does not focus specifically on the population of workers designated as qualified injured workers in the California system. The research also does not attempt to analyze differences in future earnings between those returning to alternative and modified work and those receiving additional training, counseling, and placement as part of vocational rehabilitation.

workers are entitled suggests a generous system for medical care. In addition, medical care is perhaps the largest cost of the system.

However, in practice, a large fraction of claimants accept a lump sum cash settlement in exchange for giving up the right to coverage of future medical problems associated with the injury. The WCIRB provided information about the method of resolving PPD claims. As Table 5.5 indicates, the majority of claims are resolved by compromise and release. Fewer than 3 percent of claims are resolved by court decisions either finding and award (F&A) or dismissal; about 5 percent are resolved by stipulations. The remainder are resolved by a general WCIRB category "other," which we understand includes claims settled by compromise and release that were not formally approved.

Given the findings with regard to the financial effect of injuries reported above, it is possible that, as noted in the qualitative interviews, workers are forgoing the right to future medical care out of financial need. These results suggest that the adequacy of medical care in California should be regarded as an open question.

Table 5.5

Methods for Resolving Claims

	Injury Year					
	1989	1990	1991	1992[a]	1993[a]	1994[a]
Stipulation	5.53	4.98	4.47	5.23	5.82	4.77
Find & Award	1.34	1.31	1.21	1.11	0.86	0.58
Dismissal	1.44	1.22	1.45	1.31	1.63	2.09
C&R	59.40	59.11	59.31	53.56	44.33	33.08
Other	30.30	31.11	31.51	36.73	45.25	57.12

NOTE: Percentages do not total to 100 in any year because of a small number of cases reporting other codes for resolution methods.

[a]Percentages differ for years 1992, 1993, and 1994 because those years include only 4, 3, and 2 report levels, respectively.

CONCLUSION

California provides a wide array of benefits to injured workers, including medical coverage, indemnity benefits to replace lost earnings, and vocational rehabilitation for workers unable to return to their pre-injury occupation. However, this section revealed that the wage losses of injured workers are large, from 20 to 40 percent of the wages of the control group, and they are sustained throughout the four to five years following the injury. The section also shows that time out of work subsequent to initial return to work is a common occurrence in California, contributing to the large wage losses observed. Workers' compensation indemnity in California does not keep up with wage losses of the magnitude observed: A large fraction, at least 50 percent, are not replaced by indemnity benefits.

Future research is needed to understand the causes for the wage losses observed in this section. Methodological questions need to be addressed, including determining whether a more closely matched control group is needed. Our database is of unprecedented richness, but compared to the complexity of the problem, it is decidedly limited. Data from self-insured firms, more years of post-injury data, earnings for both controls and injured workers in other states or sectors not covered by UI, and information on fringe benefits received and taxes paid would improve the analysis. When more recent data are available, the effect of the recession on the size of the wage losses should also be examined. Finally, interviews with injured workers would provide invaluable insight into the long-term effect of workplace injuries.

Additional research is needed into the availability and use of other income support and medical insurance programs. For instance, some of the increased time out of work after the injury may be compensated by unemployment insurance. Workers with severe disabilities may receive Social Security Supplemental Security Income or Disability Insurance. Our understanding of the financial implications of a workplace injury is limited if only workers' compensation benefits are considered. In addition, if injured workers are eligible to use other social services, coordination of other programs with workers' compensation could improve the targeting of resources to injured workers, particularly since all of them will initially make a workers' compensation claim.

In the next section, our evaluation of the permanent partial disability system continues with an examination of the disability rating, which is used to differentiate among disabled workers for the purpose of setting benefits. This will provide insight into the

functioning of the PPD system, as well as into the adequacy and equity
of benefits for different disability ratings.

6. THE VALIDITY AND CONSISTENCY OF DISABILITY RATINGS AND THE EQUITY OF COMPENSATION

The amount of indemnity benefits received for a permanent partial disability is determined by the disability rating. The rating is intended to collapse the multiple dimensions of disability into a single number that will allow the effect of an injury on one person to be compared to the effect of a different injury on a different person. The resulting comparison will lead to higher benefits for the one with the higher number. Given the formidable task that the rating is intended to accomplish, and its direct effect on payments of benefits, it is not surprising that it may be the most contentious part of the California permanent partial disability system.

Our interviews with participants and stakeholders in the California workers' compensation system often revealed concerns about the difficulty of determining disability ratings and inconsistencies among raters. Some critics argued that the California disability schedule was so difficult to apply and the basis for determining ratings so imprecise and indeterminate that the rating process was capricious, subject to the biases and interests of the person doing the rating. Even the less extreme critics of the California schedule were concerned that the rating process and the ratings produced by it are unpredictable and inconsistent causing increased litigation rates and rising claims' processing costs.

To evaluate the disability rating schedule, we need to consider why it is needed. PPD indemnity is intended to compensate workers for a future loss of the ability to compete in the labor market, where this loss is of unknown magnitude at the time indemnity is paid. The administrative function of the disability rating is to predict this loss. In California, the prediction is based upon objective medical findings, a doctor's assessment of the need for work restrictions and of the worker's injury-associated pain, and the age and occupation of the worker. These are then scaled and weighted to provide a number that ranks workers by disability so that the level of benefits can be set to compensate the appropriate fraction of their loss.

In this section, we examine whether the disability rating successfully predicts the loss of ability to compete in the labor market, measuring the loss as the reduction in quarterly earnings following an injury. We separate claims by disability rates and then examine proportional wage losses within each rating category. If higher disability ratings are not associated with higher levels of proportional wage loss, this is evidence that the rating method is unsuccessful at carrying out its administrative function.

We also examine reasons why ratings may not predict wage loss: The rating method may be flawed or too difficult to apply. We investigate variability in rating using a matched sample of claims from the Workers' Compensation Insurance Rating Bureau (WCIRB) and the Disability Evaluation Unit (DEU).

In the next subsection, we extend the wage loss study of the previous section to examine the ability of the rating to predict wage loss. We then examine variability in ratings for the same claim. The last section describes the *American Medical Association Guides* to rating impairment, which some system participants would prefer to the current system.

THE VALIDITY OF THE DISABILITY RATING AND THE EQUITY OF COMPENSATION

In this subsection, we examine the validity of the disability rating by investigating the relationship between proportional wage loss and disability rating. We expect that ratings under the California schedule should increase as workers' proportional wage losses increase. In other words, if higher disability ratings are associated with higher proportional wage loss, the rating system is valid. The question of validity of the rating is also related to the question of the equity of compensation. Disability ratings determine benefits. If equal proportional wage losses are associated with different disability ratings, or if workers with higher proportional wage losses receive lower disability ratings, these findings would raise questions of equity. In particular, to investigate if California's workers'

compensation benefits are allocated among PPD claimants equitably, we
will compare the proportion of wages lost to the fraction of wage loss
replaced by disability rating groups.

Validity

In Figures 6.1 and 6.2, we report the ratio of quarterly mean
before-tax earnings over time for the injured workers relative to the
controls for five disability rating categories.[1] The data are from
workers injured in 1991-1993. Only quarters when both control and
injured are working are included in Figure 6.2 (Method I), while injury-
related time out of work is included in the calculations in Figure 6.1
(Method II).[2] If the injured worker and the control have equal
earnings, as they do before the injury, the ratio will be 1.0. If the
injured worker makes less than the control, this ratio will be less than
one.

At the time of the injury, the injured workers' earnings drop for
all five disability categories in both figures. For minor injuries,
those with disability ratings 1-5, 6-10, and 11-20, the quarterly
earnings initially fall to 60-65 percent of the controls' earnings in
both figures. All three minor injury categories show some wage
improvement over time, though none of the groups experience full wage
recovery. All three minor injury groups show significant wage loss all
throughout and even at the end of the five-year period.

----

[1]In future work, a greater amount of disaggregation would be
preferable, particularly in the highest disability rating category, 36-
99. However, the sample sizes in this group are too small to allow
further disaggregation. This sample, initially the smallest of the five
to begin with, also has high rates of attrition due to the seriousness
of their injuries. Since our wage data are available only to the second
quarter of 1996, only the first two injury quarters in 1991 have a full
five years of wage data, so the results for this group in Table 6.1 for
five years are based upon only 119 injured workers.

[2]See Section 5. Figure 6.1 is based on Method I, described in the
previous chapter. Figure 6.2 is based on Method II.

- 128 -

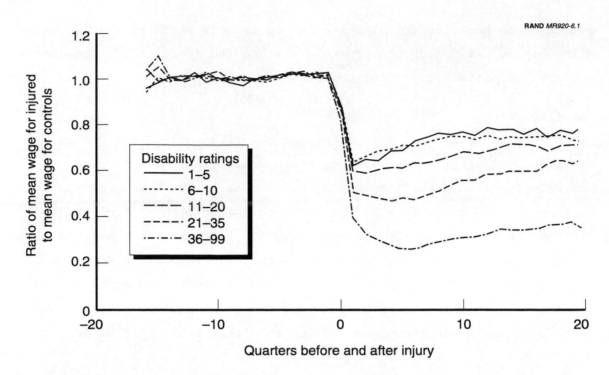

Figure 6.1--Mean Quarterly Wage Ratio, Workers Injured Between 1991
and 1993 Relative to Controls, by Disability Rating, Including
Injury-Related Time Out of Work

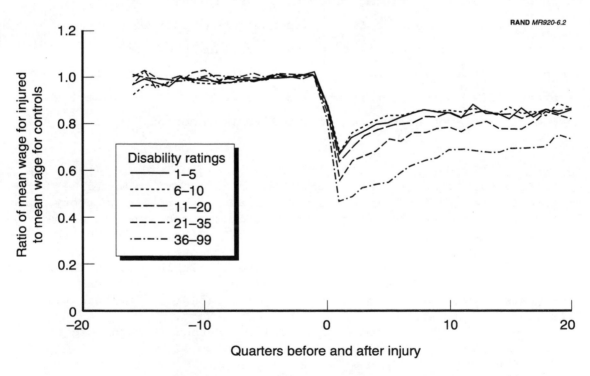

Figure 6.2--Mean Quarterly Wage Ratio, Workers Injured Between 1991
and 1993 Relative to Controls, by Disability Rating, Including
Only Quarters When Both Are Working

The figures show that, among the three lowest rating categories, proportional wage losses are very similar and therefore the validity of the disability rating for ratings below 20 is questionable. For full losses (in Figure 6.2), by five years, the lowest category (1-5) has the highest wage relative to their controls, but for the entire five years, the lowest category (1-5) and the second lowest category (6-10) are virtually indistinguishable. The third lowest category (11-20) is very similar to the two lowest categories as well. For the conservative measure (in Figure 6.1), all three lowest rating categories are indistinguishable in every quarter.

The major injury disability rating groups show more wage loss in Figure 6.1. While the 21-35 rating category shows some improvement over time, the relative wages for this group are always below the relative wages of the three minor disability rating groups. Considerably more severe wage losses are experienced by the highest disability rating category, those with disability ratings between 36 and 99. More than half of this group are out of work at the end of five years, but among the minority who are working, wages are consistently less than 40 percent of their controls.

The difference between Figures 6.1 and 6.2 can be explained by Figure 6.3. The figure shows that higher disability ratings are associated with a greater likelihood of not working in a given quarter. This figure represents the number of injured workers working in a quarter divided by the number of controls working, within disability rating categories. Prior to the injury, the ratio is approximately 1.0 for all of the rating categories. After the injury, however, the ratio drops to less than 1.0 as the injured workers experience time out of work, dropping by a greater amount the greater the disability rating. For disability ratings 1-10, approximately 90 percent of the workers are at work by 10 quarters after the injury. In contrast, for those with the highest disability ratings, those between 36 and 99, the fraction with injury-related time out of work is greater than half throughout the period after the injury.

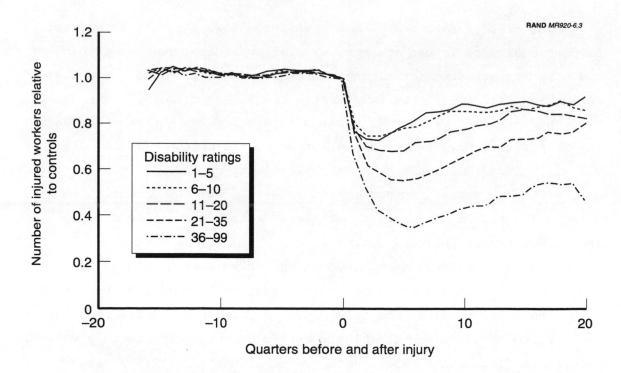

Figure 6.3--Ratio of Number of Workers Injured Between 1991 and 1993 Working in Quarter to Controls, by Disability Rating

In Table 6.1, we report the cumulative wage loss (i.e., the total loss over all years, average for workers), proportional wage loss (i.e., the wage loss as a percentage of total wages earned by the controls and that presumably would have been earned by injured workers but for their injury), and replacement rate (benefits as a percentage of wage loss) for workers injured in 1991-1993, by the same five disability rating categories. The data are reported for three, four, and five years after the injury.[3] As in Tables 5.3-5.4 of Section 5, Method I reports the conservative measure of wage loss, where the estimates are calculated including only quarters where both the injured worker and the control are working, and therefore only quarters where wages are greater than zero. Method II reports the full wage loss which includes injury-related time out of work by including zero wages in the average for the injured worker if the injured worker is not working while the control is

---

[3]As in Tables 5.3-5.4 in Section 5, the five-year wage loss includes only individuals injured in 1991. The four-year wage loss includes 1991-1992, and the three-year wage loss includes all three years.

Table 6.1

Cumulative Wage Loss, Proportional Wage Loss, and Replacement Rate, 1991-1993, by Disability Rating Category

	Disabil-ity Rating	Years from Inj.	Method I. Only Quarters with Injured and Control Working				Method II. Including Injury-Related Time Out of Work			
			Cumul. Wage Loss	Bene-fits	Prop. Wage Loss	Repl. Rate	Cumul. Wage Loss	Bene-fits	Prop. Wage Loss	Repl. Rate
1	1-5	5	20,847	2,874	18.1	13.8	29,788	3,461	29.5	11.6
2	1-5	4	17,322	2,893	18.5	16.7	26,047	3,242	30.4	12.4
3	1-5	3	13,734	2,974	18.0	21.7	19,549	3,282	28.5	16.8
4	6-10	5	20,496	5,974	16.6	29.1	31,308	6,619	28.6	21.1
5	6-10	4	17,986	5,776	17.8	32.1	27,311	6,692	29.8	24.5
6	6-10	3	12,010	5,635	15.0	46.9	19,648	6,785	27.0	34.5
7	11-20	5	21,522	10,964	17.3	50.9	39,188	13,816	32.3	35.3
8	11-20	4	19,378	10,635	18.8	42.3	32,139	13,623	33.1	42.4
9	11-20	3	14,999	10,711	18.5	71.4	25,016	13,489	32.9	53.9
10	21-35	5	29,026	19,674	24.5	67.8	56,560	28,606	45.9	50.6
11	21-35	4	24,825	20,169	23.7	81.2	44,866	26,969	44.1	60.1
12	21-35	3	18,926	19,035	35.3	100.1	35,939	24,799	44.5	69.0
13	36-99	5	33,596	28,045	33.7	83.5	90,793	43,877	69.3	48.2
14	36-99	4	32,172	26,871	35.3	83.5	72,838	37,879	66.4	52.0
15	36-99	3	27,961	22,689	35.6	81.1	57,498	30,842	65.4	53.6

working. All dollars are before-tax and converted to 1997 dollars using the Southwest Regional CPI.

The results in Table 6.1 again show that, for low-rated claims, the disability rating is not valid. The proportional wage loss of the workers with disability ratings 1-5 is consistently higher than that of the workers in the higher disability category, 6-10. For five years of wage loss in Method I (conservative method), even the disability ratings 11-20 experience lower wage loss (17.3) than the category 1-5 (18.1). It appears that disability ratings between 1 and 10 make distinctions for which there is no difference in disability, i.e., wage loss. Compared to the two lowest disability rating categories, workers who receive disability ratings between 11 and 20 suffer no greater reduction in wages when they are working, and only slightly more full wage loss when we include quarters not working. But this latter difference is not large enough that we can conclude that the disability ratings appropriately distinguish among claimants who receive a rating of 20 or lower. The category 11-20 seems to have somewhat higher wage losses,

but not consistently, and not by a large enough amount that we are
confident in concluding that the disability rating can distinguish
between it and the two lowest categories.

On the other hand, for higher-rated claims, proportional wage
losses are consistently higher. Particularly in Method II, proportional
wage losses are consistently approximately 50 percent higher for
category 21-35 than for the three lowest disability rating categories,
and more than 100 percent higher in category 36-99. This suggests that
the California disability rating process can identify and distinguish
among devastating injuries, even though it cannot distinguish among the
merely serious.

Perhaps the most prominent feature of the table is the significant
wage losses observed for even the least disabled. After three years,
every disability rating category experienced wage losses greater than
$19,000 for the full loss that counts injury-related time out of work
(Method II on Table 6.1). Using the conservative measure of wage loss,
every category has greater than $20,000 in wage losses by five years
(Method I, Table 6.1). Proportional wage loss exceeds 15 percent by
three years for every category using the conservative measure of wage
loss, and proportional wage loss exceeds 27 percent by three years for
every category when including injury-related time out of work.

Because workers' compensation benefits are modest, particularly
for low-rated claims, these large wage losses imply generally low
replacement rates. After four years, when injury-related time out of
work is included, no disability rating category has two-thirds of wage
loss replaced (Method II, Table 6.1). Therefore, even within the
highest disability rating categories, using this measure of wage loss,
benefits appear inadequate. With the conservative measure of wage loss
only, the two highest disability rating categories have adequate wage
replacement, exceeding the two-thirds standard.

The lowest disability rating category has the lowest wage
replacement. By five years, counting injury-related time out of work,
only 12 percent of wage loss is replaced. The wage losses and benefits
for this group are illustrated in Figure 6.4. This group suffers
continuing wage loss five years after the quarter of injury, but they

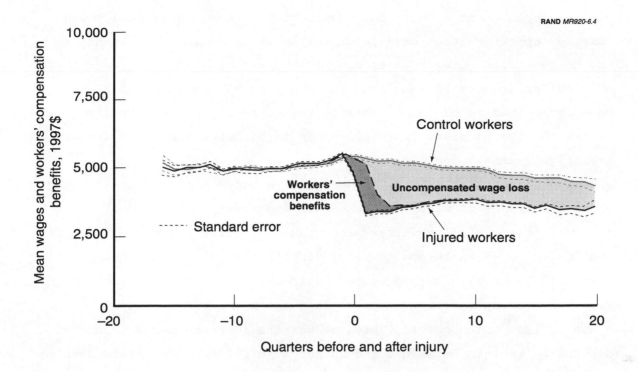

Figure 6.4--Mean Quarterly Wages and Benefits for Workers Injured Between 1991 and 1993 and Controls, Disability Ratings 1-5, Including Injury-Related Time Out of Work

have largely exhausted their benefits before one year. Even adopting the conservative measure of wage loss and examining only the first three years after the injury, Table 6.1 shows that those in the lowest disability rating category do not have 25 percent of their wage loss replaced.

Equity

In Section 3 we defined fairness using two standards, vertical equity and horizontal equity. These two standards imply several different tests of California's treatment of permanent partial disability claims. California's workers' compensation system fails each test of equity.

Horizontal equity is a standard for individuals in equal circumstances: They should be treated equally. Here, in considering wage loss, horizontal equity implies that persons with comparable amounts of wage loss should receive similar benefits and, in turn,

similar replacement rates. Our examination of horizontal equity was
somewhat opportunistic, drawing on our observation that applicants in
the three lowest categories of disability ratings (1-5, 6-10, and 11-20)
had similar amounts of wage loss yet received substantially different
benefits depending on the disability rating that they received.[4] Some
claims receive benefits that replace 35 to 51 percent of wage losses
over five years (those that receive ratings of 11 to 20) while others,
with indistinguishable wage losses, receive benefits that replace only
12 to 14 percent of wage losses (1-5 ratings).

The degree of disability--wage loss--of course differs among this
vast majority of workers with minor disabilities. But California's
disability schedule is ineffective in identifying these differences and
awards differing benefits on bases that are unrelated to actual
disabilities. Consequently, because workers in these three groups of
disability ratings between 1 and 20 received different benefits despite
the comparability of their disabilities, the California disability and
payment schedule violates horizontal equity for the vast majority of
injured workers--those with less serious injuries.

The second concept, vertical equity, looks at the equivalence or
appropriateness of treatment among persons in different circumstances.
This concept cannot be applied as directly as horizontal equity. Most
simply, vertical equity could require that applicants with differing
degrees of wage loss all be treated equivalently; that they each receive
reimbursement of the same pro rata share of their wage losses. Trusts
created to compensate work-related asbestos injuries generally adopt
this definition that vertical equity means pro rata equivalency. But
some have argued that it is fairer and more appropriate to prefer
workers with greater disabilities--giving them a higher replacement rate
than workers with lesser injuries. In this case, the vertical equity

---

[4]Typically, comparisons across disability ratings are considered to
be tests of vertical equity, because the disability rating is supposed
to measure disability and, therefore, imply different circumstances.
However we found that for low-rated claims, the disability rating is not
associated with differences in disability, i.e., wage loss, so we
combined all three low-rated claim categories for testing horizontal
equity among these claims.

standard requires consistent treatment; that if the group with the least disability receives the least, then the group with the greatest disability should receive the most. Therefore, a more general definition of vertical equity, which was adopted by Berkowitz and Burton (1987), combines these two tests of vertical equity and requires either that different injuries be treated equivalently, or that they be treated consistently.

Conclusions with regard to vertical equity depend upon whether injury-related time out of work is counted in wage loss and upon the two different standards for judging such equity. Although our test of vertical equity is concerned with benefit amounts and wage replacements for persons with differing wage loss, we use disability ratings as the basis for categorizing claims. As we have observed, wage loss differs among workers in three categories of disability ratings, 1-20, 21-35, and 36-99, increasing with disability ratings. Therefore, using the disability rating categories, we can see how benefits and wage replacement changes as wage loss increases.[5] Using the estimates from Method I, where time out of work is not counted, we find that California's system compensates a higher fraction of the wage loss for individuals with higher wage losses (associated with higher disability ratings). This finding is consistent with a standard of vertical equity that would require greater benefits for persons with greater disabilities. However, the findings are inconsistent with the simpler definition of vertical equity that would require all applicants to be treated comparably, i.e., receive comparable percentages of wage replacement at all levels of disability.

Using Method II, which counts time out of work, the replacement rate does not increase with disability (increasing wage loss associated with higher disability ratings). The wage replacement is higher for

---

[5] Categorization based on disability ratings also avoids methodological limitations inherent in the estimation of wage loss. Because the concept of wage loss is based in part on an estimate of the hypothetical wages that a worker would have earned but for the injury, analyses based on individual persons or categorizations based on individual wage loss estimates are problematic. We plan to investigate the implications of these limitations in continuing work.

workers with intermediate levels of disability (a wage replacement of 50.6 percent among those with disability ratings 21-35) than for those with lower disabilities (35.3 percent or less among those with disability ratings of 1-20). However, wage replacement is no different between workers with intermediate levels of disability (disability ratings 21-35) and those with severe disabilities (48.2 percent among those with disability ratings over 35). These results satisfy neither alternative standard of vertical equity. The simple standard is not satisfied because wage replacement is not comparable among all workers-- the vast majority with minor injuries receive much smaller benefits. The expectation that more serious injured workers should receive greater benefits is not satisfied because wage replacement does not increase for the most seriously disabled.

The focus of this analysis is the validity of ratings, and the implications for equity. We recognize that it is a limited analysis of equity. Comparisons of replacement rates for different injuries with the same ratings, or for different parts of the state, would provide further evidence on horizontal equity. Analysis of the variation in replacement rates within disability ratings groups would also provide additional information about horizontal equity. These analyses would provide critical information for evaluating the PPD system, and they are a high priority for future work. We expect to expand these analyses through continuing work.

The large wage losses among low-rated claims are surprising. We do not know if the disabilities associated with the low ratings are not as minor as the rating suggests, or if the results suggest that workplace injuries may have consequences far beyond impairment. Possible explanations are that there may be stigma associated with claiming permanent partial disability, or that a workplace injury leads to career disruption. Similar wage losses have been found in studies of the effect of layoffs (Jacobson, Lalonde, and Sullivan, 1993; Schoeni and Dardia, 1996) and job changing associated with the injury may explain some of the losses. Further research into the causes of these large wage losses for low-rated claims is required.

EFFECT OF THE 1993 BENEFIT INCREASES

As discussed in Section 5, the 1993 reforms included benefit increases for high-rated claims, 15 and above, including increases in PPD benefits, and life pensions. The data to evaluate the replacement rates for injuries in 1996 are not available. As reported in Section 6, we simulated the effect of the 1996 benefits using the 1991-1993 injury data. The results on replacement rates are reported in Table 6.2.

As expected, the largest effect of the 1993 reforms is to increase the benefits of high-rated claims. While the 1-5 and 6-10 disability rating categories are largely unaffected, the higher disability rating categories experience significant benefit increases, increasing replacement rates by 7-15 percent. Ironically, if the proportional wage loss patterns among low-rated claims are the same after the reform, this benefit adjustment further exacerbated the inequitable treatment among low-rated claims, raising benefits for those claimants with disability

Table 6.2

**Replacement Rates Using 1996 Benefits, 1991-1993
Injuries, by Disability Rating Category**

	Disability Rating	Years from Injury	Method I. Injured and Control Working	Method II. Including Time Out of Work
1	1-5	5	14.4	12.0
2	1-5	4	17.6	13.0
3	1-5	3	23.1	17.7
4	6-10	5	30.4	21.8
5	6-10	4	33.5	25.4
6	6-10	3	48.8	35.7
7	11-20	5	54.9	37.8
8	11-20	4	59.1	45.5
9	11-20	3	77.7	58.1
10	21-35	5	75.0	55.3
11	21-35	4	90.4	65.9
12	21-35	3	112.5	76.2
13	36-99	5	99.4	56.3
14	36-99	4	96.0	59.6
15	36-99	3	92.4	61.2

ratings of 15 to 20 but not raising benefits for claimants with ratings 1-14 who had comparable wage losses.

Overall, if the true replacement rate is the midpoint of the range between Methods I and II, the benefit increase led to replacement rates for the two highest disability rating categories that meet the two-thirds adequacy condition. For the two lowest rating categories, only the TTD maximum increased, and therefore the replacement rates were virtually unchanged.

VARIABILITY IN DISABILITY RATINGS

In our interviews with system participants, the unpredictability and inconsistency of disability ratings was a repeated theme. The rating process, many asserted, is too subjective, producing increased uncertainty, litigation, and expense. These criticisms imply that a single claim might receive widely varying ratings depending upon the rater or even by the same rater at different times. If this is true for minor claims, then it would provide an explanation for our finding that there is no validity to the ratings among low-rated claims. If a claim that is rated 11-20 could just as easily have been given a rating of 1-5 by a different rater, and vice versa, then we would find that the wage losses of injured workers with ratings of 1-5 would be no different than those with ratings of 11-20. In this subsection, we explore the variability of ratings using data on ratings from two different databases for the same claim.

We acquired the database developed by the Disability Evaluation Unit (DEU) of the Division of Workers' Compensation used to track all claims rated by DEU raters. The database consists of all claims rated in 1992-1994, including both summary and consultative ratings. This database provides information about injuries for claims evaluated by the DEU as well as the disability rating given by the DEU.

We matched the ratings in the DEU data with claims data for 1993 accidents from the WCIRB data (described in Section 5) using Social Security Numbers.[6] The resulting matched database included 16,591 pairs

---

[6]The sample of matched DEU-WCIRB should not be regarded as a random sample of claims. First, we only use DEU claims with positive ratings,

of ratings.[7] The WCIRB data report the rating estimated by the
adjuster, which would be calculated using much of the same information
that would be sent to the DEU. When the claim closes, the rating
reflects the actual financial settlement of the claim.[8] Prior to
closing, the adjuster provides a rating that indicates his/her best
judgment as to the disability level at which a claim will ultimately
close. This rating is used by the insurer to set an appropriate reserve
level.[9]

As noted above, insurance companies report on all PPD claims to
the WCIRB for up to five "report levels," where the first report level
is 6-18 months after the injury, and subsequent reports are submitted at
12 month intervals thereafter. We include comparisons for both the
first and the second WCIRB reports because both have limitations. The
first report level for 1993 accidents will largely occur during 1994,
and the second during 1995. We do not know the date of either the DEU
rating or the WCIRB report, but given the delay after an accident before
a claim is rated by the DEU, and given that the DEU ratings are for
1993-1994 only, we expect that many of the first report level ratings
will be contemporaneous with the DEU rating. However, the first report
is completed fairly early in a claim. Consequently, if the WCIRB rating
precedes the DEU rating, the insurance adjuster may be estimating a
reserve rating based on incomplete medical information, perhaps less
than the full evaluation available to a DEU rater. Some divergence in

---

since WCIRB claims without positive ratings are not necessarily reported
to the WCIRB, and we want to treat the two databases in a parallel
fashion. Second, the DEU tends to include more unrepresented claimants.
However, we have no reason to expect that differences in rating for this
sample would be different for another sample.

[7]In some cases, multiple ratings were included in the DEU for the
same claim. We averaged these ratings.

[8]The claim settlement may include other considerations than those
that normally enter into the calculation of a disability rating. For
instance, issues of apportionment may lead to a negotiated settlement
that is lower than the dollar amount that is predicted by the disability
rating. In that case, the final WCIRB rating will be adjusted downward
to justify the dollar amount paid.

[9]It differs from the rating the adjuster may convey to an applicant
or attorney in attempting to settle a claim--a rating made for
negotiation purposes.

ratings will therefore occur in part because each is done based on different information. The second report is received by the WCIRB approximately two years after the injury. By this time, it is likely that the DEU rating has already occurred, and therefore the adjuster would be likely to have the permanent and stationary report from the doctor and to know the DEU rating. For these reasons, the first report level may overstate the variability, but the second report level may understate it.

Conceptually, we treat the DEU rating as "true" and examine the ability of the WCIRB rating to predict the DEU rating. We use only open claims from the WCIRB since we do not want the WCIRB rating to reflect the settlement negotiation. The results of the DEU-WCIRB rating comparisons are shown in Tables 6.3 and 6.4. The tables break down the distribution of WCIRB ratings by decile and also include the 25th and 75th percentile. Column I reports the disability rating for each decile of the WCIRB. For instance, from Table 6.3, in the row labeled 10, Column I reports the value 5. This means that 10 percent of WCIRB first report level ratings from the matched sample of WCIRB and DEU ratings are less than or equal to 5. In the row labeled 75, Column I reports the value 20. Therefore, 75 percent of WCIRB first report ratings are less than or equal to 20. Similarly, from Table 6.4, it can be seen that 10 percent of WCIRB second report level ratings are less than 5, and 75 percent are less than 27.

The remainder of the columns in Tables 6.3 and 6.4 report statistics about the ratings in the sample of matched DEU ratings that correspond to the rating from the WCIRB in Column I. Column II reports the median of the ratings in the DEU for all claims in the decile for the WCIRB for that row. Column III reports the 25th percentile and Column IV reports the 75th percentile of the DEU rating. Therefore, focusing on the median of the WCIRB (the row labeled 50), we see that for a first report level median of 13, the DEU median is 14. However, 25 percent of claims rated by the DEU with WCIRB first report level ratings of 13 are rated below 9, and another 25 percent are rated above 24. At the second report level for the WCIRB, the median is 17, and the

Table 6.3

Comparison of Ratings for the Same Claims Between DEU and WCIRB First Report Level

Percent of WCIRB Rating, First Report Level	I. WCIRB Rating, First Report Level	II. Median of Matched DEU Rating	III. 25% of Matched DEU Are Below…	IV. 75% of Matched DEU Are Above…	V. IQR (Difference Between IV and III)	VI. Total Benefits Median Matched DEU (Dollar Value of II)	VII. Total Benefits for IQR (Dollar Value of V)
10	5	10	5	20	15	4,235	7,770
20	7	10	6	19	13	4,235	6,755
25	8	11	6	20	14	4,795	7,140
30	10	13	7	23	16	5,915	9,030
40	10	13	7	23	16	5,915	9,030
50	13	14	9	24	15	6,475	8,890
60	15	16	9	26	17	7,595	10,008
70	19	19	12	28	14	9,275	8,622
75	20	20	13	30	17	9,870	12,285
80	23	23	15	30	15	11,970	12,285
90	30	25	18	34	16	14,171	12,285

Table 6.4

Comparison of Ratings for the Same Claims between DEU and WCIRB Second Report Level

Percent of WCIRB Rating, Second Report Level	I. WCIRB Rating, Second Report Level	II. Median of Matched DEU Rating	III. 25% of Matched DEU Are Below…	IV. 75% of Matched DEU Are Above…	V. IQR (Difference Between IV and III)	VI. Total Benefits Median Matched DEU (Dollar Value of II)	VII. Total Benefits for IQR (Dollar Value of V)
10	5	8	4	17	13	3,360	6,545
20	9	9	5	13	8	3,780	3,850
25	10	11	6	20	14	4,795	7,140
30	11	11	8	16	8	4,795	4,410
40	14	14	10	17	7	6,475	3,920
50	17	17	13	20	7	8,155	3,955
60	20	20	12	26	14	9,870	10,008
70	25	26	17	32	15	15,059	8,622
75	27	25	17	28	11	14,171	12,285
80	30	29	22	33	11	17,723	12,285
90	40	35	24	40	16	23,828	12,285

corresponding DEU median is 17, with 25 percent below 13, and 25 percent above 20.

To measure the variability of rating, we use the "interquartile range" (IQR) which is equal to the difference between the 25th and the 75th percentile of DEU ratings, Columns III and IV. The IQR is reported in Column V. Variability in DEU ratings (as measured by the IQR) is constant as the first WCIRB disability ratings increase. If it were equally difficult to rate claims at every rating, then the DEU IQR would increase as the WCIRB rating increases. This is because the distribution of claims is skewed, with the majority of claims below approximately 15. Since the DEU IQR is constant, this suggests that for first disability ratings in the WCIRB, rating claims consistently is more difficult for low-rated claims than for high.

In Columns III and IV, we convert the DEU ratings and rating variability into dollars of indemnity benefits using the benefit schedule. Column VI reports the total dollar value of PPD indemnity for a claim with the DEU rating in Column II. In Column VII, we report the dollar value of the range in benefits in Column VII. The dollar values of the DEU IQR suggest that for individuals with a particular WCIRB rating, there is significant variability in indemnity benefits at the DEU ratings. For low-rated claims, this variability approaches twice the median indemnity value. The dollar value of the DEU IQR relative to the dollar value of the median benefit decreases as the rating increases for low-rated claims. This suggests that the variability is relatively more costly for low-rated claims.

At the second report level, there is convergence between the DEU and the WCIRB. The WCIRB rating and the corresponding median DEU rating tend to be closer. The DEU IQR tends to be smaller. The increase in the DEU IQR with the percentile of the WCIRB is also more consistent with the shape of the underlying distribution. Nonetheless, significant variability in ratings remains at the second report level.

These results suggest that the variability in rating is one reason that there is no correspondence between ratings and wage loss for low-rated claims. For low-rated claims, holding WCIRB rating constant at a particular level, the corresponding DEU rating is highly likely to be in

any of the three low-rated claim categories in Table 6.1. Even if in
theory the rating were able to predict wage loss, if it is applied
inconsistently, then observed ratings would not correspond to wage loss.

There are three reasons why the test described in this subsection
is not a true test of inter-rater reliability. First, we have not
insured that the information available to each party is the same. The
adjuster, for instance, may not have all of the medical information used
by the DEU rater. Second, we are not sure if the two ratings are
independent. The adjuster may know the DEU rating, even at the first
report level. Third, we do not know if the adjuster uses information
other than what is required to rate a claim when setting the rating. It
may be, for instance, that the adjuster is aware that issues of
compensability will lead to a lower settlement, and therefore set a
lower rating.

In summary, we have found that rating variability between the
WCIRB and the DEU is significant. To the extent that this variability
represents true inconsistency or unreliability in rating, it suggests
that, particularly among low-rated claims, this variability is costly,
undermining the validity of the rating, leading to outcomes that are
unrelated to wage loss.

THE *AMA GUIDES*

We conclude this chapter on the California disability rating system
with a discussion of the *AMA Guides*. While empirical evidence is
limited, many system participants believe the *AMA Guides* would improve
consistency. In the last subsection, we examined the inconsistency of
ratings, and noted that it can lead to ratings that are invalid. It is
important to note that validity in California is measured relative to
disability. The *AMA Guides* are not designed to measure disability--
rather, they are intended to measure impairment. Unfortunately, the
validity of the *Guides* at measuring impairment cannot be tested, since
there is no independent empirical measure of impairment like the
measures of wage loss that we used to test the validity of California
ratings.

To understand the utility and limitations of the *AMA Guides*, it is helpful to examine their description of the steps to evaluate impairment.[10] The *Guides* describe three steps for evaluating impairment. The first step is designed to accurately document the clinical status of an injured person by obtaining a medical history, conducting a medical evaluation including appropriate tests, and completing diagnostic procedures. Second, once the clinical status of a patient is documented, a physician then determines "the nature and extent of impairment or dysfunction of the affected body part or system." This step requires that the physician analyze the medical history, as well as clinical and laboratory findings for the injured person. The *Guides* then describe a third step which requires physicians to compare "results of analyses with criteria specifying guides for the particular part, system, or function." However, this third step really involves two separate determinations or steps of its own.

To carry out the third step described by the *Guides*, a physician must first determine the degree of impairment of the particular organ or system and then, using this finding, determine the "whole person impairment" which is rated on the *AMA Guides'* 100 point scale. The first two steps of the evaluation and the first part of the third step, the evaluation of an organ system impairment, are well within the normal experience and knowledge of a physician. For example, a physician may carry out the first two steps and reach a conclusion that an injured worker has a 30 percent limitation in motion for an injured wrist. The second part of the third step, the evaluation of a whole person impairment, is not an ordinary medical judgment. Indeed, it is not clear that a whole person impairment scale is meaningful. The *AMA Guides* provide no definition or justification for this scale, describing only the high end of the scale. A score of 0 presumably implies that there is no impairment because of an injury. The *Guides* define the other end of the scale as: "95 percent to 100 percent is considered to represent almost total impairment--a state that is approaching death." Unfortunately, a scale that has nothing wrong at one end and death at

---

[10]AMA (1993), p. 8.

the other is not very useful nor does it give any information about what the AMA believes to be a 50 percent impairment as opposed to a 25 percent impairment.

For example, as described on pages 154-164 of the *AMA Guides*, Fourth Edition, the example assumes a relevant history of an insulator who worked with asbestos-containing products for 30 years. The medical evaluation presumably showed moderate dyspnea (shortness of breath), the presence of pulmonary rales (a distinctive sound made during respiration), with x-ray confirmation of pulmonary opacities or scarring that is typical of asbestosis. As part of this examination, the *AMA Guides* instruct the physician to conduct spirometry, a test that measures pulmonary function. As the second step in the impairment evaluation, the *AMA Guides* require the physician to determine the injury (here a restrictive pulmonary impairment) and analyze the laboratory findings, which, for example, show that the results of a pulmonary function test produced a forced vital capacity equal to 2.0.

The *AMA Guides* then require, as a third step, that the physician determine the extent of respiratory impairment by comparing the results of the examination and tests to criteria established in the *Guides*. The *Guides* show that this worker would have, by example, a respiratory impairment of 45 percent--his pulmonary level is 55 percent of normal for a person of that age and height. Note that this impairment deals only with pulmonary impairment, not with the whole person impairment that is the objective of the *AMA Guides*. The *Guides*, however, translate the specific respiratory impairment into a whole person impairment somewhere between the range of 26 to 50 percent.

Note that all of the steps of this medical evaluation are conducted routinely by doctors up to and through the determination of degree of respiratory impairment. The fourth step, the whole person impairment, is not a matter of routine medical practice, but must be made in order to place this injured worker on a scale that can be compared to workers who suffered all other manner of injuries, such as ruptured cervical discs, amputations of fingers, or loss of sexual function.

The *AMA Guides* attempt to put all residual conditions resulting from injuries onto a one dimensional scale, assuming that the limitation on a person's activities from one type of organ system impairment can be compared to that of all other types of organ system impairments. It is not obvious that these different limitations can all be compared and ranked with each other, and there is no way to test it. Furthermore, the *AMA Guides* not only attempt to rank these disparate types of organ system impairments on one scale, but the use of this scale to determine dollar benefits implies that these rankings have some relational meaning. For example, the use of the *AMA Guides* to determine disability payments implies that the difference between an injury with an AMA rating of 40 compared to an injury with an AMA rating of 50 is the same as the difference between an injury with a rating of 30 to one with a rating of 40. It is impossible to verify whether this is true.

While the ability of the *AMA Guides* to measure impairment is unknowable, it remains possible that the *Guides* would provide a better measure of *disability* than the current California system. In other words, it is possible that the *AMA Guides* rank individuals by wage loss more effectively than the California disability rating system. We will consider this possibility and other ways to improve the disability rating process in Section 8.

7. PROCESSING PPD CLAIMS

The analyses of the last two chapters have shown how wage losses, workers' compensation benefits and the adequacy of benefits as replacement for wage losses differ between major and minor disability claims. This section presents a system level analysis of this key distinction in claims. Our analysis shows that, overwhelmingly, California's workers' compensation system for PPD claims is one for handling minor disability claims--the very claims that appear to be treated most poorly by that system.

THE PREDOMINANCE OF MINOR PPD CLAIMS

The vast majority of PPD claims filed under the California workers' compensation system involve claims with relatively low disability ratings. Figure 7.1 shows the distribution of insurance companies' initial ratings for claims filed in accident years 1989 through 1994, as shown in the WCIRB, USR database.[1] As Figure 7.1 shows, half of the claims involve disability ratings of less than 10, and 90 percent of claims involve disability ratings of 25 or less. The WCIRB defines minor claims as those with ratings below 25, and major claims as those with ratings above 25. Three percent of claims involve disability ratings that are greater than 40 (Table 7.1).

This pattern did not change in any significant way for claims filed between 1989 and 1994. Table 7.2 shows the distribution of disability ratings and the cumulative distributions for each of these accident years, broken down into disability rating groupings that we will be using throughout this section. Throughout the entire period approximately half of the claims involved disability ratings that were 10 or less and slightly less than one-third had disability ratings between 11 and 20.

---

[1]The distribution of disability ratings for claims when they close is very similar to these ratings applied when claims are first opened. There are no differences in any of the relevant factors that we discuss in this subsection.

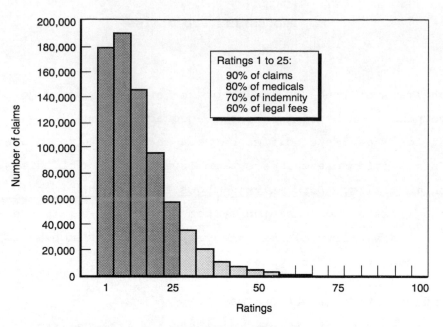

SOURCE: WCIRB Uniform Statistical Report database, 1989–1994 accident years.

Figure 7.1--The Vast Majority of PPD Claims Involve Low Ratings

Table 7.1

Number of PPD Claims at Insured Firms,
1990-1994

Injury Year	Number of Claims
1991	182,680
1991	202,497
1992	148,099
1993	101,883
1994	88,676

SOURCE: WCIRB USR database.

Many of the participants we interviewed assert that the increase in
claims rated 0-10 in the early 1990s as seen in Table 7.2, reflected
filings of stress, cumulative trauma, and claims filed by medical mills.
However, other sources might have contributed to this increase, since
(as a percentage) lowest rated claims dropped little in 1993 and 1994
when, according to interviewees, medical mills had mostly closed.   The
general stability of claim distribution is particularly interesting
given the steady reduction in the number of PPD claims reported in
California over this period of time.   While the total number of PPD

Table 7.2

Half of PPD Claims Have the Lowest 10 Percent Ratings and One-Third Have the Next Lowest 10 Percent

Initial Rating	% of Claims	Cumulative % of Claims
0-10	49.4	49.4
11-20	32.0	81.4
21-40	16.3	97.7
41-70	2.2	99.9
71-99	0.1	100.0

SOURCE: WCIRB USR database.

Distribution of Disability Ratings over Time

Injury Year	Percentages of PPD Claims by Initial Ratings				
	0-10	11-20	21-40	41-70	71-99
1989	43.3	34.2	19.7	2.7	0.1
1990	46.6	32.7	17.9	2.7	0.1
1991	50.9	31.7	15.2	2.1	0.1
1992	52.9	30.8	14.5	1.7	0.1
1993	51.3	31.4	15.5	1.5	0.1
1994	49.9	31.6	16.5	1.9	0.1

Injury Year	Cumulative Percentages for Initial Ratings				
	0-10	11-20	21-40	41-70	71-99
1989	43.3	77.5	97.2	99.9	100.0
1990	46.6	79.3	97.2	99.9	100.0
1991	50.9	82.6	97.8	99.9	100.0
1992	52.9	83.7	98.2	99.9	100.0
1993	51.3	82.7	98.2	99.9	100.0
1994	49.9	81.5	98.0	99.9	100.0

SOURCE: WCIRB USR database.

claims has dropped steadily during this period (see Table 7.1), there is no indication that this reduction is due to fewer filings of less serious injury claims. Rather the stability of the percentage distribution across all these years suggests there has been a general reduction in severity in the number of PPD claims filed.

The distinction between low- and high-rated PPD claims is not new to observers of workers' compensation. In many of its reports, the WCIRB routinely categorizes and describes PPD claims as being minor (disability ratings of less than 25) or major.[2] However, no one has thoroughly examined the differences between these groups of claims including their wage loss and the replacement of wage loss through workers' compensation benefits, nor the significance of these two groups of claims for California's workers' compensation system.

Of course the financial significance of any single minor claim, one with relatively low ratings, is far less than the financial significance of a more serious claim involving a higher disability rating. Perhaps for this reason people pay less attention to lower-rated disability claims. Nevertheless, because of their sheer numbers, these low-rated claims dominate not only the volume of claims within the workers' compensation system, but also the financial significance of PPD claims.

As Table 7.3 indicates, close to 60 percent of all indemnity benefits paid to PPD claimants are paid to those with ratings of 20 or less. Using the WCIRB's definition of minor claims (a rating of 25 percent or less), minor claims account for 70 percent of all indemnity payments. This concentration of financial significance did not change across the years covered by our WCIRB database.

The expenses for medical treatment of permanent PPD claims are also concentrated among those with low disability ratings (Table 7.4). Approximately 70 percent of all payments for medical treatment expenses

Table 7.3

Most Indemnity Benefits Are Paid in Claims Involving Lower Disability Ratings
(WCIRB: Incurred Indemnity)

Initial Rating	% of Claims	Cumulative % of Claims
0	0.6	0.6
1-10	20.8	21.4
11-20	35.3	56.7
21-40	35.8	92.5
41-70	7.1	99.6
71-99	0.4	100.0

SOURCE: WCIRB USR database.

---

[2]We generally report a more conservative classification of claims with ratings of 20 and under as minor.

Table 7.4

**Most Medical Benefits Are Paid in Claims
Involving Lower Disability Ratings**

Initial Rating	% of Claims	Cumulative % of Claims
0	0.6	0.6
1-10	31.3	31.9
11-20	36.4	68.3
21-40	27.2	95.5
41-70	4.3	99.8
71-99	0.2	100.0

SOURCE: WCIRB USR database.

are paid to claims involving disability ratings of less than 20 and approximately a third to those with disability ratings of 10 or less. Again, this pattern has not changed in any meaningful way across the several accident years included in our analysis.

Payment of temporary disability benefits is also concentrated among claims with lower disability ratings (Table 7.5). In California injured workers are entitled to receive temporary disability benefits while they are out of work because of a workplace injury. These benefits cease when an injured worker returns to work or earlier if his medical condition reaches a point of being permanent and stationary. At such time, the worker becomes eligible for permanent disability benefits.

The concentration of temporary disability benefits among minor claims occurs even though the period of temporary disability is far less

Table 7.5

**Most Temporary Disability Benefits Are Paid
to Claimants with Lower Disability
Ratings**

Initial Rating	% of Claims	Cumulative % of Claims
0	1.3	1.3
1-10	27.3	28.6
11-20	33.6	62.2
21-40	30.2	92.4
41-70	6.9	99.3
71-99	0.7	100.0

SOURCE: WCIRB USR database.

for such workers. When one considers the overwhelming number of claimants with low disability ratings, about 30 percent of temporary disability benefits are paid to claimants with disability ratings of less than 10, and over 60 percent are paid to claimants whose disability ratings are 20 or less (Table 7.5). Again, this pattern has not changed throughout the years covered by our analysis.

Rehabilitation benefits are utilized more often by workers with more serious injuries and higher disability ratings (Table 7.6). Only 16.7 percent of claims with disability ratings of less than 10 receive rehabilitation benefits and 37.5 percent of claims with disability ratings between 11 and 20 receive them. The percentage utilizing rehabilitation is far lower than the 55 to 69 percent among claimants with higher disability ratings. But again, because of the overwhelming number of claims with low disability ratings, rehabilitation benefits are concentrated among workers with minor disabilities. Approximately one-quarter of all cases that receive rehabilitation benefits involve workers with disability ratings below 10, and 64 percent of the claims receiving rehabilitation benefits have ratings of 20 or less.

However, when we consider the cost of rehabilitation benefits, the pattern described above is reversed, with benefit dollars going primarily to major claims. As Table 7.7 shows, less than one-third of all the payments for disability benefits are made to claims with

Table 7.6

**Participation in Rehabilitation Increases with Disability
Ratings, but Participation is Concentrated
Among Minor Claims**

Initial Rating	% with Rehabilitation Benefits	% of All Claims with Rehabilita- tion Benefits	Cumulative % of Claims
0	7.4	0.2	0.2
1-10	16.7	25.6	25.8
11-20	37.5	37.9	63.7
21-40	60.9	31.4	95.1
41-70	68.6	4.8	99.9
71-99	54.6	0.2	100.0
Total	32.2		

SOURCE: WCIRB USR database.

Table 7.7

**Most Vocational Rehabilitation Benefits Are Paid
to Claimants with Higher Disability Ratings**

Initial Rating	% of Claims	Cumulative % of Claims
0	0.1	0.1
1-10	8.0	8.1
11-20	23.6	31.7
21-40	32.3	64.0
41-70	35.3	99.3
71-99	0.7	100.0

SOURCE: WCIRB USR database.

disability ratings of 20 or less, approximately another third are paid to claims with disability ratings between 21 and 40, and another third to the small number of claimants with disability ratings above 40.

In summary, these results show that claims with low disability ratings dominate the volume of claims within the California workers' compensation system and absorb most of the benefit payments.

TIME TO RESOLUTION FOR PPD CLAIMS

One of the putative advantages of replacing tort litigation with an administrative process was the efficiency and speed of the latter. Early resolution of workers' compensation claims is beneficial to all parties. It allows injured workers to receive compensation much more quickly than they would through the tort litigation system. It also allows them to reassemble their lives and put behind them the hassles and stigma that might be associated with being involved in disputes about the amount of their disabilities and their benefit entitlement. Early resolution allows employers to minimize transaction costs involved with processing workers' compensation claims and, potentially, to avoid tension and reduced morale on the part of injured workers.

Of course early resolution is not by itself an objective that trumps all others. Claimants might get fast resolution by taking whatever first offer an insurer or employer makes; employers might get fast resolution by accepting any medical claim that a worker makes. But these might not be fair or desirable outcomes. Fairness and timely resolution are both important goals for California's workers' compensation system. Stated another way, even if California delivered fair outcomes for PPD claims (a matter of serious doubt judging by the prior two sections), the workers' compensation system might be criticized if it took too long and spent too much money to deliver those outcomes.

California's basis for determining permanent disability benefits should facilitate early resolution of claims. The disability schedule is supposed to determine benefits predictively, based on estimates of workers' lost ability to compete in an open labor market, rather than retrospectively, by counting up the actual wages that a worker loses. Parties do not need to wait to measure actual lost wages, but rather should be able to apply the disability schedule (i.e., make the prediction of disability) as soon as a worker's medical condition becomes permanent and stationary and an appropriate doctor has provided a useful medical evaluation.[3]

As we have seen, PPD claims appear ripe for early resolution. Minor disability claims on average leave temporary disability within five months of injury and major claims within one year. Nevertheless, despite the benefits that can be associated with early resolution of workers' compensation claims and the opportunity to do so under California's basis for determining benefits, the processing of PPD claims has become distressingly slow. Claims typically take many years to be resolved--long after temporary disability payments end. These delays not only deny the possible benefits associated with early resolution but have forced new state policies, such as requiring that advances be made on PPD payments, that might not be necessary if the PPD system were faster.

In this subsection of our study, we look at several issues involving the time to resolution of PPD claims. These analyses were drawn from the WCIRB's USR claims database which provides information about the timing and characteristics of claims.

_____

[3]Early resolution would be inappropriate and likely against a claimant's interests if disability ratings were determined and claims resolved before the worker's medical condition has stabilized. The parties would not know what the worker's final medical outcome will be and the claimant's condition might worsen after the claim is resolved.

The WCIRB requires that insurers provide annual reports for a PPD claim as long as there are changes in the status of that claim from the prior reporting period. Insurers must report all PPD claims filed under a policy within 18 months of the beginning date of that policy. For example, for workers' compensation policies that began on January 1, 1996, and ran through December 12, 1996, the insurer would have to report claims filed under that policy by July 1, 1997. This first report for the 1996 policy year might include injuries that occurred as many as 18 months prior to the filing of the report--January 1, 1996--as well as injuries that occurred as recently as six months prior to filing of the report--December 31, 1996. If injuries occur in an even distribution throughout the policy year, injuries will have occurred on average approximately one year prior to the filing of the first report. After this initial report, an insurer must provide new information in a report filed twelve months after the first report. In other words, the second report is filed 30 months after the date of the beginning of the policy year.

Insurers continue to file reports through the fifth level on 12 month anniversaries following the date of filing of the initial report. Thus the fifth report includes information through five and one-half years after the beginning of the policy year. Because there is inevitably some lag in WCIRB processing and preparation of data files describing these reports, we have data on all five reporting levels only for claims in policy years 1989 and 1990 and only two report levels of information for claims filed in 1993.

At each report level, the WCIRB reports the status of a claim--open or closed. As Table 7.8 indicates, few claims are reported closed during the first report level, which covers the period up to 18 months after the beginning of the policy year. Across the five years examined in this report, only about 6 percent to 9 percent of the claims are reported to have closed during the first year. Even after the fifth reporting level, five and a half years after the beginning of the policy year, about 11 percent of claims remain unresolved (1989 and 1990 data only).

Table 7.8

**Report Level at Which PPD Claims Close As a Percentage of
Claims in Injury Year**

Injury	Report Level					Lost	Open
Year	1	2	3	4	5	Claims	Last RLV
1989	6.8	17.7	19.5	14.8	13.6	16.6	11.1
1990	6.0	14.7	16.4	18.2	17.1	16.6	11.0
1991	5.8	14.8	21.5	23.9		16.1	18.0
1992	6.8	19.9	30.0			12.1	31.2
1993	8.5	29.4				7.7	54.4

**Report Level at Which PPD Claims Close,
Cumulative As a Percentage of Claims
in Injury Year**

Injury	Report Level				
Year	1	2	3	4	5
1989	6.8	24.6	44.0	58.8	72.4
1990	6.0	20.7	37.1	55.3	72.4
1991	5.8	20.5	42.1	65.9	
1992	6.8	26.7	56.7		
1993	8.5	37.9			

However, Table 7.8 also shows one of the anomalies in the WCIRB database: A substantial number of claims are never reported as having been closed, but disappear from the WCIRB reporting system. We have labeled these as "lost" claims, although we do not believe these claims are truly lost. We assume they are claims that were effectively resolved, but without the formalities of a release, or whose resolution was not reported to the WCIRB.[4] In addition, some of these claims may have been abandoned by the applicants. These lost claims represent about one-sixth of all claims in 1989 and 1990. The somewhat smaller number of lost claims in subsequent years probably reflects the fact that the data cover fewer report levels. Thus some claims that we report as open for later accident years would eventually become lost claims.

If these lost claims really are closed, but without formal documents, we would underestimate the rate at which claims actually

---

[4]The WCIRB does not require reports of claims resolved for less than $5,000 of indemnity. However, insurers can and often do report final resolutions for many claims below this $5,000 requirement.

resolve unless we add lost claims in each year to the number of claims formally closed in that year. In Table 7.9, we have made this addition. Assuming, as seems likely, that most claims are resolved when they disappear, the resolution rate looks somewhat more favorable. Now, about one-seventh of claims are resolved in the first report level within 18 months after the beginning of the policy year, and more than a third of claims are resolved in either the first or second report level (cumulative), within 30 months of the beginning of the policy year.[5] Yet even with this assumption about the treatment of lost claims, three years pass before more than half of PPD claims are resolved (cumulative claims closed injury years 1989-1992).

Table 7.9

Report Level at Which Claims Close or Disappear As a Percentage of Claims in Injury Year

| Injury | Report Level | | | | | Open |
Year	1	2	3	4	5	Last RLV
1989	14.3	22.1	22.1	16.9	13.6	11.1
1990	14.2	19.1	18.9	19.8	17.1	11.0
1991	14.7	19.0	24.4	23.9		18.0
1992	14.5	24.2	30.0			31.2
1993	16.2	29.4				54.4

Report Level at Which Claims Close or Disappear, Cumulative As a Percentage of Claims in Injury Year

| Injury | Report Level | | | | | Open |
Year	1	2	3	4	5	Last RLV
1989	14.3	36.4	58.5	75.4	88.9	100.0
1990	14.2	33.2	52.1	71.9	89.0	100.0
1991	14.7	33.7	58.1	82.0		100.0
1992	14.5	38.7	68.8			100.0
1993	16.2	45.6				100.0

---

[5]Note that the number of claims reported resolved at the last report level for 1991 through 1993 when we have less than the full five years of information are higher than the comparable report level for 1989 and 1990 when we have the full five years. This increase probably reflects in part the fact that if we had obtained a subsequent report some of the claims reported closed in those years would actually have remained open. Alternatively, this could also indicate a sharp increase in the diligence of the parties in resolving claims in the last year for which data were provided to WCIRB and to us.

We conducted several further analyses to identify claims that are
taking a long time to resolve. Table 7.10 shows the time to resolution
for 1990 claims within the several categories of disability ratings,
treating lost claims as resolved in the year they disappear.[6] The
patterns indicated on Table 7.10 are similar for all other years and are
also similar when we disaggregate claims by the final disability rating
as opposed to the initial disability rating.

The speed of resolution is related to the level of disability in a
claim. The most serious claims take substantially longer to resolve.
About 5 percent of claims with disability ratings above 21 are resolved
by the first report level and only about 20 percent are resolved by the
end of the second report level. About one in seven of these 1990 policy
year claims remains open after the fifth report level--on average five
years after the date of the injury.

But even minor disability claims take a surprisingly long time to
resolve. About a fifth of disability claims with ratings of 10 or below
are resolved in each of the first two years. Only 30 percent of claims
with disability ratings between 11 and 20 are resolved within the first
two years. About 10 percent of these low-rated claims remain open after
the end of the fifth reporting level. Thus even though these claims

Table 7.10

**Major Claims Take Years But Even Minor Claims Resolve
Slowly (report level at which claims close or
disappear as a percentage of claims in each
disability rating category)**

| Report | Initial Disability Rating | | | | |
Level	1-10	11-20	21-40	41-70	71-100
1	21.5	9.9	5.8	4.6	4.5
2	21.1	20.5	17.3	15.3	13.1
3	17.9	21.1	21.8	20.7	20.7
4	17.0	20.4	21.8	21.8	21.4
5	12.7	16.6	20.4	23.6	24.4
Still open	9.9	11.5	13.0	14.0	15.9

SOURCE: WCIRB 1990 policy year.

[6]We use 1990 as the last year for which we have five years of
information. Table 7.11 below provides information for 1993 policy
year.

involve relatively low stakes and leave temporary disability within months of the injury, they typically take many years to resolve.

Early data for the 1993 policy claims suggest there may have been some improvement in the speed of resolving PPD claims (Table 7.11).[7] Data from 1993 also allow us to examine how speed of resolution is related to whether or not an applicant is represented, since the WCIRB changed its reporting requirements in 1993 to get better information about representation. The data indicate that over half of the 1993 claims with ratings below 10 are resolved within the first two report levels, a number that reaches 60 percent among unrepresented applicants (41 percent of unrepresented and 50 percent of represented open after two years). Indeed, 37 percent of unrepresented applicants with claims involving a disability rating of 10 or less are resolved within the first report level. Still, most minor claims, with disability ratings of 20 or less, are not resolved within the first two report levels. Indeed, 68 percent of unrepresented claims with disability ratings between 11 and 20 are still open after two report levels. Except for those with ratings of 10 or less, applicants who are represented have a greater chance of having their claims resolved early (i.e., a smaller

Table 7.11

Few Claims Resolved Within 30 Months with or Without an Attorney (percentage of claims grouped by ratings and representation that close at each report level)

1993 Policy Claims
Rating at Last Report

Report Level	1-10 Not Rep	1-10 Rep	11-20 Not Rep	11-20 Rep	21-40 Not Rep	21-40 Rep	41-70 Not Rep	41-70 Rep	71-100 Not Rep	71-100 Rep
1	37	17	14	8	5	3	3	2	2	2
2	22	33	18	34	17	32	16	27	12	22
Open	41	50	68	58	78	65	81	71	86	76

[7]As we noted above, this may be an artifact of having only two report levels of data for the 1993 claims.

percentage of open claims after two years). But even among represented applicants, fewer than half of claims are resolved within the first two years (i.e., open claims are 50 percent or greater for all ratings).

Workers are protected to some extent from delay in resolving claims. They receive temporary disability payments (typically for a relatively brief part of this delay) and (recently) advance payments of PPD benefits. For most other system participants, delays are costly. Employers and insurers must pay for carrying open claims. Taxpayers bear added costs as claims repeatedly involve the formal processes of the WCAB, the DEU, and other portions of the DWC. Payments to applicants' lawyers are delayed until claims close.

COSTS OF PPD CLAIMS RELATIVE TO BENEFITS

Finally we turn to a rough consideration of the relative costs of processing PPD claims, analyzing this separately for our several categories of disability ratings. Our measure of costs represents a limited subset of all the actual costs and claims because the only data available to us are the costs of applicants' and defense lawyers' fees. We calculated the total amount of legal fees as a percentage of incurred indemnity (i.e., temporary, plus permanent, plus rehabilitation indemnity and plan costs). The first column in Table 7.12 shows these percentages across 1989-1994. If we added to this the costs to insurers and employers of carrying and processing claims, we would expect a much higher ratio of costs to benefits than we display on Table 7.12.

Table 7.12

Ratio of Legal Costs to Benefits Is Highest
for Lowest-Rated Claims

Last Reported Disability Rating	Lawyer Fees as % of Indemnity	Fees in Each Rating Category as % of Total Fees
1-10	26	33
11-20	12	26
21-40	7	29
41-70	6	11
71-99	4	2

SOURCE: WCIRB, closed claims 1989-1994.
NOTE: Percentage calculated across all closed claims whether or not lawyers participated.

Table 7.12 shows another perverse effect of California's treatment of minor disability claims. The table shows that lawyers' fees represent far greater proportions of indemnity payments among claims for minor disabilities than for major claims, even though lawyers are involved in a far smaller percentage of minor claims.[8] Legal fees (defense and applicant) exceed 25 percent of the indemnity payments for claims with disability ratings of 10 or below. In contrast, among claims with disability ratings of 21 or greater, legal fees represent less than 7 percent of indemnity costs.

We also looked at the total amount of legal fees across all PPD claims and determined what percentage of that total amount was spent on claims involving disability ratings within each of the disability categories (the last column in Table 7.12). This analysis revealed that 33 percent of all legal fees was spent on claims involving disability ratings of 10 or less, and almost 60 percent of all legal fees were spent on claims involving disability ratings of 20 or less. In short, these relatively minor disability claims not only consume most of the medical treatment and indemnity dollars within the workers compensation system, but they also consume most of the legal fees and, possibly, an even greater share of all other transaction costs.

PPD BENEFITS FOR PARTICULAR CATEGORIES OF INJURIES

In this section, we have described various costs associated with the claims process, particularly for low-rated claims. We have found that, in comparison to the average stakes involved (as measured by average indemnity benefits) the costs of low-rated claims are considerable. However, the average stakes may not be the most useful standard to measure against transactions costs. Particularly for litigation costs such as legal fees and the cost from delays in closing claims or employers' and insurers' costs in carrying open cases, the stakes may better be measured by the range of paid benefits, since this measures what can be gained by disputing a claim. In this subsection,

------

[8]We calculated Column I as the mean legal fees for each category, including zeros, divided by the mean indemnity.

we examine the range of benefits by injury categories. These analyses
provide background to our later recommendation of a two-track system for
resolving low-rated claims.

Table 7.13 shows the benefit levels and the number of claims for
13 general categories of injuries indicated in the WCIRB database that
were selected because they involve large numbers of claims and modest
compensation benefits. The table also shows for comparison a fourteenth
category, ruptured disc, that involves more serious disabilities and
larger payments. The thirteen claims were selected because they
typically involve modest benefits, median benefits ranging from $3,100
to $7,500. More interestingly, the range of payments between the 25th
and 50th percentiles is narrow for each of these types of injuries. For
example, for the 25 percent of claimants with mental stress claims
between the 25th and 50th percentile, the difference in benefit levels
is only $1,600. The difference in payments for claims with carpal
tunnel injuries is $3,300 for those claims between the 25th and 50th
percentiles. The range of payments between the 50th and the 75th and
the full interquartile range (difference between 25th to 75th
percentiles of payments, known as "IQR") are wider.

Table 7.13

Many Injuries PPD Benefits Have Narrow Range

| Injury Group | Range of Benefits | | | |
	25th	50th	75th	Number
Mental stress	1,500	3,150	6,724	30,764
Finger amputation	1,785	3,608	7,562	4,528
Upper ext. contusion	2,000	4,515	9,901	10,095
Head contusion	2,100	4,700	10,059	4,317
Foot sprain	1,500	4,240	10,374	5,223
Carpal tunnel	2,500	5,810	11,670	34,904
Neck strain	2,500	5,915	12,501	5,618
Neck/trunk contusion	2,500	5,923	12,000	6,949
Upper back strain	2,500	6,000	12,000	8,650
Lower ext. contusion	2,100	5,667	12,670	13,159
Multiple contusion	2,999	6,776	13,949	10,253
Lower back strain	3,360	7,500	15,303	106,891
Neck sprain	2,310	7,035	16,905	690
Ruptured disc	16,835	25,725	39,621	875

Without a full accounting of the costs associated with the claims process, it is difficult to evaluate whether it is worthwhile for parties to bear costs of litigation and delay in order to change outcomes in the ranges shown on Table 7.13 for these claims. Moreover, these costs are not symmetrical for applicants and employers/insurers. Because legal fees for applicants' lawyers are fixed and modest, it may be worthwhile for applicants to assume such costs even to obtain the modest increments in fees that might be derived for these claims. The biggest costs to applicants may be the delay and hassles of continued litigation. Employers' and insurers' costs are likely to be higher: Average defense lawyers fees are greater than those for applicant lawyers and employers and insurers also must pay costs of administering claims.

This comparison of litigation costs to ranges of benefits suggests that parties might expect better outcomes if they spend more on litigation. We do not know that this is so. The results that workers get greater benefits in some cases or that employers have to pay less in some cases may have little to do with whether or not the worker or employer hires a lawyer and whether or not they fully press litigation. We cannot examine this issue within data available to us. However, our analyses of inconsistency in the rating process, described in Section 6 in Tables 6.3 and 6.5, suggest that outcomes at the 25th percentile or the 75th percentile for these claims is substantially a matter of chance.

We compared the range of payments for minor injuries as shown on Table 7.13 with the range in ratings (and therefore benefits) generated by inconsistency in ratings between the WCIRB and the DEU, as discussed in Section 6. We found that the range in payments between the 25th and 75th percentile is roughly the same as the range in payments from inconsistencies in the rating process--differences in ratings that are made by different raters for the same case. For example, the median benefit for upper extremity contusion as shown on Table 7.13 is $4,515, equivalent to a disability rating of 10.5. The interquartile range (IQR) for this injury, calculated by subtracting the 25th from the 75th percentile in Table 7.13, is $7,901. We compared this range in payment to the range in benefits resulting from inconsistency in the rating process. Table 6.3 in Section 6 showed the dollar amount associated with the range of disability ratings given by the DEU for particular values in the WCIRB. For WCIRB ratings of 10, we found that the dollar value for the interquartile range of DEU ratings is $9,030, greater than the observed range of payments for upper extremity contusions.

In general, the comparison of Table 7.13 in this section and Table 6.3 in the last section suggests that for many of the minor injuries in Table 7.13, the IQR is similar to the range reported for the DEU ratings that correspond to a set of constant WCIRB ratings. This suggests that for the 13 types of minor injuries shown on Table 7.13 whether a claim is resolved as low as the 25th percentile or as high as the 75th percentile may depend to a great degree upon who is doing the rating or upon the inherent inconsistency in California's rating process.

This suggests that much of the variability in payments is driven by inter-rater inconsistency. Combined with the results regarding legal fees and the time to closure, this suggests that "system costs" are a large fraction of the range of benefits paid.

Like the thirteen minor injury claims shown on Table 7.13, the majority of PPD claims within the California workers' compensation system, have generally low ranges of disputes with regard to indemnity benefits with amounts in dispute at most only a bit greater than the transaction costs for disputing their indemnity payments. In contrast, a smaller number of claims with more serious injuries, such as those based on an applicant's ruptured disc, have greater benefits and involve a range of benefits that greatly exceeds any for the thirteen injury groups that have lower disability ratings (and far greater numbers of claims). If system costs do not increase proportionately with the size of the claim, as one would expect for many administrative costs, and as our results with regard to legal fees and time to closure suggest, then for these high-rated claims, disputes about benefits involve stakes that exceed the transaction costs for such disputes.

These comparisons suggest that solely from considerations of costs, litigation for most minor claims is not appropriate but litigation for the relatively small number of higher-stakes claims is appropriate. It would be cost-effective to resolve the majority of minor disability claims (but not high-disability claims) simply by offering the average payment received by such claims in order to forgo transaction costs. Furthermore, because the range in most payments for minor claims seems to be substantially determined by inconsistency in the rating process, the resolution of most claims for the average would represent a fairer resolution. Since much of the current difference in these payments is without reason, it would be better if most claims could be resolved for the same amount. The offer of an average payment should not be unattractive to applicants. Because much of the variation in payment for minor claims results from the inconsistency in the rating process, claimants cannot know in advance whether they will receive, by example, the 25th percentile or the 75th percentile payment. By waiting and litigating, they might get either, primarily due to chance. An offer of the average payment would have the same expected value and a chance at the 25th or 75th percentile, but through a quicker and easier process.

In practice, the categories shown on Table 7.13 might be refined to narrow the range of payments within a category of claims so that an offer of the average claim value would be more attractive. Each of the low rated categories of claims on Table 7.13 involves broad, simple categories that may encompass a variety of injuries with different levels of severity and disability. Ranges of benefits would be smaller if we had data for and could categorize injuries into more homogeneous groups, such as the number of amputated fingers or types and severity of back strains. Because we do not have these data, we cannot examine how much the range of payments might be reduced by such details.

However, as a proxy for that analysis, we looked at two injuries--carpal tunnel and lower back strain--comparing the range of benefits between (a) all claims with the injury and (b) a subset of those claims where medical treatment costs were below the 70th percentile. The amount of medical benefits is one indication of the severity of an injury, so we would expect that claims with medical treatment below the 70th percentile are less serious injuries and would have a narrower range of benefits.

When we limit our consideration to those claims with medical treatment costs below the 70th percentile, the range in benefits decreases substantially (Table 7.14). Among carpal tunnel claims, the range in benefits between the 25th and 50th percentiles decreases from $3,300 to $2,100. For claimants with lower back strains, the range in benefits decreases from $4,200 among all claims to $2,800 among those claims with medical benefits below the 70th percentile. If data were available to categorize these claims on the basis of meaningful medical indicators appropriate to each category, we would observe narrower ranges of benefits.

Table 7.14

Range of Benefits Becomes Smaller As We Define More Specific Injuries (e.g., claims with medical benefits less than 70th percentile)

Injury Group	Range of Benefits			
	25th%	50th%	75th%	Number
Carpal tunnel				
All claims	2,500	5,810	11,670	34,904
<70th percentile	2,100	4,250	9,041	21,871
Lower back strain				
All claims	3,360	7,500	15,303	106,891
<70th percentile	2,100	4,935	10,000	58,871

SUMMARY

The various workers' compensation databases available to us were not designed to support either research or policy analysis of the treatment of PPD claims within the California workers' compensation system and cannot answer all the questions we have about the treatment of those claims. Nevertheless, these data provide significant insights into the treatment of PPD claims.

As we have seen, although the individual benefits within claims are low for low-rated claims, the aggregate costs of those claims dominate the workers' compensation system, because the vast majority of all claims have low ratings. In contrast, the stakes of any individual high-rated claim are great and are more likely to entail litigation. But the aggregate costs and aggregate benefits associated with high-rated claims are small proportions of the financial stakes of the workers' compensation system in California. In every way that we could consider, PPD claims in California's workers' compensation system constitute mostly minor claims.

8. POLICY ISSUES AND RECOMMENDATIONS

Our stakeholder and participant interviews as well as our analysis of workers' compensation and wage loss data suggest potential reforms for California's treatment of permanent partial disability claims. In this section we briefly summarize key problems identified in our analyses and then describe policy recommendations for addressing them.

SUMMARY OF KEY PROBLEM AREAS

Our research provides a mixed picture of California's PPD process, disability schedule, and the adequacy of benefits. Almost every person we interviewed expressed concerns about the PPD system and made suggestions for reform. Our quantitative analyses suggest that many of the criticisms raised by interviewees were applicable to only part of California's PPD system and were not accurate descriptions of the entire system. On the other hand, our quantitative studies suggest basic inefficiencies and problems with the PPD system that are broader and more systematic than most interviewees noted.

When we integrate our qualitative and quantitative findings, the following problem areas emerge.

Low-Rated PPD Claims: Need for a Simple Process

California's present PPD process is poorly suited to deal with minor injury claims, which dominate the numbers, the claims process, and every element of cost except rehabilitation. These claims, which involved relatively low stakes, should be resolved quickly and easily. Nevertheless, they go through the same process as the more complex, higher-stakes, serious disability claims and consume most of the legal fees (and presumably, other transaction expenses) involved in handling PPD claims. This process produces disability ratings for minor claims that do not seem to be consistently determined and that have little relation to the wages lost by workers. The failure to recognize and deal effectively with low-rated PPD claims not only burdens injured workers and employers, but also clogs the entire workers' compensation system in California.

High-Rated Claims--Need to Validate the Disability Schedule

Our wage loss analysis shows greater validity to ratings for high-rated claims, yet our analyses of DEU and WCIRB ratings suggest that different raters substantially disagree about ratings for the same case.

The relatively low predictability of ratings indicates that parties must be uncertain about the appropriate disability rating for these serious claims--a lack of certainty that probably contributes to litigation. Uncertainty and unpredictability allow parties to manipulate the rating process. The high financial stakes of indemnity payments for serious disability claims provide an incentive to do so. Both applicant and defense lawyers reported to us that they can and do manipulate the present rating process.

Limited Wage Recovery for All Injured Workers

Our wage loss analyses indicate that under the current workers' compensation system there are substantial wage losses for workers at all disability levels and only limited wage recoveries. When we consider both injured workers who leave the labor force as well as the reduced level of wages among those who return, indemnity payments available through the California workers' compensation system seem inadequate for workers at all levels of disability. On the other hand, when we consider only the relative wages of workers who return to work, the indemnity payments approach reasonable compensation for workers with the most serious injuries. Under either analysis, the amount of compensation for workers with less serious injuries seems neither related to the amount of their wage loss nor adequate to compensate wages lost.

The Problem of Return to Work

The wage loss analysis also indicates that the return of injured workers to work is a significant and complex problem, one that is not well addressed by the current workers' compensation system in California. Many injured workers, even those with relatively minor injuries, permanently exit the California workplace. Many others intermittently enter, leave, and re-enter the workforce after their workplace injuries. These losses to the workforce represent not only wage losses to injured workers, but also a loss of productivity and output for California's economy.

Improving the Utility of Medical Evaluations

The process for obtaining medical evaluations of injured workers and the quality of medical evaluation reports are of concern to almost everyone we interviewed. California's current reliance on treating doctors as the principal source of evaluations was broadly criticized because (1) treating doctors are often unfamiliar with the language and needs of the workers' compensation system, (2) treating physicians are perceived by some to be biased, and (3) the legal presumption of correctness for a treating doctor's evaluation creates an arbitrary tactical advantage to the party selecting that doctor. Because treating doctors are at times chosen more for their forensic than their treating skills, some interviewees are concerned that the quality of a worker's medical care is compromised.

Reducing Burdens on the WCAB

Our interviews with participants and stakeholders suggest that the WCAB court system is poorly utilized and burdened by unnecessary paperwork and litigation issues.

Obtaining Needed Information

Finally, both our analysis of existing workers' compensation data as well as our efforts at proposing feasible reforms confront a pressing need to develop comprehensive and useful claims-level data for PPD claims. The databases that we used in this report provide valuable, but limited, information. They were not designed to support research, are inadequate for needed analysis of the California PPD system, and limit changes that could improve the treatment of PPD claims.

POLICY RECOMMENDATIONS

We developed policy recommendations to address these concerns about treatment of PPD claims within the California workers' compensation system. We propose these recommendations as a program of related policy change that should support and supplement each other. Many recommendations depend upon the successful implementation of other recommendations in order to be effective.

Summary of Policy Recommendations

We make the following policy recommendations:

1. Form a task force that combines technical and analytic expertise along with political oversight reflecting major interest groups concerned about California's treatment of PPD workers' compensation claims. The task force would be responsible for reviewing and implementing a number of the study's recommendations.

2. Develop and implement an elective fast-track system for processing and compensating minor PPD claims.

3. Continue RAND's current wage loss study and implement additional research to review the adequacy of present PPD payments.

4. Revise the California PPD schedule, base ratings on empirical measures of wage loss, and clarify and simplify the medical categories within the schedule.

5. Initiate a program by the DEU to improve the consistency and predictability of disability ratings.

6. Provide a workers' compensation closed-claims database to WCAB judges, DEU raters, and all other parties.

7. Develop policies to increase return to work, drawing on continuing strategies undertaken by other states.

8. Implement procedures to expedite litigation in the WCAB.

9. Limit the use of C&Rs.

10. Improve the utility of medical evaluations.

Detailed Discussions of Recommendations

Form a Task Force. We recommend that a task force be created that combines technical and analytic expertise and reflects major interest groups concerned about California's treatment of PPD workers' compensation claims. Many of our other recommendations require technical study and development that can be carried out by the task force. The task force can also provide the forum for balancing various interests affected by the recommended reforms and for obtaining the political support necessary for their implementation. The task force, which could be developed by the Commission on Health and Safety and Workers' Compensation or by a new entity, should provide both openness and political balance in reviewing and implementing policy changes. Ideally, its recommendations should be developed in detail by a working group of persons who have technical knowledge and an analytic approach to dealing with policy issues in the area of workers' compensation.

The task force should be responsible for reviewing and implementing the first five policy recommendations described below.

Revise the PPD Schedule. Our interviews with participants and stakeholders in the California workers' compensation system indicated broad interest in revising the PPD schedule, although there was substantial disagreement as to the nature of such revisions. In particular, employers and insurers see the PPD schedule as being too indeterminate, resulting in capricious and inconsistent ratings that generate unnecessary litigation. On the other hand, many lawyers, both applicant and defense, find this indeterminacy useful. Indeed, they believe it serves their clients' interest because it gives attorneys flexibility and discretion in the way they rate and handle claims.

Our research leads to mixed conclusions about the PPD schedule. On its face, the document is opaque, complex, and hard for lay persons, either injured workers or employers, to understand. Interviewees indicated that the terms and application of the schedule are far from clear even to medical professionals. Yet the results of our comparisons of different ratings for the same cases suggest that for most PPD claims--the vast majority with ratings under 20--differences in ratings may be greatly a matter of chance.

More fundamentally, our wage loss study raises concerns about the validity of ratings reached by applying the California PPD schedule. Again, for the vast majority of claims that involve minor injuries we saw no correspondence between the ratings placed on claims and the amount of actual wage loss experienced by injured workers. Although claims with the highest ratings had greater wage losses than lower-rated

claims, this conclusion was based solely on observing differences in the
mean wage loss among workers with various disability ratings. Given the
great inconsistency in disability ratings observed even among workers
with the highest ratings, it is likely that there are substantial ranges
of wage losses *within* the broad disability rating categories.

It is not surprising that the ratings under the California PPD
schedule are not systematically related to differences among workers'
wage losses. Although disability benefits are intended to compensate
injured workers' losses of wage earning capacity, the PPD schedule was
not developed specifically to link disability ratings and loss of wage
earning capacity. Rather, the disability schedule evolved from a series
of political compromises among interest groups based upon a consensus
about how various types of injuries, within various occupations, are
likely to be related to a worker's loss of income. At best, the
document was developed to have a certain apparent or "face" validity.
At worst, it is a document that reflects only repeated political
compromises.

The California PPD schedule can be revised through two
complementary processes. The first process is to clarify and improve
the objective findings and other factors that are used to classify or
sort claims into different disability levels. These are the factors
that doctors should look for and report on in making their medical
evaluations. This process should draw on the knowledge and experience
of the IMC and respected forensic doctors. It should draw on a
systematic and regular examination of the consistency of DEU ratings
(see the discussion of recommended DEU study of rating reliability,
below) that can identify elements of the schedule that confuse and
produce inconsistent ratings. And the process should look to other
learned sources, such as the compilation of medical findings that the
AMA Guides list as related to impairments. The second process would
develop a new schedule that starts with this improved list of medical
findings and other factors to determine which have a relationship with
injured workers' actual wage losses (as discussed in detail in the next
subsection). This empirical link could be established by elaborating,
refining, and adapting the wage loss studies described in this report.

Develop an Empirical Disability Schedule Based on Wage Loss. The
fundamental problem with the disability rating schedule is that it was
not developed through a process most likely to insure that the schedule
met its statutory objectives: to set disability ratings that are
systematically related to a worker's reduced ability to compete in the
open labor market. PPD benefits in California are not based on a
worker's *actual* wage losses because it may take years to determine the
actual amount of wages lost by an injured worker, well past the time
when benefits must be determined. Furthermore, payment of workers'
compensation benefits based on a worker's actual wage losses could
create undesirable incentives for the worker to remain out of work to
maximize the amount of wage loss and, therefore, benefits. Rather, like
many workers' compensation schemes throughout the country, California's
disability schedule attempts to predict how much wage loss an injured
worker will suffer and then provide benefits that are related to the
worker's *predicted* wage loss.

But California has not developed a schedule that actually predicts
disability, that has a demonstrated, empirically derived relationship to
actual wage losses. In effect, the disability schedule passes as a
predictive system, but without evidence that it really measures what it
is supposed to predict.

In principle, developing a California disability schedule is no
different from developing any of the predictive devices such as those
used, perhaps most notably, as standardized tests to determine
admissions to college or graduate and professional schools. Such
predictive devices have the same basic elements.

First, a set of predictors is defined--characteristics that can be
objectively identified and measured. In the case of the disability
schedule, predictors might include workers' injuries, restrictions and
other residuals in their physical capabilities, their occupation, age,
education, and gender. These predictors are now identified in the
current schedule and in other documents such as the *AMA Guides*.

Second, measurements of these predictors are compared to a
numerical scale that measures the outcome one wants to predict, known as

the "criterion" variable. For the disability schedule, the criterion is the amount of wage loss that injured workers have suffered.

As a part of these numerical comparisons, statistical tests are used to identify sets of predictors that are systematically related to the criterion. In the case of the disability schedule, such tests would make it possible to identify sets of medical findings and other related matters that are historically and predictably related to wage loss and which should be the factors used by medical evaluators and raters. The tests would identify other factors that are not related to wage loss, which should be ignored. And, finally, the tests would indicate how much wage loss occurred historically for particular groups of injuries, in order to establish the ratings for such injuries.

This process--identifying predictors and the statistical testing of the relationship between those predictors and wage loss--would yield an empirically derived predictive model of wage losses that could be used to fashion a new disability schedule for rating and paying PPD benefits.

The California disability schedule was not developed in this way. Similarly, alternative schedules that claim to measure impairment, such as the *AMA Guides*, have no empirically demonstrated relationship to disabilities or lost wages. Portions of the *AMA Guides*--e.g., identification of tests, diagnostic procedures, and limitations for particular body parts or systems--might contribute significantly to the development of a new disability schedule for California. However, the impairment evaluations that come out of the *AMA Guides* are not likely to be useful either in developing a new schedule for California or as an interim schedule until the state can derive an empirical schedule based on wage loss. The *Guides* provide sophisticated and well thought out descriptions of injuries that might be related to impairment or disability, but they provide no justification or explanation for the impairment scale that is central to the *Guides'* use.

Table 8.1 summarizes the important features of the present California disability schedule, the *AMA Guides*, and an empirically derived schedule based on wage loss analyses. The empirical wage loss analyses would develop a schedule that is fitted to and measures actual wages lost by injured workers. On such a schedule, the order of ratings

for injuries would be consistent with the amount of wages lost by
workers with various injuries. Furthermore, because the scale is
derived from a measure of dollars, it allows arithmetic comparisons; for
example, it is reasonable to assume that one injury is twice as
disabling as another because it generates twice as much wage loss.

Table 8.1

Utility of Alternative Schedules

Present Schedule	AMA Guides	Wage-Loss Analysis
Designed to predict "average" wage loss	Designed to measure "average" impairment	Designed to predict "average" wage loss
Design not empirical	Design not empirical	Empirical design
Scale: 1. Meaningful 2. Ordinal, some support 3. Relational, unsupported	Scale: 1. Questionable meaning 2. Ordinal, unsupported 3. Relational, unsupported	Scale: 1. Meaningful, empirical 2. Ordinal 3. Relational
Classify claims based on medical opinions and common sense	Classify claims based on medical consensus	Classify claims based on AMA guidelines, ratings experience, and empirical testing
Validity of ratings: tested, some support	Validity of ratings: untestable, no independent criterion	Validity of ratings: testable, scale based on relationship to validating criterion
Rating process: trained raters	Rating process: doctors, some trained (depending on state)	Rating process: automated or trained raters
Consistency: some	Consistency: some, lower than claimed	Consistency: high

In developing a wage-loss-based disability scale, the task force
could build upon RAND's current wage loss analysis. By linking the DEU
database to the income information that RAND has obtained from the EDD
for those workers, the task force could examine elements of how the
current PPD schedule is related to wage loss. It would be useful to

supplement current information about medical conditions, residuals, and occupations--for example, by drawing selected samples of injured workers for whom EDD wage information has already been obtained.

The content of such a supplemental database is critical to developing a wage-loss-based disability schedule. First, data should be collected for all elements of the present PPD schedule that the task force believes might be related to a worker's wage loss. Second, medical findings, tests, and other medical judgments used by the *AMA Guides* might appropriately be considered as elements of the revised schedule.[1] Third, the task force should work with experienced raters, adjusters, and applicants' lawyers in order to identify medical matters that are routinely used to evaluate and rate claims under the PPD schedule.

The review of these three sources will identify a substantial list of items that might be included as predictors in developing a PPD schedule based on wage loss. However, most items of medical information are needed only for a limited set of claims. Thus, rather than collecting a broad set of information for every claim, the data collection strategy should be modular, collecting for each type of injury only the information likely to be important for determining disability for that kind of claim.

Revisions of the disability schedule should be sensitive to how changes might affect the return to work and the retention of injured workers. As we suggest below, California should develop policies aimed at increasing return and retention. Changes in the disability schedule should complement and not undercut such policies.

Once it is developed, the workers' compensation schedule should not be treated as a static document. The relationships between particular injuries and wage losses are likely to change over time, particularly if California develops effective policies for returning and retaining injured workers. The task force, the DWC, or another appropriate entity should periodically update the wage loss study, obtaining new

---

[1]Using the *AMA Guides* to identify elements to be included in the wage loss study does not suggest that the *Guides* should be adopted as a rating schedule.

information about wages and testing the validity of the then-current
schedule. We expect that these updates will lead to periodic
adjustments and changes in the schedule.

Conduct a Follow-Up Survey to Review the Adequacy of PPD Payments.
California's Labor Code prescribes that the amount of benefits for
permanent partial disability should be related to a worker's loss of
ability to compete in an open labor market, with an expectation that the
level of indemnity payments should compensate workers for two-thirds of
their wage losses, subject to a statutory maximum. The results of our
wage loss study suggest that PPD indemnity payments fall short of this
goal for workers with all levels of permanent disabilities. The
shortfall is particularly striking for workers with disability ratings
of 20 percent or less. The apparent inadequacy of PPD indemnity
payments for workers with the least serious injuries is not surprising
since California has not adjusted PPD indemnity payments for minor
injuries since 1983.

These results suggest that PPD indemnity payments should be
increased, particularly for workers with minor injuries. However,
before recommending such increases, the task force should verify the
wage loss findings and explore (1) why so many injured workers,
particularly those with minor injuries, fail to return to permanent
work, and (2) why wages for workers who do return fail to recover even
over extended periods of time.

To help decisionmakers understand more completely the forces
driving wage losses for injured California workers, we recommend
extending the wage loss study. For example, the inquiry might be
furthered by surveying a sample of workers who suffered injuries several
years ago and whose injuries and wage losses are already included in the
current wage loss study. The survey could document their work
experience and sources of income since their injuries as well as their
perceptions of the workers' compensation system. It might also be
useful to survey the workers' employers to learn about workers'
adaptations to their injuries and their ability to meet work
requirements after the injury. Interviews with employers should be
conducted in a manner that would not violate workers' confidences or

adversely affect workers. Finally, a survey of some of the workers used as controls in our wage loss study could enhance our understanding of the wage loss results.

If the survey results support the observation of the current study that substantial post-injury wage losses go uncompensated, then such findings would present a strong argument for increasing PPD indemnity benefits.

Improve Consistency and Predictability of Ratings. The DWC and DEU can improve the consistency and predictability of the rating process by instituting routine procedures for testing the consistency of DEU raters. Other entities that perform rating, coding, or data entry processes like those performed by the DEU have often implemented procedures in which multiple employees independently rate or code the same case. The DEU's adoption of such reliability checks could serve multiple purposes.

First, such checks would provide a measure of the overall reliability and consistency of the DEU rating process.

Second, they would identify troublesome areas of the disability schedule or problematic types of claims for which the consistency of ratings is comparatively low. The DEU could improve the rating process for these claims by having raters identify best rating practices and by developing training programs focused specifically on cases that are more difficult to rate.

Third, these reliability checks will identify raters whose practices differ from those of most other raters. The DEU could provide additional education or support to help these raters bring their practices into line with their colleagues.

Fourth, the DEU could draw upon these reliability checks to develop educational materials to train new raters, to provide continuing education to present raters, and to provide training sessions for other professionals, lawyers, and adjusters. Such standardized training could improve rating consistency.

To perform these reliability checks, cases would be submitted to multiple raters to be evaluated. Cases could be selected randomly or chosen to focus on the types of cases that appear to be creating problems. Raters should not be told that they are rating a claim that has been sent to multiple raters. Data from these multiple-rated cases would then be used to promote the four goals stated above.

Create Elective Fast Track for Minor Claims. Our research results argue for adopting different procedures to deal more efficiently and fairly with minor PPD claims. Minor PPD claims--those with disability ratings under 20 or 25--dominate the PPD claims volume, the indemnity and medical compensation paid, as well as processing costs. Particularly among minor claims, ratings differ for similar claims. They often go through a contentious, expensive, and time consuming process in which parties fight over small differences in benefits-- differences that are only weakly related to the real wage losses that workers sustain.

We propose a new, elective, fast-track system designed to deal with minor PPD claims. The fast track would create a simple, objectively based administrative system that provides fixed and certain payments to claimants who meet certain specified criteria. Such a system should limit litigation for the vast majority of PPD claims.

Our proposal is similar to systems in other states that operate two-track systems (see Section 5 for a discussion of states with two systems, typically for scheduled and unscheduled injuries). However, to avoid problems experienced by other states, our proposed fast track would provide similar benefit levels under either system and give applicants the choice of electing either the present system or the simplified administrative fast-track system.

The proposed fast-track system would be available only to claimants with low-rated claims--those with ratings below 20 or 25, and only to those who have admitted injuries (an injury that the employer admits is work-related). Although the fast-track system is elective for applicants, employers could force a summary process to resolve AOE/COE disputes. The summary process would be handled quickly to insure that applicants are not denied the principal advantage of the fast-track system, early resolution of their claims. An applicant electing the fast track could proceed with his/her claim only if the summary process determined that the injury was work-related.

The fast track would be based upon a schedule that lists categories
of injuries defined by specific, objective medical findings. Each
scheduled injury would have an associated non-negotiable flat payment.
Applicants whose medical conditions fit within an injury category would
be entitled to receive that fixed payment. An applicant's eligibility
for payment within any category would be determined by an evaluation
from a treating doctor.

If an employer disputes the treating doctor's evaluation, the claim
would be referred and processed under the current, three-doctor QME
panel process. If an applicant did not accept the QME's evaluation,
he/she could withdraw from the fast track and proceed along the normal
workers' compensation track.

Payment of the fast-track amount would serve as a final resolution
of the indemnity rights for a particular claim. The claim could not be
reopened for the same injury or event. We believe the fast-track system
should operate independently of determinations of workers' rights to
medical treatment and rehabilitation benefits; however, some type of
summary processes might be appropriate for medical and rehabilitation
benefits for at least some cases.

The task force should be responsible for determining both the
categories of injuries in the fast-track schedule and the payment
amounts. For example, it could identify injury categories that can be
characterized by objective medical findings and that historically have
received relatively homogeneous PPD payments. Initially, these might be
developed jointly from existing databases (WCIRB, DEU, and WCAB) in
conjunction with the judgments of technical members of the task force
about appropriate categorization. Payment schedules should be developed
using current payment patterns and information generated by the wage
loss study about actual wage losses associated with particular types of
injuries.[2]

_____

[2]Because we also recommend an empirical revision of the disability
rating schedule based on the wage loss study, the wage-loss-based
revisions to both the fast-track payment schedule and the main rating
schedule should be completed in tandem, so that payment disparities
between the two schedules do not provide perverse financial incentives
to claimants to process through one channel rather than the other.

Because the fast track must operate as an attractive alternative to the main system, the payments should approximate the average payments that claimants would anticipate receiving if they proceeded through the main system.

The task force, in conjunction with the DWC, should develop simple descriptive materials to inform applicants about the two systems. Claimants should be able to use applicant attorneys for counseling and advice regarding their choice to use the fast track. The amount of compensation for such services should be set so that attorneys are financially indifferent to an applicant's choice of tracks. This implies a modestly lower rate of compensation for advising applicants under the fast-track system, since attorneys will be able to represent many more fast-track claims than those requiring ordinary litigation.

The fast-track schedule should be revised as more detailed medical information becomes available through the revised claims-level database presently proposed by the DWC and as information is developed to support the revised empirical, wage-loss-based disability schedule. Furthermore, as scheduled ratings under the main disability schedule shift with adoption of a wage-loss-based schedule, the task force should make similar modifications to the fast-track schedule.

The task force will also need to consider how the availability of a fast, easy, and certain payment program will affect the number of workers who apply for PPD benefits. The task force might look to a follow-up wage-loss survey we propose to help estimate the number and likely characteristics of additional applicants whom the fast track might bring into the PPD process. The task force should consider not only how many additional applicants the fast-track process might generate, but also whether or not these additional applicants should receive PPD benefits. If necessary, the task force might contemplate barriers that might discourage inappropriate additional applications for the fast-track system.

Finally, the task force should consider how the fast-track system will change the financial demands placed upon employers. As part of this inquiry, the task force should try to identify costs for processing minor injury claims under the present system and estimate the cost savings that could be achieved by using the fast-track system.

Provide Workers' Compensation Closed Claim Information. Claims-level data that track how claims are being resolved in the PPD system would help claimants make more informed decisions and help all parties arrive at more consistent settlements. These data would provide feedback to lawyers, applicants, employers, and insurance adjusters about historical patterns in claims resolution, thus guiding decisionmaking and setting reasonable expectations about resolving new claims. Such data would help ensure more informed and consistent practices and resolutions in the workers' compensation system, operating either under the present schedule or under a revised wage-loss-based schedule.

Develop Strategies for Increasing Return to Work. The task force can draw upon both the wage loss study as well as a possible follow-up study of applicants and employers in order to better understand the problems of low rates of return to work and episodic periods of employment and unemployment after injured workers return to work. The task force should consider strategies for increasing return to work and employment stability after injury. As part of this consideration, the task force should monitor the effects of statutory attempts in other states to encourage return to work.

Reduce Inappropriate Use of Compromise and Release. Our interviews with workers' compensation participants raised concerns about inappropriate use of the C&R process. Some were concerned that the lump sum C&R payments were inadequate recompense for the forgone rights to future medical treatment; others felt that the waiver of future medical treatments may shift the obligations for paying for medical treatment to taxpayers, unions, or other parties. Even participants who were not critical of the C&R process recognized the strong allure of the lump sum payment in a system that does not otherwise provide them.

The task force may be able to investigate the C&R issue by looking to research that RAND is proposing to an independent funding source. This study would provide additional information about workers' utilization of social welfare and support programs, including state disability insurance, social security benefit programs, Medicare, Medicaid, and general welfare payments. Among other things, the proposed study may reveal how workers' election of C&Rs is related to their subsequent participation in these various social support programs.

Should the task force conclude that there is an over-reliance on the C&R process, ways to reduce C&Rs could be considered. For example, applicants might be allowed to take limited lump sum indemnity payments without court approval. This might reduce the attractiveness of C&Rs as the only potential source for lump sum payments.

Expedite Litigation. The WCAB and the individual workers' compensation courts are central in every way to the treatment of PPD claims within California. The courts may be the only office of the state with which injured workers interact; thus, workers' respect for and satisfaction with the entire workers' compensation process will be in large part determined by their experiences with the court. In addition, decisions by the courts directly or indirectly determine the results of all workers' compensation claims. Even the vast majority of workers' compensation claims that are compromised and "released" are settled in light of the parties' expectations about decisions that might be undertaken by the courts. Finally, courts set the time frame for resolution of workers' compensation claims; like all types of litigation, workers' compensation claims are more likely to be resolved when they are scheduled for resolution by the court.

Given this central role, the WCAB court system must be able to operate expeditiously, efficiently, and fairly and to treat all parties with dignity. Our interviews with participants and stakeholders as well as our own observations of the court system indicate that courts are burdened with unnecessary clerical and judicial functions. WCAB courts are awash in paper but funds to support clerical work are scarce. For example, documents submitted to the Los Angeles WCAB are filed by persons serving community service sentences for criminal convictions.

We believe that the adoption of the elective fast-track system would reduce some of the burdens on the WCAB, allowing courts to focus resources on the remaining cases. However, other initiatives to expedite litigation are necessary.

A substantial part of the problem could be alleviated by mandating the electronic filing of papers with the WCAB. Most filings to the WCAB are on standardized forms that could be easily submitted electronically. Even forms submitted by unrepresented applicants could be entered electronically by using optical scanning machines and bar codes that indicate the nature of the form. Electronic filing would not only alleviate a substantial burden on the WCAB, but it would also protect against the misfiling that must inevitably result from inexperienced personnel dealing with documents in places such as Los Angeles. Furthermore, electronic filing will allow lawyers, insurers, and third party administrators to verify that forms have been received and properly filed.

Two further recommendations deal with reducing substantive burdens on WCAB courts. First, we recommend eliminating judicial review of C&Rs for represented applicants. Second, we recommend that WCAB consider appointing hearing officers for medical lien issues who are trained in matters of medical accounting and medical economics. The number of persons with knowledge about medical billing practices and medical accounting has burgeoned in recent years. The WCAB could utilize such experts to hear and resolve many issues with regard to lien claims, freeing judges to deal with matters for which they are more appropriately trained.

In light of our qualitative interviews, we also recommend that the state increase its efforts to limit variability in paperwork and procedural requirements across the various boards. This problem was noted by participants in a number of the stakeholder groups.

Improve the Utility of Medical Evaluations. Our interviews revealed broad dissatisfaction with the current processes for obtaining and using medical evaluations. The current presumption of correctness for evaluations made by treating doctors was criticized on the grounds that treating doctors are generally less informed about issues of forensic medicine and not well prepared to provide useful medical evaluations. In addition, current rules allow parties to manipulate the selection of the treating doctor. Employers monopolize selection of treating doctors early in a claim; represented applicants can do so

later. Each side appreciates the tactical advantage of selecting the
treating doctor and is, in turn, dissatisfied when the other party gets
to enjoy this advantage.

Several arguments are made in support of the presumption of
correctness for the treating doctor's evaluation. First, the present
presumption (and the medical-legal limits on the compensability of
multiple evaluations) reduces the number of evaluations that workers
must undergo and that insurer/employers then must pay. Second, treating
doctors are said to be relatively less biased in their medical
evaluations.

As we noted in our discussion of the qualitative interviews, views
on the bias of treating physicians were mixed. Some argued that
treating doctors may be overly generous to injured workers because of
their past relationships with their patients, others argued that
treating doctors may be less likely to recognize residual injuries
because they are confident that the medical treatment they provided is
effective.

Attempts by the IMC to educate treating doctors by exposing them to
courses on the workers' compensation process have been relatively
unsuccessful. These courses have been poorly attended because they
typically present a broad range of information, only a portion of which
is useful to each medical specialty. This problem is not unique to
California. Other states, both those that use the *AMA Guides* and those
using other kinds of schedules, continue to struggle with how to
adequately train treating physicians to complete suitable evaluations.

We feel this knowledge gap could be substantially narrowed if
medical reports were filed electronically. We recommend that all
medical evaluations, whether performed by treating or forensic doctors,
be submitted to the parties, to the DEU, and to the WCAB electronically.
This filing could be done through an interactive process in which an
"expert system" played a key role. (An expert system is a special
purpose computer program that encapsulates knowledge about a particular
area. A user can query the system for information and be prompted by it
to provide information.) The expert system component could inform
doctors of tests and evaluations that are central to rating the

particular kind of injury at issue, inform the doctor of issues of judgment relative to the rating, and provide working definitions of how particular words and phrases are to be used in the rating process. Such interactive electronic filing procedures provide a more effective way to communicate required information than do broad training courses.

If treating doctors can be informed of workers' compensation issues through such an interactive process, their medical evaluations may well be the most informed and unbiased basis of judgments for PPD claims. For this reason, we suggest that evaluations by treating doctors form the basis for scheduling claims under the fast-track system.

However, the presumption of correctness for the treating doctor's evaluation seems inappropriate for the claims that proceed through the main workers' compensation track. Issues involving medical evaluations are almost always the primary factual issues in a workers' compensation claim. It is inappropriate to prejudge the reliability of this critical information through the presumption of correctness, particularly when this presumption can be manipulated by the party that appoints the treating doctor. Litigation is an adversarial process. The parties should be able to control the factual information they present. Therefore, we recommend that each party be able to retain one treating or forensic doctor as its primary source for medical evaluations, and that the parties and the workers' compensation judges be free to assess the relative credibility of those reports as they see fit.

IMPLEMENTATION OF RAND'S RECOMMENDATIONS

Many of our recommendations can be implemented directly by the DWC. Indeed the DWC is contemplating or has begun to implement many of them-- for example, development of a new claims-level database and institution of procedures to test rating reliability within the DEU. Implementing these policies requires careful planning and execution. Policies that require information from parties, such as a claims-level database, or that change the way participants interact with the workers' compensation system, such as the electronic and interactive filing systems, should be implemented in ways that minimize the burdens upon system participants and that provide direct benefits to the parties. The elements of databases and interactive electronic systems must be carefully designed to insure that they collect information both for processing individual claims as well as for supporting broader reform efforts, such as the elective fast-track system and development of a new wage-loss-based schedule. The DWC should supplement its own expertise with outside experts in designing data collection, developing interactive expert systems, and designing procedures for measuring the reliability of ratings processes.

Our proposals with regard to further evaluation and reform of the disability schedule and rating process involve fundamental changes in the workers' compensation system that require both technical work and political cooperation. Our proposals for a survey to follow up the wage loss study, the development of a revised wage-loss-based disability schedule and a fast-track system require quantitative analyses, additional data collection, feasibility studies, and thoughtful design of procedures.

Finally, effectively implementing these policies requires the broad input of participants and interest groups in the workers' compensation system. We have proposed establishing a task force to carry out the necessary technical work, provide input, and facilitate cooperative efforts among the many interest groups. To accomplish these goals, the task force must have both technical expertise and political balance. The latter will help ensure that new policies are fair, and that they have the political support necessary to be implemented successfully.

Appendix A

COMMISSION ON HEALTH AND SAFETY AND WORKERS' COMPENSATION

James J. Hlawek, 1997 Commission Chairman, County Administrative Officer, County of San Bernardino. Appointed by the Governor to represent public agency employers.

Leonard McLeod, Finance Committee Chair, California Correctional Peace Officers' Association. Appointed by the Governor to represent labor.

Gerald O'Hara, Director, California Teamsters Public Affairs Council. Appointed by the Speaker of the Assembly to represent labor.

Tom Rankin, President, California Labor Federation, AFL-CIO. Appointed by the Senate Rules Committee to represent labor.

Kristen Schwenkmeyer, Secretary-Treasurer, Gordon and Schwenkmeyer. Appointed by the Senate Rules Committee to represent employers.

Robert B. Steinberg, Senior Partner, Law Offices of Rose, Klein and Marias. Appointed by the Speaker of the Assembly to represent employers.

Darrel "Shorty" Thacker, Director-Field Support Operations, Bay Counties District Council of Carpenters. Appointed by the Governor to represent labor.

Gregory Vach, Director of Workers' Compensation, Interstate Brands Company. Appointed by the Governor to represent employers.

Commission Staff

Christine Baker, Executive Officer

Kirsten Strvmberg, Research Program Specialist

Evonne Jolls, Staff Services Analyst

Janice Yapdiangco, Office Technician

Appendix B

ADVISORY GROUP TO THE COMMISSION ON HEALTH AND SAFETY
AND WORKERS' COMPENSATION

Mark Ashcraft, Manager, Self-Insurance Plans, State of California

Dave Bellusci, Senior Vice President and Chief Actuary, Workers'
Compensation Insurance Rating Bureau

Dr. Doug Benner, Medical Care Program, Kaiser Permanente

Dr. Joseph Bernstein, Private Practice

Carlyle Brakensiek, Esq., Executive Vice President, California Society
of Industrial Medicine and Surgery

Julianne Broyles, Director of Insurance and Employee Relations,
California Chamber of Commerce

Neil Burraston, Consultant, California Senate Industrial Relations
Committee

Sharon Collins, Area Supervisor, Central California, Disability
Evaluation Unit, Division of Workers' Compensation, State of
California

Yvette De Lucia, Workers' Compensation Administrator, Daugherty and
Company

Jill Dulich, Regional Director, Marriott International

John Frailing, Esq., California Applicants' Attorneys Association

Dr. Lloyd Friesen, California Chiropractic Association

Mark Gerlach, Esq., Consultant, California Applicants' Attorneys
Association

Ted Hanf, Past President, California Workers' Compensation Defense
Attorneys Association

Philip Harber, Professor of Medicine, University of California, Los
Angeles

Brian Hatch, Director of Governmental Affairs, California Professional
Firefighters

Molly Hillis, Consultant, Joint Committee on Workers' Compensation

Peggy Jones, Deputy Administrative Director, Division of Workers'
Compensation, State of California

Lori Kammerer, Managing Director, Californians for Compensation Reform

Dr. Craig Little, California Chiropractic Association

Dr. Allan MacKenzie, Executive Medical Director, Industrial Medical Council, State of California

Geri Madden, Government Relations Officer, State Compensation Insurance Fund

Joe Markey, President, California Self-Insurers Association

Blair Megowan, Manager, Disability Evaluation Unit, Division of Workers' Compensation, State of California

John Middagh, Manager of Workers' Compensation, Walt Disney Company

Theresa Muir, Manager, Workers' Compensation Division, Southern California Edison

Nick Murphy, Systems Administrator, State Compensation Insurance Fund

Diane Przepiorski, Executive Director, California Orthopaedic Association

Merle Rabine, Esq., California Applicants' Attorneys Association

Dr. Linda Rudolph, Manager, Managed Care Unit, Division of Workers' Compensation, State of California

Pam Schroeder, Workers' Compensation and Systems Manager, The Transamerica Corporation

Rich Schultz, Communications and Education Center Manager, State Compensation Insurance Fund

Bob Sniderman, Past President, CARRP

Dr. Gail A. Walsh, Co-Chair, Industrial Medical Council, State of California

John Wilson, Executive Director, Schools Excess Liability Fund

Edward Woodward, President, California Workers' Compensation Institute

Casey Young, Administrative Director, Division of Workers' Compensation, State of California

Richard Younkin, Assistant Chief, Division of Workers' Compensation, State of California

BIBLIOGRAPHY

American Medical Association (AMA), *AMA Guides to the Evaluation of Permanent Impairment,* fourth edition, 1993.

Antonakes, John A., "Claims Cost of Back Pain," *Best's Review* (Prop/Casualty), Vol. 82, No. 5, September 1981, pp. 36-40, 129.

Appel, David A., "Health Care Costs in Workers' Compensation," *Benefits Quarterly*, Vol. 9, No. 4, Fourth Quarter 1993, pp. 6-8.

Baker, Laurence C., and Alan B. Krueger, "Medical Costs in Workers' Compensation Insurance," *Journal of Health Economics*, Vol. 14, 1995, pp. 531-549.

Ball, Christopher, *How to Handle Your Workers' Compensation Claim: A Complete Guide for Employees*, Nolo Press, 1995.

Barth, Peter S., and Carol A. Telles, *Workers' Compensation in California: An Administrative Inventory*, Workers' Compensation Research Institute, December 1992.

Barth, Peter S., and Stacey Eccelston, *Revising Worker's Compensation in Texas: Administrative Inventory*, Workers' Compensation Research Institute, 1995.

Battista, Mark, "Guides to the Evaluation of Permanent Impairment," *The Journal of the American Medical Association*, Vol. 261, No. 17, May 5, 1989, pp. 2558-2559.

Beane, Reginald E., and Larry N. Joseph, "Why Medical Cost Management Programs Make Good Business Sense," *Risk Management*, Vol. 41, No. 5, May 1994, pp. 48-51.

Benedict, Mary Ellen, and Kathryn Shaw, "The Impact of Pension Benefits on the Distribution of Earned Income," *Industrial and Labor Relations Review*, Vol. 48, No. 4, 1995, pp. 740-757.

Berkowitz, Monroe, and John F. Burton, Jr., *Permanent Disability Benefits in Workers' Compensation*, W. E. Upjohn Institute for Employment Research, Kalamazoo, MI, 1987.

Berreth, Charles, "Workers' Compensation Laws: Significant Changes in 1993," *Monthly Labor Review*, Vol. 117, January 1994, pp. 53-65.

Boden, Les, *Reducing Litigation: Evidence from Wisconsin*, Workers' Compensation Research Bureau, 1988.

Boden, Leslie I., *The AMA Guides in Maryland*, WC-92-5, Workers' Compensation Research Institute, September 1992.

Boden, Leslie I., and Richard A. Victor, "Models for Reducing Workers' Compensation Litigation," *Journal of Risk and Insurance*, Vol. 61, No. 3, 1994, pp. 458-475.

Bound, John, "The Health and Earnings of Rejected Disability Insurance Applicants," *American Economic Review*, Vol. 79, No. 3, June 1989, pp. 482-503.

Bresnitz, Eddy A., Howard Frumkin, Lawrence Goldstein, David Neumark, Michael Hodgson, and Carolyn Needleman, "Occupational Impairment and Disability among Applicants for Social Security Disability Benefits in Pennsylvania," *American Journal of Public Health*, Vol. 84, No. 11, November 1994, pp. 1786-1790.

Bruce, Christopher J., and Frank J. Atkins, "Efficiency Effects of Premium-Setting Regimes under Workers' Compensation: Canada and the United States," *Journal of Labor Economics*, Vol. 11, No. 1(2), 1993, pp. S38-S69.

Burton, Jr., John F., "Workers' Compensation Costs, 1960-1992: The Increases, the Causes and the Consequences," *Workers' Compensation Monitor,* March/April 1993, pp. 1-23.

Butler, Richard J., "Economic Determinants of Workers' Compensation Trends," *Journal of Risk and Insurance*, Vol. 61, No. 3, 1994, pp. 383-401.

Butler, Richard J., David L. Durbin, and Nurhan M. Helvacian, "Increasing Claims for Soft Tissue Injuries in Workers' Compensation: Cost Shifting and Moral Hazard, *Journal of Risk and Uncertainty*, Vol. 13, 1996, pp. 73-87.

Butler, Richard J., William G. Johnson, and Marjorie L. Baldwin, "Managing Work Disability: Why First Return to Work Is Not a Measure of Success," *Industrial & Labor Relations Review*, Vol. 48, No. 3, April 1995, pp. 452-469.

Butler, Richard J., and John D. Worrall, "Work Injury Compensation and the Duration of Nonwork Spells," *The Economic Journal*, Vol. 95, September 1985, pp. 714-724.

California Commission on Health and Safety and Workers' Compensation, *Permanent Disability Fact-Finding Hearing: Executive Summary and Written Testimony*, Los Angeles, 18 January 1996.

California Workers' Compensation Institute (CWCI), *Economic Consequences of Job Injury: A Report to the Industry*, 1984.

California Workers' Compensation Research Institute, "Physician Costs Under the Official Medical Fee Schedule: Unit Price vs. Utilization," *CWCI Research Update*, September 1992.

Card, David, and Brian McCall, "Is Workers' Compensation Covering Uninsured Medical Costs? Evidence from the 'Monday Effect,'" *Industrial & Labor Relations Review*, Vol. 49, No. 4, July 1996, p. 690.

Carrol, Anne M., "The Role of Regulation in the Demand for Workers' Compensation Self-Insurance," *Journal of Insurance Regulation*, Vol. 13, No. 2, Winter 1994, pp. 168-184.

Cerne, Frank, "Lowering the Boom on Workers' Comp," *Hospitals & Health Networks*, Vol. 68, No. 16, August 20, 1994, pp. 50-52.

Cheadle, Allen, Franklin Gary, Carl Wolfhagen, and James Savarino, "Factors Influencing the Duration of Work-Related Disability: A Population-Based Study of Washington State Workers' Compensation, *American Journal of Public Health*, Vol. 84, No. 2, February 1994, pp. 190-197.

Chelius, James, Book Review, "Economic and Social Security and Substandard Working Conditions," *Industrial & Labor Relations Review*, Vol. 46, No. 1, October 1992, p. 199.

Chelius, J. R., and K. Kavanaugh, "Workers' Compensation and the Level of Injuries," *The Journal of Risk and Insurance*, Vol. 2, 1988, pp. 315-323.

Citizens for Tax Justice, *Who Pays? A Distributional Analysis of the Tax Systems in All 50 States*, June 1996.

Commission on Health and Safety and Workers' Compensation, *Vocational Rehabilitation Benefit: An Analysis of Costs, Characteristics, and the Impact of the 1993 Reforms*, August 1997.

Cullinane, Danielle, *Compensation for Work-Related Injury and Illness*, RAND, N-3343-FMP, 1992.

Culver, Charles, Michael Marshall, and Constance Connolly, "Analysis of Construction Accidents: The Workers' Compensation Database," *Professional Safety*, Vol. 38, No. 3, March 1993, pp. 22-27.

Dahl, S., and J. R. Jepsen, "Reported Occupational Diseases. A 5-Year Follow-Up Study from the County of Ribe," *Ugeskrift for Laeger*, Vol. 156, No. 19, May 9, 1994, pp. 2902-2907.

Darling-Hammond, Linda, and Thomas J. Kniesner, *The Law and Economics of Workers' Compensation: Policy Issues and Research Needs*, RAND, R-2716-ICJ, 1980.

Dennen, Taylor, "The Savings Potential of 24-Hour Coverage," *Risk Management*, Vol. 39, No. 9, September 1992, pp. 71-76.

Department of Consumer and Business Services, *Monitoring the Key Components of Legislative Reform,* 3rd edition, February 1997.

Department of Labor and Industries, Health Service Analysis Section, *Provider Bulletin,* #95-07, 1995.

Department of Labor and Industries, *Medical Examiners Handbook,* June 1996a.

Department of Labor and Industries, *Attending Doctors Handbook,* October 1996b.

Department of Labor and Industries, *Long Term Disability and Prevention Pilots, Annual Report to the Legislature,* December 1996c.

Dillingham, Alan E., "The Effort of Labor Force Age Distribution on Workers' Compensation Costs," *The Journal of Risk and Insurance,* Vol. 50, No. 2, June 1983, pp. 235-248.

"Discrepancies in Impairment Ratings by Types of Doctors," *Texas Monitor,* Vol. 1, No. 4, Winter 1996, p. 7.

Durbin, David, "The Cost of Treating Injured Workers: The Changing Workers' Compensation Landscape," *Benefits Quarterly,* Vol. 9, No. 4, Fourth Quarter 1993, pp. 9-21.

Durbin, David, and D. Appel, "The Impact of Fee Schedules and Employer Choice of Physician," *NCCI Digest,* Vol. 6, No. 3, September 1991, pp. 19-38.

Durbin, David L., Dan Corro, and Nurhan Helvacian, "Workers' Compensation Medical Expenditures: Price vs. Quantity," *Journal of Risk and Insurance,* Vol. 63, No. 1, 1996, pp. 13-33.

Farinella, Michael A., "Workers' Compensation Shows Great Strength: 1994 Results Are Boosted by Lower Losses, Reforms," *Best's Review P/C,* November 1995, p. 46.

Fenn, Paul, "Sickness Duration, Residual Disability, and Income Replacement: An Empirical Analysis," *The Economic Journal,* Vol. 91, March 1981, pp. 158-173.

Feuerstein, M., S. Callan-Harris, P. Hickey, D. Dyer, W. Armbruster, and A. M. Carosella, "Multidisciplinary Rehabilitation of Chronic Work-Related Upper Extremity Disorders. Long-Term Effects," *Journal of Occupational Medicine,* Vol. 35, No. 4, April 1993, pp. 396-403.

Fletcher, Meg, "Carpal Tunnel Claims May Soar," *Business Insurance,* Vol. 30, No. 32, August 5, 1996, p. 44.

Galizzi, Monica, and Leslie I. Boden, *What Are the Most Important Factors Shaping Return to Work? Evidence from Wisconsin*, Workers' Compensation Research Institute, WC-96-6, October 1996.

Gardner, John A., *Return to Work Incentives: Lessons for Policymakers from Economic Studies*, Workers' Compensation Research Institute, 1989.

Gerlach, M. J., *Summary and Analysis of WCIRB Permanent Disability Claim Summary*, prepared for the California Applicants' Attorneys Association, January 1997.

Gice, Jon, "Permanent Partial Disability: Good Intentions Gone Bad," *CPCU Journal*, Vol. 47, No. 3, September 1994, pp. 152-158.

Gice, Jon, "The Relationship Between Job Satisfaction and Workers' Compensation Claims," *CPCU Journal*, Vol. 48, No. 3, September 1995, pp. 178-184.

Hall, Robert, Fred McFarlane, Anne Nelson, and Tom Siegfried, *Evaluation of Permanent Disability and Workers' Compensation: Methodology, Public Law and Policy, and Reemployment of the Injured Worker*, prepared by Interwork Institute, the Work and Health Technologies Center, San Diego State University, 1996.

Heckman, James J., Hidehiko Ichimura, and Petra Todd, "Matching as an Econometric Estimator," University of Pittsburgh Department of Economics Working Paper No. 315, July 1997.

Hennessey, John C., and Janice M. Dykacz, "A Comparison of the Recovery Termination Rates of Disabled-Worker Beneficiaries Entitled in 1972 and 1985," *Social Security Bulletin*, Vol. 56, No. 2, Summer 1993, pp. 58-69.

Hennessey, John C., and L. Scott Muller, "The Effect of Vocational Rehabilitation and Work Incentives on Helping the Disabled-Worker Beneficiary Back to Work," *Social Security Bulletin*, Vol. 58, No. 1, Spring 1995, pp. 15-28.

Herlick, Stanford D., *California Workers' Compensation Law*, Fifth Edition, Vols. 1 and 2, Parker Publications Division, Carlsbad, CA, 1995.

Hirsch, Barry T., David A. MacPherson, and J. Michael Dumond, "Workers' Compensation Recipiency in Union and Nonunion Workplaces," *Industrial and Labor Relations Review*, Vol. 50, No. 2, 1997, pp. 213-236

Holness, D. L., and J. R. Nethercott, "Work Outcome in Workers with Occupational Skin Disease," *American Journal of Industrial Medicine*, Vol. 27, No. 6, June 1995, pp. 807-815.

Huffman, Dennis L., "Developing Work Injury Disability Provider Networks," *Risk Management*, Vol. 41, No. 11, November 1994, pp. 49-56.

Infante-Rivard, C., and M. Lortie, "Prognostic Factors for Return to Work after a First Compensated Episode of Back Pain," *Occupational and Environmental Medicine*, Vol. 53, No. 7, July 1996, pp. 488-494.

Jacobson, L. S., R. J. Lalonde, and D. G. Sullivan, "Earnings Losses of Displaced Workers," *American Economic Review,* Vol. 83, No. 4, 1993, pp. 685-709.

Johnson, William G., John F. Burton, Lisa Thornquist, and Brian Zaidman, "Why Does Workers' Compensation Pay More for Health Care?" *Benefits Quarterly*, Vol. 9, No. 4, Fourth Quarter 1993, pp. 22-31.

Johnson, William G., Paul R. Cullinan, and William P. Curington, "The Adequacy of Workers' Compensation Benefits," *Research Report of the Interdepartmental Workers' Task Force*, Vol. 6, Government Printing Office, Washington, D.C., 1979.

Juliff, Ronald J., and Phillip L. Polakoff, "An Integrated Approach to Disability Management," *Risk Management*, Vol. 41, No. 4, April 1994, pp. 91-98.

Kasdan, M. L., M. I. Vender, K. Lewis, S. P. Stallings, and J. M. Melhorn, "Carpal Tunnel Syndrome: Effects of Litigation on Utilization of Health Care and Physician Workload," *Journal of the Kentucky Medical Association*, Vol. 94, No. 7, July 1996, pp. 287-290.

Katz, Jeffrey N., Laura Punnett, Barry P. Simmons, Anne H. Fossel, Nancy Mooney, and Robert B. Keller, "Workers' Compensation Recipients with Carpal Tunnel Syndrome: The Validity of Self-Reported Health Measures," *American Journal of Public Health*, Vol. 86, No. 1, January 1996, pp. 52-56.

King, C., J. Pavone, and S. Marshall, *Return-to-Work Patterns and Programs for Injured Workers Covered by Texas Workers' Compensation Insurance*, Texas Workers' Compensation Research Center, 1993.

Kochhar, Satya, and Charles G. Scott, "Disability Patterns Among SSI Recipients," *Social Security Bulletin*, Vol. 58, No. 1, Spring 1995, pp. 3-14.

Kralj, Boris, "Employer Responses to Workers' Compensation Insurance Experience Rating," *Industrial Relations-Quebec*, Vol. 49, No. 1, Winter 1994, pp. 41-59.

Krause, Niklas, Lisa Dansinger, and Andrew Wiegand, *Does Modified Work Facilitate Return to Work for Temporarily or Permanently Disabled Workers: A Review of the Literature,* September 1997.

Krueger, Alan B., Book Review, "Permanent Disability Benefits in Workers' Compensation," *Journal of Economic Literature*, Vol. 24, December 1991, pp. 1774-1776.

Krueger, Alan B., "Incentive Effects of Workers' Compensation Insurance," *Journal of Public Economics*, Vol. 41, 1990, pp. 73-99.

Krueger, Alan, "Workers' Compensation Insurance and Duration of Workplace Injuries," *NBER Working Paper* No. 3253, 1990.

Krueger, Alan B., and John F. Burton, Jr., "The Employers' Costs of Workers' Compensation Insurance: Magnitudes, Determinants, and Public Policy," *Review of Economics and Statistics*, Vol. 72, May 1990, pp. 228-240.

Levy, David, and Ted Miller, "Hospital Rate Regulations, Fee Schedules, and Workers' Compensation Medical Payments," *Journal of Risk & Insurance*, Vol. 63, No. 1, March 1996, pp. 35-48.

Loeser, John D., Stephen E. Henderlite, and Douglas A. Conrad, "Incentive Effects of Workers' Compensation Benefits: A Literature Synthesis," *Medical Care Research and Review*, Vol. 52, No. 1, March 1995, pp. 34-59.

McCunney, Robert J., and Cheryl Barbanel, "Auditing Workers' Compensation Claims Targets Expensive Injuries, Job Tasks," *Occupational Health & Safety*, Vol. 62, No. 10, October 1993, pp. 75-78.

Meyer, Bruce, W. Kip Viscusi, and David L. Durbin, "Workers' Compensation and Injury Duration: Evidence from a Natural Experiment," *American Economic Review,* Vol. 85, No. 3, 1995.

Milliman & Robertson, Inc., *Colorado Workers' Compensation Closed Claim Study: 1996*, January 1997.

Minnesota Department of Labor and Industry, *COMPAct*, July 1995.

Mitchell, Olivia S., "The Relation of Age to Workplace Injuries," *Monthly Labor Review*, July 1988, pp. 8-13.

Moore, Michael J., and W. Kip Viscusi, *Compensation Mechanisms for Job Risks: Wages, Workers' Compensation, and Product Liability*, Princeton University Press, NJ, 1990.

Morgan, Barbara, "Factors Influencing Return to Work After Injury," A paper prepared for presentation at the Annual Meeting of the American Economic Association, New Orleans, January 1997.

Muller, L. Scott, "Disability Beneficiaries Who Work and Their Experience Under Program Work Incentives," *Social Security Bulletin*, Vol. 55, No. 2, Summer 1992, pp. 2-19.

Muller, L. Scott, Charles G. Scott, and Barry V. Bye, "Labor-Force Participation and Earnings of SSI Disability Recipients: A Pooled

Cross-Sectional Time Series Approach to the Behavior of Individuals," *Social Security Bulletin*, Vol. 59, No. 1, Spring 1996, pp. 22-42.

Narendranathan, W., S. Nickell, and J. Stern, "Unemployment Benefits Revisited," *The Economic Journal*, Vol. 95, June 1985, pp. 307-329.

Nelson, Jr., William J., "Workers' Compensation: Coverage, Benefits, and Costs, 1990-91," *Social Security Bulletin*, Vol. 56, No. 3, Fall 1993, pp. 68-74.

Neuhauser, Frank, and Andrew Koehler, *Evaluating the Reforms of the Medical-Legal Process Using the WCIRB Permanent Disability Survey*, prepared for the Commission on Health and Safety and Workers' Compensation by UC DATA/Survey Research Center, UC Berkeley, July 1996.

Oregon Department of Consumer and Business Services, *Reconsideration of Claim Closures, Calendar Year 1996,* May 1997.

Pozzebon, Silvana, "Medical Cost Containment under Workers' Compensation," *Industrial & Labor Relations Review*, Vol. 48, October 1994, p. 153.

Pozzebon, Silvana, and Terry Thomason, "Medical Benefit Costs in Canadian Workers' Compensation Programs: A Comparative Perspective," *Benefits Quarterly*, Vol. 9, No. 4, Fourth Quarter 1993, pp. 32-41.

Price, Daniel N., "Workers' Compensation: 1976-80 Benchmark Revisions," *Social Security Bulletin*, Vol. 47, No. 7, July 1984, pp. 3-23.

Pryor, Ellen Smith, "Flawed Promises: A Critical Evaluation of the American Medical Association's Guides to the Evaluation of Permanent Impairment," *Harvard Law Review*, Vol. 103, 1990, pp. 964-976.

Reed, Presley, "Disability Management: Lessons from California (California State Disability Insurance Program)," *HR Focus*, Vol. 72, No. 11, November 1995, pp. 10-12.

Research and Oversight Council on Workers' Compensation, *Severely Injured Workers: Supplemental Income Benefits in the Texas Workers' Compensation System,* 1996a.

Research and Oversight Council on Workers' Compensation, *Annual Nonsubscription Survey--1996 Estimates,* 1996b.

Roberts, Karen, and Susan Zonia, "Workers' Compensation Cost Containment and Health Care Provider Income Maintenance Strategies," *Journal of Risk and Insurance*, Vol. 61, No. 1, 1994, pp. 117-131.

Root, Normal, "Fewer Injuries Among Older Workers," *Monthly Labor Review*, March 1981, pp. 30-34.

Rudolph, Linda, "Managed Care in California's Workers' Compensation System: A Survey of Current Practices," prepared by the Medical Director and staff of the Managed Care Program, the California Division of Workers' Compensation, February 1996.

Rupp, Kalman, and Charles G. Scott, "Length of Stay on the Supplemental Security Income Disability Program," *Social Security Bulletin*, Vol. 58, No. 1, Spring 1995, pp. 29-47.

Rupp, Kalman, and Charles G. Scott, "Trends in the Characteristics of DI and SSI Disability Awardees and Duration of Program Participation," *Social Security Bulletin*, Vol. 59, No. 1, Spring 1996, pp. 3-21.

Rupp, Kalman, and David Stapleton, "Determinants of the Growth in the Social Security Administration's Disability Programs--An Overview," *Social Security Bulletin*, Vol. 58, No. 4, Winter 1995, pp. 43-70.

Ruser, John W., "Workers' Compensation Insurance, Experience Rating, and Occupational Injuries, *RAND Journal of Economics*, Vol. 16, No. 4, 1985, pp. 487-503.

Ryan, Darian, "California's Workers' Compensation: Breaking Away from Rate Regulation," *Best's Review P/C*, November 1995, p. 57.

Sauer, Susan M., "Using Performance Guarantees to Contain Workers' Compensation Costs," *Risk Management*, Vol. 41, No. 4, April 1994, pp. 75-80.

Schmulowitz, Jack, "Worker's Compensation: Coverage, Benefits, and Costs, 1992-93," *Social Security Bulletin*, Vol. 58, No. 2, Summer 1995, pp. 51-57.

Schoeni, Robert F., and Michael Dardia, "Wage Losses of Displaced Workers in the 1990s," RAND, DRU-1474-RC, 1996.

Schultz, Paul T., and Karen L. Looram, "Managing Workers' Compensation Medical Costs: A State-by-State Guide," *Employee Relations Law Journal*, Vol. 19, No. 3, 1993/1994, pp. 251-267.

Shor, Glenn Merrill, *Evolution of WC Policy in California, 1911-1990*, a dissertation submitted to the Graduate Division, University of California at Berkeley.

Shulman, Marvin L., "Workers' Compensation Shows Great Strength: But Outlook Is Only Fair as Competition Heats Up," *Best's Review P/C*, November 1995, p. 47.

Solomon, Barbara, "Using Managed Care to Control Workers' Compensation Costs," *Compensation & Benefits Review*, Vol. 25, No. 5, September/ October 1993, pp. 59-65.

Stone, Deborah, *The Disabled State*, Temple University Press, Philadelphia, 1988.

Sum, Juliann, *Navigating the California Workers' Compensation System: The Injured Worker's Experience, An Evaluation of Services to Inform and Assist Injured Workers in California*, prepared for the Commission on Health and Safety and Workers' Compensation by the Labor Occupational Health Program, UC Berkeley, July 1996.

Swedlow, Alex, Gregory Johnson, Neil Smithline, and Arnold Milstein, "Increased Costs and Rates of Use in the California Workers' Compensation System as a Result of Self-Referral by Physicians," *New England Journal of Medicine*, Vol. 327, No. 21, November 19, 1992, pp. 1502-1506.

Telles, Carol A., "An Overview of Medical Cost Containment in Workers' Compensation," *Benefits Quarterly*, Vol. 9, No. 4, Fourth Quarter 1993, pp. 42-50.

Telles, Carol A., and Sharon E. Fox, *Workers' Compensation in Colorado: Administrative Inventory*, Workers' Compensation Research Institute, 1996.

Texas Workers' Compensation Commission, *Texas Workers' Compensation System Data Report,* 1997.

Thomason, Terry, "Permanent Partial Disability in Workers' Compensation: Probability and Costs," *Journal of Risk and Insurance*, Vol. 60, No. 4, 1993, pp. 570-590.

Thomason, Terry, and John F. Burton, Jr., "Economic Effects of Workers' Compensation in the United States: Private Insurance and the Administration of Compensation Claims," *Journal of Labor Economics*, Vol. 11, 1(2), 1993, pp. S1-S37.

Thompson, Mark, Book Review, "Income and Social Security and Substandard Working Conditions," *Industrial & Labor Relations Review*, Vol. 49, No. 4, July 1996, p. 756.

Tompkins, Neville C., "Action at the State Level: The New Round of Workers' Compensation Controls," *Compensation & Benefits Review*, Vol. 27, No. 3, May/June 1995, pp. 45-50.

Toward a More Cost-Effective System of Dispute Resolution: A Panel Discussion, International Workers' Compensation Repository, Shawnee Mission, Kansas, 1996.

Trolin, Brenda, "Workable Workers' Comp," *State Legislatures*, Vol. 19, No. 6, June 1993, pp. 38-42.

Victor, Richard, and C. Fleischman, *How Choice of Provider and Recessions Affect Medical Costs in Workers' Compensation*, Workers' Compensation Research Institute, Cambridge, MA, 1990.

Viscusi, W. Kip, *Employment Hazards: An Investigation of Market Performance*, Harvard University Press, Cambridge, MA, 1979.

Wendelken, G., "Managed Care in Workers' Compensation: Current Practices and Considerations for Future Policy," *NCCI Monograph*, May 1993.

Wilkie, Dana, "Workers' Comp on the Mend," *State Legislatures*, Vol. 21, No. 8, September 1995, pp. 12-18.

Workers' Compensation Insurance Rating Bureau, *1989 Reform Act--Cost Monitoring Report*, February 6, 1997.

Young, Casey L., "Beyond Workers' Compensation: A New Vision," *Benefits Quarterly*, Vol. 8, No. 3, 1992, pp. 56-65.

ICJ PUBLICATIONS

OUTCOMES

General

Carroll, S. J., with N. M. Pace, *Assessing the Effects of Tort Reforms*, R-3554-ICJ, 1987. $7.50.

Galanter, M., B. Garth, D. Hensler, and F. K. Zemans, *How to Improve Civil Justice Policy*, RP-282. (Reprinted from *Judicature*, Vol. 77, No. 4, January/February 1994.) Free.

Hensler, D. R., *Summary of Research Results on the Tort Liability System*, P-7210-ICJ, 1986. (Testimony before the Committee on Commerce, Science, and Transportation, United States Senate, February 1986.) $4.00.

_____ , *Trends in California Tort Liability Litigation*, P-7287-ICJ, 1987. (Testimony before the Select Committee on Insurance, California State Assembly, October 1987.) $4.00.

_____ , *Researching Civil Justice: Problems and Pitfalls*, P-7604-ICJ, 1988. (Reprinted from *Law and Contemporary Problems*, Vol. 51, No. 3, Summer 1988.) $4.00.

_____ , *Reading the Tort Litigation Tea Leaves: What's Going on in the Civil Liability System?* RP-226. (Reprinted from *The Justice System Journal*, Vol. 16, No. 2, 1993.) Free.

_____ , *Why We Don't Know More About the Civil Justice System—and What We Could Do About It*, RP-363, 1995. (Reprinted from *USC Law*, Fall 1994.) Free.

Hensler, D. R., and E. Moller, *Trends in Punitive Damages: Preliminary Data from Cook County, Illinois, and San Francisco, California*, DRU-1014-ICJ, 1995. Free.

Hensler, D. R., M. E. Vaiana, J. S. Kakalik, and M. A. Peterson, *Trends in Tort Litigation: The Story Behind the Statistics*, R-3583-ICJ, 1987. $4.00.

Hill, P. T., and D. L. Madey, *Educational Policymaking Through the Civil Justice System*, R-2904-ICJ, 1982. $4.00.

Lipson, A. J., *California Enacts Prejudgment Interest: A Case Study of Legislative Action*, N-2096-ICJ, 1984. $4.00.

Moller, E., *Trends in Punitive Damages: Preliminary Data from California*, DRU-1059-ICJ, 1995. Free.

Shubert, G. H., *Some Observations on the Need for Tort Reform*, P-7189-ICJ, 1986. (Testimony before the National Conference of State Legislatures, January 1986.) $4.00.

_____ , *Changes in the Tort System: Helping Inform the Policy Debate*, P-7241-ICJ, 1986. $4.00.

Jury Verdicts

Bailis, D. S., and R. J. MacCoun, *Estimating Liability Risks with the Media as Your Guide*, RP-606, 1996. (Reprinted from *Law and Human Behavior*, Vol. 20, No. 4, 1996, pp. 419–429.) Free.

Carroll, S. J., *Jury Awards and Prejudgment Interest in Tort Cases*, N-1994-ICJ, 1983. $4.00.

_____ , *Punitive Damages in Financial Injury Jury Verdicts*, CT-143, June 1997. (Written statement delivered on June 24, 1997, to the Judiciary Committee of the United States Senate.) $5.00.

Chin, A., and M. A. Peterson, *Deep Pockets, Empty Pockets: Who Wins in Cook County Jury Trials*, R-3249-ICJ, 1985. $10.00.

Dertouzos, J. N., E. Holland, and P. A. Ebener, *The Legal and Economic Consequences of Wrongful Termination*, R-3602-ICJ, 1988. $7.50.

Hensler, D. R., *Summary of Research Results on the Tort Liability System*, P-7210-ICJ, 1986. (Testimony before the Committee on Commerce, Science, and Transportation, United States Senate, February 1986.) $4.00.

Hensler, D. R., and E. Moller, *Trends in Punitive Damages: Preliminary Data from Cook County, Illinois, and San Francisco, California*, DRU-1014-ICJ, 1995. Free.

MacCoun, R. J., *Getting Inside the Black Box: Toward a Better Understanding of Civil Jury Behavior*, N-2671-ICJ, 1987. $4.00.

_____ , *Experimental Research on Jury Decisionmaking*, R-3832-ICJ, 1989. (Reprinted from *Science*, Vol. 244, June 1989.) $4.00.

_____ , *Inside the Black Box: What Empirical Research Tells Us About Decisionmaking by Civil Juries*, RP-238, 1993. (Reprinted from Robert E. Litan, ed., *Verdict: Assessing the Civil Jury System*, The Brookings Institution, 1993.) Free.

_____ , *Is There a "Deep-Pocket" Bias in the Tort System?* IP-130, October 1993. Free.

_____ , *Blaming Others to a Fault?* RP-286. (Reprinted from *Chance*, Vol. 6, No. 4, Fall 1993.) Free.

_____ , *Improving Jury Comprehension in Criminal and Civil Trials*, CT-136, July 1995. $5.00.

Moller, E., *Trends in Punitive Damages: Preliminary Data from California*, DRU-1059-ICJ, 1995. Free.

_____ , *Trends in Civil Jury Verdicts Since 1985*, MR-694-ICJ, 1996. $15.00.

Moller, E., N. M. Pace, and S. J. Carroll, *Punitive Damages in Financial Injury Jury Verdicts*, MR-888-ICJ, 1997. $9.00.

_____ , *Punitive Damages in Financial Injury Jury Verdicts: Executive Summary*, MR-889-ICJ, 1997. $15.00.

Peterson, M. A., *Compensation of Injuries: Civil Jury Verdicts in Cook County*, R-3011-ICJ, 1984. $7.50.

_____ , *Punitive Damages: Preliminary Empirical Findings*, N-2342-ICJ, 1985. $4.00.

_____ , *Summary of Research Results: Trends and Patterns in Civil Jury Verdicts*, P-7222-ICJ, 1986. (Testimony before the Subcommittee on Oversight, Committee on Ways and Means, United States House of Representatives, March 1986.) $4.00.

_____ , *Civil Juries in the 1980s: Trends in Jury Trials and Verdicts in California and Cook County, Illinois*, R-3466-ICJ, 1987. $7.50.

Peterson, M. A., and G. L. Priest, *The Civil Jury: Trends in Trials and Verdicts, Cook County, Illinois, 1960–1979*, R-2881-ICJ, 1982. $7.50.

Peterson, M. A., S. Sarma, and M. G. Shanley, *Punitive Damages: Empirical Findings*, R-3311-ICJ, 1987. $7.50.

Selvin, M., and L. Picus, *The Debate over Jury Performance: Observations from a Recent Asbestos Case*, R-3479-ICJ, 1987. $10.00.

Shanley, M. G., and M. A. Peterson, *Comparative Justice: Civil Jury Verdicts in San Francisco and Cook Counties, 1959–1980*, R-3006-ICJ, 1983. $7.50.

_____ , *Posttrial Adjustments to Jury Awards*, R-3511-ICJ, 1987. $7.50.

Costs of Dispute Resolution

Dunworth, T., and J. S. Kakalik, Preliminary Observations on Implementation of the Pilot Program of the Civil Justice Reform Act of 1990, RP-361, 1995. (Reprinted from Stanford Law Review, Vol. 46, No. 6, July 1994.) Free.

Hensler, D. R., Does ADR Really Save Money? The Jury's Still Out, RP-327, 1994. (Reprinted from The National Law Journal, April 11, 1994.) Free.

Hensler, D. R., M. E. Vaiana, J. S. Kakalik, and M. A. Peterson, Trends in Tort Litigation: The Story Behind the Statistics, R-3583-ICJ, 1987. $4.00.

Kakalik, J. S., and A. E. Robyn, Costs of the Civil Justice System: Court Expenditures for Processing Tort Cases, R-2888-ICJ, 1982. $7.50.

Kakalik, J. S., and R. L. Ross, Costs of the Civil Justice System: Court Expenditures for Various Types of Civil Cases, R-2985-ICJ, 1983. $10.00.

Kakalik, J. S., P. A. Ebener, W. L. F. Felstiner, and M. G. Shanley, Costs of Asbestos Litigation, R-3042-ICJ, 1983. $4.00.

Kakalik, J. S., P. A. Ebener, W. L. F. Felstiner, G. W. Haggstrom, and M. G. Shanley, Variation in Asbestos Litigation Compensation and Expenses, R-3132-ICJ, 1984. $7.50.

Kakalik, J. S., and N. M. Pace, Costs and Compensation Paid in Tort Litigation, R-3391-ICJ, 1986. $15.00.

_____ , Costs and Compensation Paid in Tort Litigation, P-7243-ICJ, 1986. (Testimony before the Subcommittee on Trade, Productivity, and Economic Growth, Joint Economic Committee of the Congress, July 1986.) $4.00.

Kakalik, J. S., E. M. King, M. Traynor, P. A. Ebener, and L. Picus, Costs and Compensation Paid in Aviation Accident Litigation, R-3421-ICJ, 1988. $10.00.

Kakalik, J. S., M. Selvin, and N. M. Pace, Averting Gridlock: Strategies for Reducing Civil Delay in the Los Angeles Superior Court, R-3762-ICJ, 1990. $10.00.

Kakalik, J. S., T. Dunworth, L. A. Hill, D. McCaffrey, M. Oshiro, N. M. Pace, and M. E. Vaiana, Just, Speedy, and Inexpensive? An Evaluation of Judicial Case Management Under the Civil Justice Reform Act, MR-800-ICJ, 1996. $8.00.

- 209 -

_____ , Implementation of the Civil Justice Reform Act in Pilot and Comparison Districts, MR-801-ICJ, 1996. $20.00.

_____ , An Evaluation of Judicial Case Management Under the Civil Justice Reform Act, MR-802-ICJ, 1996. $20.00.

_____ , An Evaluation of Mediation and Early Neutral Evaluation Under the Civil Justice Reform Act, MR-803-ICJ, 1996. $20.00.

Lind, E. A., Arbitrating High-Stakes Cases: An Evaluation of Court-Annexed Arbitration in a United States District Court, R-3809-ICJ, 1990. $10.00.

MacCoun, R. J., E. A. Lind, D. R. Hensler, D. L. Bryant, and P. A. Ebener, Alternative Adjudication: An Evaluation of the New Jersey Automobile Arbitration Program, R-3676-ICJ, 1988. $10.00.

Peterson, M. A., New Tools for Reducing Civil Litigation Expenses, R-3013-ICJ, 1983. $4.00.

Priest, G. L., Regulating the Content and Volume of Litigation: An Economic Analysis, R-3084-ICJ, 1983. $4.00.

DISPUTE RESOLUTION

Court Delay

Adler, J. W., W. L. F. Felstiner, D. R. Hensler, and M. A. Peterson, *The Pace of Litigation: Conference Proceedings*, R-2922-ICJ, 1982. $10.00.

Dunworth, T., and J. S. Kakalik, *Preliminary Observations on Implementation of the Pilot Program of the Civil Justice Reform Act of 1990*, RP-361, 1995. (Reprinted from *Stanford Law Review*, Vol. 46, No. 6, July 1994.) Free.

Dunworth, T., and N. M. Pace, *Statistical Overview of Civil Litigation in the Federal Courts*, R-3885-ICJ, 1990. $7.50.

Ebener, P. A., *Court Efforts to Reduce Pretrial Delay: A National Inventory*, R-2732-ICJ, 1981. $10.00.

Kakalik, J. S., *Just, Speedy, and Inexpensive? Judicial Case Management Under the Civil Justice Reform Act*, RP-635, 1997. (Reprinted from *Judicature*, Vol. 80, No. 4, January-February 1997, pp. 184-189.) Free.

Kakalik, J. S., M. Selvin, and N. M. Pace, *Averting Gridlock: Strategies for Reducing Civil Delay in the Los Angeles Superior Court*, R-3762-ICJ, 1990. $10.00.

_____ , *Strategies for Reducing Civil Delay in the Los Angeles Superior Court: Technical Appendixes*, N-2988-ICJ, 1990. $10.00.

Kakalik, J. S., T. Dunworth, L. A. Hill, D. McCaffrey, M. Oshiro, N. M. Pace, and M. E. Vaiana, *Just, Speedy, and Inexpensive? An Evaluation of Judicial Case Management Under the Civil Justice Reform Act*, MR-800-ICJ, 1996. $8.00.

_____ , *Implementation of the Civil Justice Reform Act in Pilot and Comparison Districts*, MR-801-ICJ, 1996. $20.00.

_____ , *An Evaluation of Judicial Case Management Under the Civil Justice Reform Act*, MR-802-ICJ, 1996. $20.00.

_____ , *An Evaluation of Mediation and Early Neutral Evaluation Under the Civil Justice Reform Act,* MR-803-ICJ, 1996. $20.00.

Lind, E. A., *Arbitrating High-Stakes Cases: An Evaluation of Court-Annexed Arbitration in a United States District Court*, R-3809-ICJ, 1990. $10.00.

MacCoun, R. J., E. A. Lind, D. R. Hensler, D. L. Bryant, and P. A. Ebener, *Alternative Adjudication: An Evaluation of the New Jersey Automobile Arbitration Program*, R-3676-ICJ, 1988. $10.00.

Resnik, J., *Managerial Judges*, R-3002-ICJ, 1982. (Reprinted from the *Harvard Law Review*, Vol. 96, No. 374, December 1982.) $7.50.

Selvin, M., and P. A. Ebener, *Managing the Unmanageable: A History of Civil Delay in the Los Angeles Superior Court*, R-3165-ICJ, 1984. $15.00.

Alternative Dispute Resolution

Adler, J. W., D. R. Hensler, and C. E. Nelson, with the assistance of G. J. Rest, *Simple Justice: How Litigants Fare in the Pittsburgh Court Arbitration Program*, R-3071-ICJ, 1983. $15.00.

Bryant, D. L., *Judicial Arbitration in California: An Update*, N-2909-ICJ, 1989. $4.00.

Ebener, P. A., and D. R. Betancourt, *Court-Annexed Arbitration: The National Picture*, N-2257-ICJ, 1985. $25.00.

Hensler, D. R., *Court-Annexed Arbitration in the State Trial Court System*, P-6963-ICJ, 1984. (Testimony before the Judiciary Committee Subcommittee on Courts, United States Senate, February 1984.) $4.00.

_____ , *Reforming the Civil Litigation Process: How Court Arbitration Can Help*, P-7027-ICJ, 1984. (Reprinted from the *New Jersey Bell Journal*, August 1984.) $4.00.

_____ , *What We Know and Don't Know About Court-Administered Arbitration*, N-2444-ICJ, 1986. $4.00.

_____ , *Court-Ordered Arbitration: An Alternative View*, RP-103, 1992. (Reprinted from *The University of Chicago Legal Forum*, Vol. 1990, 1990.) Free.

_____ , *Science in the Court: Is There a Role for Alternative Dispute Resolution?* RP-109, 1992. (Reprinted from *Law and Contemporary Problems*, Vol. 54, No. 3, Summer 1991.) Free.

_____ , *Does ADR Really Save Money? The Jury's Still Out*, RP-327, 1994. (Reprinted from *The National Law Journal*, April 11, 1994.) Free.

_____ , *A Glass Half Full, a Glass Half Empty: The Use of Alternative Dispute Resolution in Mass Personal Injury Litigation*, RP-446, 1995. (Reprinted from *Texas Law Review*, Vol. 73, No. 7, June 1995.) Free.

Hensler, D. R., A. J. Lipson, and E. S. Rolph, *Judicial Arbitration in California: The First Year*, R-2733-ICJ, 1981. $10.00.

_____ , *Judicial Arbitration in California: The First Year: Executive Summary*, R-2733/1-ICJ, 1981. $4.00.

Hensler, D. R., and J. W. Adler, with the assistance of G. J. Rest, *Court-Administered Arbitration: An Alternative for Consumer Dispute Resolution*, N-1965-ICJ, 1983. $4.00.

Kakalik, J. S., T. Dunworth, L. A. Hill, D. McCaffrey, M. Oshiro, N. M. Pace, and M. E. Vaiana, *An Evaluation of Mediation and Early Neutral Evaluation Under the Civil Justice Reform Act*, MR-803-ICJ, 1996. $20.00.

Lind, E. A., *Arbitrating High-Stakes Cases: An Evaluation of Court-Annexed Arbitration in a United States District Court*, R-3809-ICJ, 1990. $10.00.

Lind, E. A., R. J. MacCoun, P. A. Ebener, W. L. F. Felstiner, D. R. Hensler, J. Resnik, and T. R. Tyler, *The Perception of Justice: Tort Litigants' Views of Trial, Court-Annexed Arbitration, and Judicial Settlement Conferences*, R-3708-ICJ, 1989. $7.50.

MacCoun, R. J., *Unintended Consequences of Court Arbitration: A Cautionary Tale from New Jersey*, RP-134, 1992. (Reprinted from *The Justice System Journal*, Vol. 14, No. 2, 1991.) Free.

MacCoun, R. J., E. A. Lind, D. R. Hensler, D. L. Bryant, and P. A.
    Ebener, *Alternative Adjudication: An Evaluation of the New Jersey
    Automobile Arbitration Program*, R-3676-ICJ, 1988. $10.00.

MacCoun, R. J., E. A. Lind, and T. R. Tyler, *Alternative Dispute
    Resolution in Trial and Appellate Courts*, RP-117, 1992. (Reprinted
    from *Handbook of Psychology and Law*, 1992.) Free.

Moller, E., E. S. Rolph, and P. Ebener, *Private Dispute Resolution in
    the Banking Industry*, MR-259-ICJ, 1993. $13.00.

Resnik, J., *Many Doors? Closing Doors? Alternative Dispute Resolution
    and Adjudication*, RP-439, 1995. (Reprinted from *The Ohio State
    Journal on Dispute Resolution*, Vol. 10, No. 2, 1995.) Free.

Rolph, E. S., *Introducing Court-Annexed Arbitration: A Policymaker's
    Guide*, R-3167-ICJ, 1984. $10.00.

Rolph, E. S., and D. R. Hensler, *Court-Ordered Arbitration: The
    California Experience*, N-2186-ICJ, 1984. $4.00.

Rolph, E. S., and E. Moller, *Evaluating Agency Alternative Dispute
    Resolution Programs: A Users' Guide to Data Collection and Use*,
    MR-534-ACUS/ICJ, 1995. $13.00.

Rolph, E. S., E. Moller, and L. Petersen, *Escaping the Courthouse:
    Private Alternative Dispute Resolution in Los Angeles*, MR-472-
    JRHD/ICJ, 1994. $15.00.

Special Issues

Kritzer, H. M., W. L. F. Felstiner, A. Sarat, and D. M. Trubek, *The
    Impact of Fee Arrangement on Lawyer Effort*, P-7180-ICJ, 1986.
    $4.00.

Priest, G. L., *Regulating the Content and Volume of Litigation: An
    Economic Analysis*, R-3084-ICJ, 1983. $4.00.

Priest, G. L., and B. Klein, *The Selection of Disputes for Litigation*,
    R-3032-ICJ, 1984. $7.50.

Resnik, J., *Managerial Judges*, R-3002-ICJ, 1982. (Reprinted from the
    Harvard Law Review, Vol. 96, No. 374, December 1982.) $7.50.

_____ , *Failing Faith: Adjudicatory Procedure in Decline*, P-7272-ICJ,
    1987. (Reprinted from the *University of Chicago Law Review*,
    Vol. 53, No. 2, 1986.) $7.50.

_____ , *Due Process: A Public Dimension*, P-7418-ICJ, 1988. (Reprinted
    from the *University of Florida Law Review*, Vol. 39, No. 2, 1987.)
    $4.00.

_____ , *Judging Consent*, P-7419-ICJ, 1988. (Reprinted from the *University of Chicago Legal Forum*, Vol. 1987.) $7.50.

_____ , *From "Cases" to "Litigation,"* RP-110, 1992. (Reprinted from *Law and Contemporary Problems*, Vol. 54, No. 3, Summer 1991.) Free.

_____ , *Whose Judgment? Vacating Judgments, Preferences for Settlement, and the Role of Adjudication at the Close of the Twentieth Century*, RP-364, 1995. (Reprinted from *UCLA Law Review*, Vol. 41, No. 6, August 1994.) Free.

AREAS OF LIABILITY

Auto Personal Injury Compensation

Abrahamse, A., and S. J. Carroll, *The Effects of a Choice Auto Insurance Plan on Insurance Costs*, MR-540-ICJ, 1995. $13.00.

_____ , *The Effects of a Choice Automobile Insurance Plan Under Consideration by the Joint Economic Committee of the United States Congress*, DRU-1609-ICJ, April 1997. Free.

_____ , *The Effects of Proposition 213 on the Costs of Auto Insurance in California*, IP-157, September 1996. Free.

Carroll, S. J., *Effects of an Auto-Choice Automobile Insurance Plan on Costs and Premiums*, CT-141-1, March 1997. (Written statement delivered on March 19, 1997, to the Joint Economic Committee of the United States Congress.) $5.00.

_____ , *Effects of a Choice Automobile Insurance Plan on Costs and Premiums: Testimony Presented to the Senate Commerce, Science, and Transportation Committee, July 1997*, CT-144, July 1997. (Written statement delivered on July 17, 1997, to the Commerce, Science, and Transportation Committee of the United States Senate.) $5.00.

Carroll, S. J., and A. Abrahamse, *The Effects of a Proposed No-Fault Plan on the Costs of Auto Insurance in California: An Updated Analysis*, IP-146-1, January 1996. Free.

Carroll, S. J., and J. S. Kakalik, *No-Fault Approaches to Compensating Auto Accident Victims*, RP-229, 1993. (Reprinted from *The Journal of Risk and Insurance*, Vol. 60, No. 2, 1993.) Free.

Carroll, S. J., A. Abrahamse, and M. E. Vaiana, *The Costs of Excess Medical Claims for Automobile Personal Injuries*, DB-139-ICJ, 1995. $6.00.

Carroll, S. J., J. S. Kakalik, N. M. Pace, and J. L. Adams, *No-Fault Approaches to Compensating People Injured in Automobile Accidents*, R-4019-ICJ, 1991. $20.00.

Carroll, S. J., and J. S. Kakalik, with D. Adamson, *No-Fault Automobile Insurance: A Policy Perspective*, R-4019/1-ICJ, 1991. $4.00.

Hammitt, J. K., *Automobile Accident Compensation, Volume II, Payments by Auto Insurers*, R-3051-ICJ, 1985. $10.00.

Hammitt, J. K., and J. E. Rolph, *Limiting Liability for Automobile Accidents: Are No-Fault Tort Thresholds Effective?* N-2418-ICJ, 1985. $4.00.

Hammitt, J. K., R. L. Houchens, S. S. Polin, and J. E. Rolph, *Automobile Accident Compensation: Volume IV, State Rules*, R-3053-ICJ, 1985. $7.50.

Houchens, R. L., *Automobile Accident Compensation: Volume III, Payments from All Sources*, R-3052-ICJ, 1985. $7.50.

MacCoun, R. J., E. A. Lind, D. R. Hensler, D. L. Bryant, and P. A. Ebener, *Alternative Adjudication: An Evaluation of the New Jersey Automobile Arbitration Program*, R-3676-ICJ, 1988. $10.00.

O'Connell, J., S. J. Carroll, M. Horowitz, and A. Abrahamse, *Consumer Choice in the Auto Insurance Market*, RP-254, 1994. (Reprinted from the *Maryland Law Review*, Vol. 52, 1993.) Free.

O'Connell, J., S. J. Carroll, M. Horowitz, A. F. Abrahamse, and P. Jamieson, *The Comparative Costs of Allowing Consumer Choice for Auto Insurance in All Fifty States,* RP-518, 1996. Free.

O'Connell, J., S. J. Carroll, M. Horowitz, A. Abrahamse, and D. Kaiser, *The Costs of Consumer Choice for Auto Insurance in States Without No-Fault Insurance*, RP-442, 1995. (Reprinted from *Maryland Law Review*, Vol. 54, No. 2, 1995.) Free.

Rolph, J. E., with J. K. Hammitt, R. L. Houchens, and S. S. Polin, *Automobile Accident Compensation: Volume I, Who Pays How Much How Soon?* R-3050-ICJ, 1985. $4.00.

Asbestos

Hensler, D. R., *Resolving Mass Toxic Torts: Myths and Realities*, P-7631-ICJ, 1990. (Reprinted from the *University of Illinois Law Review*, Vol. 1989, No. 1, 1989.) $4.00.

_____ , *Asbestos Litigation in the United States: A Brief Overview*, P-7776-ICJ, 1992. (Testimony before the Courts and Judicial Administration Subcommittee, United States House Judiciary Committee, October 1991.) $4.00.

_____ , *Assessing Claims Resolution Facilities: What We Need to Know*, RP-107, 1992. (Reprinted from *Law and Contemporary Problems*, Vol. 53, No. 4, Autumn 1990.) Free.

_____ , *Fashioning a National Resolution of Asbestos Personal Injury Litigation: A Reply to Professor Brickman*, RP-114, 1992. (Reprinted from *Cardozo Law Review*, Vol. 13, No. 6, April 1992.) Free.

Hensler, D. R., W. L. F. Felstiner, M. Selvin, and P. A. Ebener, *Asbestos in the Courts: The Challenge of Mass Toxic Torts*, R-3324-ICJ, 1985. $10.00.

Kakalik, J. S., P. A. Ebener, W. L. F. Felstiner, and M. G. Shanley, *Costs of Asbestos Litigation*, R-3042-ICJ, 1983. $4.00.

Kakalik, J. S., P. A. Ebener, W. L. F. Felstiner, G. W. Haggstrom, and M. G. Shanley, *Variation in Asbestos Litigation Compensation and Expenses*, R-3132-ICJ, 1984. $7.50.

Peterson, M. A., *Giving Away Money: Comparative Comments on Claims Resolution Facilities*, RP-108, 1992. (Reprinted from *Law and Contemporary Problems*, Vol. 53, No. 4, Autumn 1990.) Free.

Peterson, M. A., and M. Selvin, *Resolution of Mass Torts: Toward a Framework for Evaluation of Aggregative Procedures*, N-2805-ICJ, 1988. $7.50.

_____ , *Mass Justice: The Limited and Unlimited Power of Courts*, RP-116, 1992. (Reprinted from *Law and Contemporary Problems*, No. 3, Summer 1991.) Free.

Selvin, M., and L. Picus, *The Debate over Jury Performance: Observations from a Recent Asbestos Case*, R-3479-ICJ, 1987. $10.00.

Aviation Accidents

Kakalik, J. S., E. M. King, M. Traynor, P. A. Ebener, and L. Picus, *Costs and Compensation Paid in Aviation Accident Litigation*, R-3421-ICJ, 1988. $10.00.

_____ , *Aviation Accident Litigation Survey: Data Collection Forms*, N-2773-ICJ, 1988. $7.50.

King, E. M., and J. P. Smith, *Computing Economic Loss in Cases of Wrongful Death*, R-3549-ICJ, 1988. $10.00.

_____ , *Economic Loss and Compensation in Aviation Accidents*, R-3551-ICJ, 1988. $10.00.

_____ , *Dispute Resolution Following Airplane Crashes*, R-3585-ICJ, 1988.
$7.50.

Executive Summaries of the Aviation Accident Study, R-3684, 1988.
$7.50.

Environment: California's Clean-Air Strategy

Dixon, L. S., and S. Garber, California's Ozone-Reduction Strategy for
Light-Duty Vehicles: Direct Costs, Direct Emission Effects and
Market Responses, MR-695-ICJ, 1996. $13.00.

_____ , Economic Perspectives on Revising California's Zero-Emission
Vehicle Mandate, CT-137, March 1996. $5.00.

Dixon, L. S., S. Garber, and M. E. Vaiana, California's Ozone-Reduction
Strategy for Light-Duty Vehicles: An Economic Assessment, MR-
695/1-ICJ, 1996. $15.00.

_____ , Making ZEV Policy Despite Uncertainty: An Annotated Briefing
for the California Air Resources Board, DRU-1266-1-ICJ, 1995.
Free.

Environment: Superfund

Acton, J. P., Understanding Superfund: A Progress Report, R-3838-ICJ,
1989. $7.50.

Acton, J. P., and L. S. Dixon with D. Drezner, L. Hill, and S. McKenney,
Superfund and Transaction Costs: The Experiences of Insurers and
Very Large Industrial Firms, R-4132-ICJ, 1992. $7.50.

Dixon, L. S., RAND Research on Superfund Transaction Costs: A Summary
of Findings to Date, CT-111, November 1993. $5.00.

_____ , Fixing Superfund: The Effect of the Proposed Superfund Reform
Act of 1994 on Transaction Costs, MR-455-ICJ, 1994. $15.00.

_____ , Superfund Liability Reform: Implications for Transaction Costs
and Site Cleanup, CT-125, 1995. $5.00.

Dixon, L. S., D. S. Drezner, and J. K. Hammitt, Private-Sector Cleanup
Expenditures and Transaction Costs at 18 Superfund Sites, MR-204-
EPA/RC, 1993. $13.00.

Reuter, P., The Economic Consequences of Expanded Corporate Liability:
An Exploratory Study, N-2807-ICJ, 1988. $7.50.

- 217 -

Law and the Changing American Workplace

Darling-Hammond, L., and T. J. Kniesner, *The Law and Economics of Workers' Compensation*, R-2716-ICJ, 1980. $7.50.

Dertouzos, J. N., E. Holland, and P. A. Ebener, *The Legal and Economic Consequences of Wrongful Termination*, R-3602-ICJ, 1988. $7.50.

Dertouzos, J. N., and L. A. Karoly, *Labor-Market Responses to Employer Liability*, R-3989-ICJ, 1992. $7.50.

Peterson, Mark A., Robert T. Reville, and Rachel Kaganoff Stern, with Peter Barth, *Compensating Permanent Workplace Injuries: A Study of the California System*, MR-920-ICJ, 1997. $20.00.

Stern, Rachel Kaganoff, Mark A. Peterson, Robert T. Reville, and Mary Vaiana, *Findings and Recommendations on California's Permanent Partial Disability System: Executive Summary*, MR-919-ICJ, 1997. $8.00.

Victor, R. B., *Workers' Compensation and Workplace Safety: The Nature of Employer Financial Incentives*, R-2979-ICJ, 1982. $7.50.

Victor, R. B., L. R. Cohen, and C. E. Phelps, *Workers' Compensation and Workplace Safety: Some Lessons from Economic Theory*, R-2918-ICJ, 1982. $7.50.

Medical Malpractice

Bailis, D. S., and R. J. MacCoun, *Estimating Liability Risks with the Media as Your Guide*, RP-606, 1996. (Reprinted from *Law and Human Behavior*, Vol. 20, No. 4, 1996, pp. 419-429.) Free.

Danzon, P. M., *Contingent Fees for Personal Injury Litigation*, R-2458-HCFA, 1980. $4.00.

_____ , *The Disposition of Medical Malpractice Claims*, R-2622-HCFA, 1980. $7.50.

_____ , *Why Are Malpractice Premiums So High—Or So Low?* R-2623-HCFA, 1980. $4.00.

_____ , *The Frequency and Severity of Medical Malpractice Claims*, R-2870-ICJ/HCFA, 1982. $7.50.

_____ , *New Evidence on the Frequency and Severity of Medical Malpractice Claims*, R-3410-ICJ, 1986. $4.00.

_____ , *The Effects of Tort Reform on the Frequency and Severity of Medical Malpractice Claims: A Summary of Research Results*, P-7211,

1986. (Testimony before the Committee on the Judiciary, United States Senate, March 1986.) $4.00.

Danzon, P. M., and L. A. Lillard, *The Resolution of Medical Malpractice Claims: Modeling the Bargaining Process*, R-2792-ICJ, 1982. $7.50.

_____ , *Settlement Out of Court: The Disposition of Medical Malpractice Claims*, P-6800, 1982. $4.00.

_____ , *The Resolution of Medical Malpractice Claims: Research Results and Policy Implications*, R-2793-ICJ, 1982. $4.00.

Kravitz, R. L. , J. E. Rolph, K. A. McGuigan, *Malpractice Claims Data as a Quality Improvement Tool: I. Epidemiology of Error in Four Specialties*, N-3448/1-RWJ, 1991. $4.00.

Lewis, E., and J. E. Rolph, *The Bad Apples? Malpractice Claims Experience of Physicians with a Surplus Lines Insurer*, P-7812, 1993. $4.00.

Rolph, E. S., *Health Care Delivery and Tort: Systems on a Collision Course?* Conference Proceedings, Dallas, June 1991, N-3524-ICJ, 1992. $10.00.

Rolph, J. E., *Some Statistical Evidence on Merit Rating in Medical Malpractice Insurance*, N-1725-HHS, 1981. $4.00.

_____ , *Merit Rating for Physicians' Malpractice Premiums: Only a Modest Deterrent*, N-3426-MT/RWJ/RC, 1991. $4.00.

Rolph, J. E., R. L. Kravitz, and K. A. McGuigan, *Malpractice Claims Data as a Quality Improvement Tool: II. Is Targeting Effective?* N-3448/2-RWJ, 1991. $4.00.

Williams, A. P., *Malpractice, Outcomes, and Appropriateness of Care*, P-7445, May 1988. $4.00.

Product Liability

Bailis, D. S., and R. J. MacCoun, *Estimating Liability Risks with the Media as Your Guide,* RP-606, 1996. (Reprinted from *Law and Human Behavior,* Vol. 20, No. 4, 1996, pp. 419-429.) Free.

Dunworth, T., *Product Liability and the Business Sector: Litigation Trends in Federal Courts*, R-3668-ICJ, 1988. $7.50.

Eads, G., and P. Reuter, *Designing Safer Products: Corporate Responses to Product Liability Law and Regulation*, R-3022-ICJ, 1983. $15.00.

_____ , *Designing Safer Products: Corporate Responses to Product Liability Law and Regulation*, P-7089-ICJ, 1985. (Reprinted from the *Journal of Product Liability*, Vol. 7, 1985.) $4.00.

Garber, S., *Product Liability and the Economics of Pharmaceuticals and Medical Devices*, R-4285-ICJ, 1993. $15.00.

Hensler, D. R., *Summary of Research Results on Product Liability*, P-7271-ICJ, 1986. (Statement submitted to the Committee on the Judiciary, United States Senate, October 1986.) $4.00.

_____ , *What We Know and Don't Know About Product Liability*, P-7775-ICJ, 1993. (Statement submitted to the Commerce Committee, United States Senate, September 1991.) $4.00.

Moller, E., *Trends in Civil Jury Verdicts Since 1985*, MR-694-ICJ, 1996. $15.00.

Peterson, M. A., *Civil Juries in the 1980s: Trends in Jury Trials and Verdicts in California and Cook County, Illinois*, R-3466-ICJ, 1987. $7.50.

Reuter, P., *The Economic Consequences of Expanded Corporate Liability: An Exploratory Study*, N-2807-ICJ, 1988. $7.50.

Punitive Damages

Carroll, S. J., *Punitive Damages in Financial Injury Jury Verdicts*, CT-143, June 1997. (Written statement delivered on June 24, 1997, to the Judiciary Committee of the United States Senate.) $5.00.

Garber, S., *Product Liability and the Economics of Pharmaceuticals and Medical Devices*, R-4285-ICJ, 1993. $15.00.

Hensler, D. R., and E. Moller, *Trends in Punitive Damages: Preliminary Data from Cook County, Illinois, and San Francisco, California*, DRU-1014-ICJ, 1995. Free.

Kakalik, J. S., P. A. Ebener, W. L. F. Felstiner, G. W. Haggstrom, and M. G. Shanley, *Variation in Asbestos Litigation Compensation and Expenses*, R-3132-ICJ, 1984. $7.50.

MacCoun, R. J., *Inside the Black Box: What Empirical Research Tells Us About Decisionmaking by Civil Juries*, RP-238, 1993. (Reprinted from Robert E. Litan, ed., *Verdict: Assessing the Civil Jury System*, The Brookings Institution, 1993.) Free.

Moller, E., *Trends in Civil Jury Verdicts Since 1985*, MR-694-ICJ, 1996. $15.00.

_____ , *Trends in Punitive Damages: Preliminary Data from California*, DRU-1059-ICJ, 1995. Free.

Moller, E., N. M. Pace, and S. J. Carroll, *Punitive Damages in Financial Injury Jury Verdicts*, MR-888-ICJ, 1997. $9.00.

_____ , *Punitive Damages in Financial Injury Jury Verdicts: Executive Summary*, MR-889-ICJ, 1997. $15.00.

Moller, E., E. S. Rolph, and P. Ebener, *Private Dispute Resolution in the Banking Industry*, MR-259-ICJ, 1993. $13.00.

Peterson, M. A., *Punitive Damages: Preliminary Empirical Findings*, N-2342-ICJ, 1985. $4.00.

Peterson, M. A., S. Sarma, and M. G. Shanley, *Punitive Damages: Empirical Findings*, R-3311-ICJ, 1987. $7.50.

Selvin, M., and L. Picus, *The Debate over Jury Performance: Observations from a Recent Asbestos Case*, R-3479-ICJ, 1987. $10.00.

Shubert, G. H., *Some Observations on the Need for Tort Reform*, P-7189-ICJ, 1986. (Testimony before the National Conference of State Legislatures, January 1986.) $4.00.

MASS TORTS AND CLASS ACTIONS

Hensler, D. R., *Resolving Mass Toxic Torts: Myths and Realities*, P-7631-ICJ, 1990. (Reprinted from the *University of Illinois Law Review*, Vol. 1989, No. 1.) $4.00.

_____ , *Asbestos Litigation in the United States: A Brief Overview*, P-7776-ICJ, 1992. (Testimony before the Courts and Judicial Administration Subcommittee, United States House Judiciary Committee, October 1991.) $4.00.

_____ , *Assessing Claims Resolution Facilities: What We Need to Know*, RP-107, 1992. (Reprinted from *Law and Contemporary Problems*, Vol. 53, No. 4, Autumn 1990.) Free.

_____ , *Fashioning a National Resolution of Asbestos Personal Injury Litigation: A Reply to Professor Brickman*, RP-114, 1992. (Reprinted from *Cardozo Law Review*, Vol. 13, No. 6, April 1992.) Free.

_____ , *A Glass Half Full, a Glass Half Empty: The Use of Alternative Dispute Resolution in Mass Personal Injury Litigation*, RP-446, 1995. (Reprinted from *Texas Law Review*, Vol. 73, No. 7, June 1995.)   Free.

Hensler, D. R., W. L. F. Felstiner, M. Selvin, and P. A. Ebener, *Asbestos in the Courts: The Challenge of Mass Toxic Torts*, R-3324-ICJ, 1985. $10.00.

Hensler, D. R., J. Gross, E. Moller, and N. Pace, *Preliminary Results of the RAND Study of Class Action Litigation*, DB-220-ICJ, 1997. $6.00.

Hensler, D. R., and M. A. Peterson, *Understanding Mass Personal Injury Litigation: A Socio-Legal Analysis*, RP-311, 1994. (Reprinted from *Brooklyn Law Review*, Vol. 59, No. 3, Fall 1993.) Free.

Kakalik, J. S., P. A. Ebener, W. L. F. Felstiner, G. W. Haggstrom, and M. G. Shanley, *Variation in Asbestos Litigation Compensation and Expenses*, R-3132-ICJ, 1984. $7.50.

Kakalik, J. S., P. A. Ebener, W. L. F. Felstiner, and M. G. Shanley, *Costs of Asbestos Litigation*, R-3042-ICJ, 1983. $4.00.

Peterson, M. A., *Giving Away Money: Comparative Comments on Claims Resolution Facilities*, RP-108, 1992. (Reprinted from *Law and Contemporary Problems*, Vol. 53, No. 4, Autumn 1990.) Free.

Peterson, M. A., and M. Selvin, *Resolution of Mass Torts: Toward a Framework for Evaluation of Aggregative Procedures*, N-2805-ICJ, 1988. $7.50.

_____ , *Mass Justice: The Limited and Unlimited Power of Courts*, RP-116, 1992. (Reprinted from *Law and Contemporary Problems*, Vol. 54, No. 3, Summer 1991.) Free.

Selvin, M., and L. Picus, *The Debate over Jury Performance: Observations from a Recent Asbestos Case*, R-3479-ICJ, 1987. $10.00.

TRENDS IN THE TORT LITIGATION SYSTEM

Carroll, S. J., *Punitive Damages in Financial Injury Jury Verdicts*, CT-143, June 1997. (Written statement delivered on June 24, 1997, to the Judiciary Committee of the United States Senate.) $5.00.

Galanter, M., B. Garth, D. Hensler, and F. K. Zemans, *How to Improve Civil Justice Policy*, RP-282. (Reprinted from *Judicature*, Vol. 77, No. 4, January/February 1994.) Free.

Hensler, D. R., *Summary of Research Results on the Tort Liability System*, P-7210-ICJ, 1986. (Testimony before the Committee on Commerce, Science, and Transportation, United States Senate, February 1986.) $4.00.

_____ , *Trends in California Tort Liability Litigation*, P-7287-ICJ, 1987. (Testimony before the Select Committee on Insurance, California State Assembly, October 1987.) $4.00.

_____ , *Reading the Tort Litigation Tea Leaves: What's Going on in the Civil Liability System?* RP-226. (Reprinted from *The Justice System Journal*, Vol. 16, No. 2, 1993.) Free.

_____ , *A Glass Half Full, a Glass Half Empty: The Use of Alternative Dispute Resolution in Mass Personal Injury Litigation*, RP-446, 1995. (Reprinted from *Texas Law Review*, Vol. 73, No. 7, June 1995.) Free.

Hensler, D. R., and E. Moller, *Trends in Punitive Damages: Preliminary Data from Cook County, Illinois, and San Francisco, California*, DRU-1014-ICJ, 1995. Free.

Hensler, D. R., M. E. Vaiana, J. S. Kakalik, and M. A. Peterson, *Trends in Tort Litigation: The Story Behind the Statistics*, R-3583-ICJ, 1987. $4.00.

Moller, E., *Trends in Punitive Damages: Preliminary Data from California*, DRU-1059-ICJ, 1995. Free.

_____ , *Trends in Civil Jury Verdicts Since 1985*, MR-694-ICJ, 1996. $15.00.

Moller, E., N. M. Pace, and S. J. Carroll, *Punitive Damages in Financial Injury Jury Verdicts*, MR-888-ICJ, 1997. $9.00.

_____ , *Punitive Damages in Financial Injury Jury Verdicts: Executive Summary*, MR-889-ICJ, 1997. $15.00.

Peterson, M. A., *Summary of Research Results: Trends and Patterns in Civil Jury Verdicts*, P-7222-ICJ, 1986. (Testimony before the Subcommittee on Oversight, Committee on Ways and Means, United States House of Representatives, March 1986.) $4.00.

_____ , *Civil Juries in the 1980s: Trends in Jury Trials and Verdicts in California and Cook County, Illinois*, R-3466-ICJ, 1987. $7.50.

Peterson, M. A., and G. L. Priest, *The Civil Jury: Trends in Trials and Verdicts, Cook County, Illinois, 1960–1979*, R-2881-ICJ, 1982. $7.50.

ECONOMIC EFFECTS OF THE LIABILITY SYSTEM

General

Carroll, S. J., A. Abrahamse, M. S. Marquis, and M. E. Vaiana, *Liability System Incentives to Consume Excess Medical Care*, DRU-1264-ICJ, 1995. Free.

Johnson, L. L., *Cost-Benefit Analysis and Voluntary Safety Standards for Consumer Products*, R-2882-ICJ, 1982. $7.50.

Reuter, P., *The Economic Consequences of Expanded Corporate Liability: An Exploratory Study*, N-2807-ICJ, 1988. $7.50.

Product Liability

Dunworth, T., Product Liability and the Business Sector: Litigation Trends in Federal Courts, R-3668-ICJ, 1988. $7.50.

Eads, G., and P. Reuter, Designing Safer Products: Corporate Responses to Product Liability Law and Regulation, R-3022-ICJ, 1983. $15.00.

_____ , Designing Safer Products: Corporate Responses to Product Liability Law and Regulation, P-7089-ICJ, 1985. (Reprinted from the Journal of Product Liability, Vol. 7, 1985.) $4.00.

Garber, S., Product Liability and the Economics of Pharmaceuticals and Medical Devices, R-4285-ICJ, 1993. $15.00.

Hensler, D. R., Summary of Research Results on Product Liability, P-7271-ICJ, 1986. (Statement submitted to the Committee on the Judiciary, United States Senate, October 1986.) $4.00.

_____ , What We Know and Don't Know About Product Liability, P-7775-ICJ, 1993. (Statement submitted to the Commerce Committee, United States Senate, September 1991.) $4.00.

Peterson, M. A., Civil Juries in the 1980s: Trends in Jury Trials and Verdicts in California and Cook County, Illinois, R-3466-ICJ, 1987. $7.50.

Punitive Damages

Carroll, S. J., *Punitive Damages in Financial Injury Jury Verdicts*, CT-143, June 1997. (Written statement delivered on June 24, 1997, to the Judiciary Committee of the United States Senate.) $5.00.

Garber, S., *Product Liability and the Economics of Pharmaceuticals and Medical Devices*, R-4285-ICJ, 1993. $15.00.

Hensler, D. R., and E. Moller, *Trends in Punitive Damages: Preliminary Data from Cook County, Illinois, and San Francisco, California*, DRU-1014-ICJ, 1995. Free.

Kakalik, J. S., P. A. Ebener, W. L. F. Felstiner, G. W. Haggstrom, and M. G. Shanley, *Variation in Asbestos Litigation Compensation and Expenses*, R-3132-ICJ, 1984. $7.50.

MacCoun, R. J., *Inside the Black Box: What Empirical Research Tells Us About Decisionmaking by Civil Juries*, RP-238, 1993. (Reprinted from Robert E. Litan, ed., *Verdict: Assessing the Civil Jury System*, The Brookings Institution, 1993.) Free.

Moller, E., *Trends in Civil Jury Verdicts Since 1985*, MR-694-ICJ, 1996. $15.00.

_____ , *Trends in Punitive Damages: Preliminary Data from California*, DRU-1059-ICJ, 1995. Free.

Moller, E., N. M. Pace, and S. J. Carroll, *Punitive Damages in Financial Injury Jury Verdicts*, MR-888-ICJ, 1997. $9.00.

_____ , *Punitive Damages in Financial Injury Jury Verdicts: Executive Summary*, MR-889-ICJ, 1997. $15.00.

Moller, E., E. S. Rolph, and P. Ebener, *Private Dispute Resolution in the Banking Industry*, MR-259-ICJ, 1993. $13.00.

Peterson, M. A., *Punitive Damages: Preliminary Empirical Findings*, N-2342-ICJ, 1985. $4.00.

Peterson, M. A., S. Sarma, and M. G. Shanley, *Punitive Damages: Empirical Findings*, R-3311-ICJ, 1987. $7.50.

Selvin, M., and L. Picus, *The Debate over Jury Performance: Observations from a Recent Asbestos Case*, R-3479-ICJ, 1987. $10.00.

Shubert, G. H., *Some Observations on the Need for Tort Reform*, P-7189-ICJ, 1986. (Testimony before the National Conference of State Legislatures, January 1986.) $4.00.

Law and the Changing American Workplace

Darling-Hammond, L., and T. J. Kniesner, *The Law and Economics of Workers' Compensation*, R-2716-ICJ, 1980. $7.50.

Dertouzos, J. N., E. Holland, and P. A. Ebener, *The Legal and Economic Consequences of Wrongful Termination*, R-3602-ICJ, 1988. $7.50.

Dertouzos, J. N., and L. A. Karoly, *Labor-Market Responses to Employer Liability*, R-3989-ICJ, 1992. $7.50.

Peterson, Mark A., Robert T. Reville, and Rachel Kaganoff Stern, with Peter Barth, *Compensating Permanent Workplace Injuries: A Study of the California System,* MR-920-ICJ, 1997. $20.00.

Stern, Rachel Kaganoff, Mark A. Peterson, Robert T. Reville, and Mary Vaiana, *Findings and Recommendations on California's Permanent Partial Disability System: Executive Summary,* MR-919-ICJ, 1997. $8.00.

Victor, R. B., *Workers' Compensation and Workplace Safety: The Nature of Employer Financial Incentives*, R-2979-ICJ, 1982. $7.50.

Victor, R. B., L. R. Cohen, and C. E. Phelps, *Workers' Compensation and Workplace Safety: Some Lessons from Economic Theory*, R-2918-ICJ, 1982. $7.50.

COMPENSATION SYSTEMS

System Design

Darling-Hammond, L., and T. J. Kniesner, *The Law and Economics of Workers' Compensation*, R-2716-ICJ, 1980. $7.50.

Hammitt, J. K., R. L. Houchens, S. S. Polin, and J. E. Rolph, *Automobile Accident Compensation: Volume IV, State Rules*, R-3053-ICJ, 1985. $7.50.

Hammitt, J. K., and J. E. Rolph, *Limiting Liability for Automobile Accidents: Are No-Fault Tort Thresholds Effective?* N-2418-ICJ, 1985. $4.00.

Hensler, D. R., *Resolving Mass Toxic Torts: Myths and Realities*, P-7631-ICJ, 1990. (Reprinted from the *University of Illinois Law Review*, Vol. 1989, No. 1, 1989.) $4.00.

_____ , *Assessing Claims Resolution Facilities: What We Need to Know*, RP-107, 1992. (Reprinted from *Law and Contemporary Problems*, Vol. 53, No. 4, Autumn 1990.) Free.

King, E. M., and J. P. Smith, *Computing Economic Loss in Cases of Wrongful Death,* R-3549-ICJ, 1988. $10.00.

Peterson, Mark A., Robert T. Reville, and Rachel Kaganoff Stern, with Peter Barth, *Compensating Permanent Workplace Injuries: A Study of the California System,* MR-920-ICJ, 1997. $20.00.

Peterson, M. A., and M. Selvin, *Resolution of Mass Torts: Toward a Framework for Evaluation of Aggregative Procedures*, N-2805-ICJ, 1988. $7.50.

Rolph, E. S., *Framing the Compensation Inquiry*, RP-115, 1992. (Reprinted from the *Cardozo Law Review*, Vol. 13, No. 6, April 1992.) Free.

Stern, Rachel Kaganoff, Mark A. Peterson, Robert T. Reville, and Mary Vaiana, *Findings and Recommendations on California's Permanent Partial Disability System: Executive Summary*, MR-919-ICJ, 1997. $8.00.

Victor, R. B., *Workers' Compensation and Workplace Safety: The Nature of Employer Financial Incentives*, R-2979-ICJ, 1982. $7.50.

Victor, R. B., L. R. Cohen, and C. E. Phelps, *Workers' Compensation and Workplace Safety: Some Lessons from Economic Theory*, R-2918-ICJ, 1982. $7.50.

Performance

Abrahamse, A., and S. J. Carroll, *The Effects of a Choice Auto Insurance Plan on Insurance Costs*, MR-540-ICJ, 1995. $13.00.

Carroll, S. J., and A. Abrahamse, *The Effects of a Proposed No-Fault Plan on the Costs of Auto Insurance in California: An Updated Analysis*, IP-146-1, January 1996. Free.

Carroll, S. J., and J. S. Kakalik, *No-Fault Approaches to Compensating Auto Accident Victims*, RP-229, 1993. (Reprinted from *The Journal of Risk and Insurance*, Vol. 60, No. 2, 1993.) Free.

Carroll, S. J., A. Abrahamse, and M. E. Vaiana, *The Costs of Excess Medical Claims for Automobile Personal Injuries*, DB-139-ICJ, 1995. $6.00.

Carroll, S. J., A. Abrahamse, M. S. Marquis, and M. E. Vaiana, *Liability System Incentives to Consume Excess Medical Care*, DRU-1264-ICJ, 1995. Free.

Carroll, S. J., J. S. Kakalik, N. M. Pace, and J. L. Adams, *No-Fault Approaches to Compensating People Injured in Automobile Accidents*, R-4019-ICJ, 1991. $20.00.

Carroll, S. J., and J. S. Kakalik, with D. Adamson, *No-Fault Automobile Insurance: A Policy Perspective*, R-4019/1-ICJ, 1991. $4.00.

Hensler, D. R., M. S. Marquis, A. Abrahamse, S. H. Berry, P. A. Ebener, E. G. Lewis, E. A. Lind, R. J. MacCoun, W. G. Manning, J. A.

Rogowski, and M. E. Vaiana, *Compensation for Accidental Injuries in the United States*, R-3999-HHS/ICJ, 1991. $20.00.

_____ , *Compensation for Accidental Injuries in the United States: Executive Summary*, R-3999/1-HHS/ICJ, 1991. $4.00.

_____ , *Compensation for Accidental Injuries: Research Design and Methods*, N-3230-HHS/ICJ, 1991. $15.00.

King, E. M., and J. P. Smith, *Economic Loss and Compensation in Aviation Accidents*, R-3551-ICJ, 1988. $10.00.

O'Connell, J., S. J. Carroll, M. Horowitz, and A. Abrahamse, *Consumer Choice in the Auto Insurance Market*, RP-254, 1994. (Reprinted from the *Maryland Law Review*, Vol. 52, 1993.) Free.

O'Connell, J., S. J. Carroll, M. Horowitz, A. Abrahamse, and D. Kaiser, *The Costs of Consumer Choice for Auto Insurance in States Without No-Fault Insurance*, RP-442, 1995. (Reprinted from *Maryland Law Review*, Vol. 54, No. 2, 1995.) Free.

Peterson, M. A., *Giving Away Money: Comparative Comments on Claims Resolution Facilities*, RP-108, 1992. (Reprinted from *Law and Contemporary Problems*, Vol. 53, No. 4, Autumn 1990.) Free.

Peterson, M. A., and M. Selvin, *Mass Justice: The Limited and Unlimited Power of Courts*, RP-116, 1992. (Reprinted from *Law and Contemporary Problems*, Vol. 54, No. 3, Summer 1991.) Free.

Rolph, J. E., with J. K. Hammitt, R. L. Houchens, and S. S. Polin, *Automobile Accident Compensation: Volume I, Who Pays How Much How Soon?* R-3050-ICJ, 1985. $4.00.

SPECIAL STUDIES

Hensler, D. R., and M. E. Reddy, California Lawyers View the Future: A Report to the Commission on the Future of the Legal Profession and the State Bar, MR-528-ICJ, 1994. $13.00.

Merz, J. F., and N. M. Pace, Trends in Patent Litigation: The Apparent Influence of Strengthened Patents Attributable to the Court of Appeals for the Federal Circuit, RP-426, 1995. (Reprinted from Journal of the Patent and Trademark Office Society, Vol. 76, No. 8, August 1994.) Free.

An annotated bibliography, CP-253 (12/97), provides a list of
RAND publications in the civil justice area through 1997. To request
the bibliography or to obtain more information about the Institute for
Civil Justice, please write the Institute at this address: The
Institute for Civil Justice, RAND, 1700 Main Street, P.O. Box 2138,
Santa Monica, California 90407-2138, or call (310) 393-0411, x6916.